Postcolonial Fiction and Colonial Time

Postcolonial Fiction and Colonial Time

Waiting for Now

Amanda Lagji

Edinburgh University Press is one of the leading university presses in the UK. We publish academic books and journals in our selected subject areas across the humanities and social sciences, combining cutting-edge scholarship with high editorial and production values to produce academic works of lasting importance. For more information visit our website: edinburghuniversitypress.com

© Amanda Lagji 2023, 2024

Edinburgh University Press Ltd
The Tun – Holyrood Road
12(2f) Jackson's Entry
Edinburgh EH8 8PJ

First published in hardback by Edinburgh University Press 2023

Typeset in 10.5/13 Adobe Sabon
by Manila Typesetting Company

A CIP record for this book is available from the British Library

ISBN 978 1 4744 9020 7 (hardback)
ISBN 978 1 4744 9021 4 (paperback)
ISBN 978 1 4744 9022 1 (webready PDF)
ISBN 978 1 4744 9023 8 (epub)

The right of Amanda Lagji 2023 to be identified as the author of this work has been asserted in accordance with the Copyright, Designs and Patents Act 1988, and the Copyright and Related Rights Regulations 2003 (SI No. 2498).

Contents

Acknowledgements	vi
Introduction	1
1. Waiting at the Heart of Colonial Time Regimes	33
2. Projects and Promissory Notes: The Waiting Rooms of V. S. Naipaul and Nadine Gordimer	58
3. Marooned Time: Disruptive Waiting and Idleness	91
4. Gendered Timescapes of Waiting: Patience and Urgency in Novels of Disillusionment	121
5. 'Strategic Waiting' and Reconciliation in the Aftermath of Conflict	159
Conclusion	199
Bibliography	215
Index	232

Acknowledgements

I acknowledge with deep gratitude the following sources of inspiration, support and critique during the long years that have led to this book's publication. First and foremost, I thank Stephen Clingman for his guidance and mentorship at the University of Massachusetts, Amherst, where I began my work on postcolonial fiction and time. In an email in summer 2013, I wrote to him that I had started to notice the temporalities of waiting in the fiction I was reading for my qualifying exams, and Stephen wrote back to say it was an intriguing observation to investigate further. And here we are: the culmination of that investigation, which Stephen has seen develop across countless drafts, beginning with exam papers, articles, a dissertation and now a book. I am grateful for the feedback and mentorship of the Asha Nadkarni and Britt Rusert, who joined my dissertation committee and offered recommendations for strengthening the relationship between the chapters and their theoretical framework.

At Pitzer College, I had the good fortune to work with Leo Kajfez and Esme Fairbairn, my research assistants who reviewed my entire manuscript during summer 2021. I am thankful for their thorough, critical feedback, which concerned recommendations for framing chapters, suggestions for the close readings, additional resources, formatting and language. I am fortunate to have worked with assistants who could work on such disparate scales all at once.

I also thank the staff at Edinburgh University Press, and especially editor Jackie Jones, whose initial warm reception of the proposal (and her incredibly incisive comments on the introduction in particular) convinced me that Edinburgh University Press would be a wonderful home for the book. It has been a pleasure to work first with Ersev Ersoy and then Susannah Butler through the publication process. I thank the anonymous reviewers of my proposal and book manuscript, who offered challenging and helpful remarks that have greatly improved the book's arguments and interventions.

Because the writing, drafting and revising of this project spans many years, I have in turn many debts to individuals, organisations and institutions that afforded me brilliant and generous interlocutors. I thank specifically the organisers (Christoph Singer and Olaf Berwald) and attendees of the interdisciplinary conference on Waiting as Cultural Practice in summer 2016, where I presented an excerpt from Chapter 5. I also thank the organisers and attendees of the Temporal Belongings conference on the Social Life of Time in summer 2018, where I presented new work that would eventually be incorporated into Chapter 1. I thank Pitzer College, which granted a generous publication award that funded and supported the indexing process; I also thank Amanda Speake for her work on the index. I worked on the final drafts of my book proposal during summer 2020 with the support of a writing group organised at Pitzer College by Shelva Paulse, and I thank her for creating a (virtual) supporting environment.

I am forever grateful to have been hired at Pitzer College with Jessica Kizer and Steffanie Guillermo. Their support and friendship have been integral to my professional and personal life, and I am fortunate to have such sources of camaraderie, humour, commiseration and enthusiasm. I was also hired with colleagues across the 5C consortium who have become wonderful friends and interlocutors as well: Alexandra Papoutsaki, David Seitz, Ambereen Dadabhoy and Brian Shuve.

An early version of Chapter 3 appeared in *Safundi* as 'Marooned Time: Disruptive Waiting and Idleness in Carpentier and Coetzee' (vol. 19, no. 2, 2018, pp. 190–211). I thank the Taylor & Francis Group for the permission to reproduce this material. Chapter 4 was drafted originally as two separate articles, appearing in *South Asian Review* as '"Now" is Here: Disillusionment and Urgency in Anita Desai's *Cry, the Peacock*' (vol. 37, no. 3, 2016, pp. 89–110) and in *African Literature Today 34: Diaspora & Returns in Fiction* as 'Wait No Longer? The Temporality of Return in Ayi Kwei Armah's *Fragments*', edited by Helen Cousins and Pauline Dodgson-Katiyo (vol. 34, November 2016, pp. 28–47). I thank the Taylor & Francis Group for the permission to reproduce material on Desai, and I thank Boydell & Brewer for permission to reproduce aspects of the argument on Armah. I want also to thank the editors and anonymous reviewers of these publications for engaging with my work and offering constructive and incisive suggestions.

Lastly, I thank my family, especially my husband Genti, who reminds me of the rewards of waiting. The timely arrival of our daughter Era, who was born not only in between book proposal and final manuscript, but also in the midst of a global pandemic, is a poignant reminder of the paradox of time: how it can slow and accelerate all at once.

Introduction

> For years now I have heard the word 'Wait!'. . . . This 'wait' has almost always meant 'never'. We must come to see with the distinguished jurist of yesterday that 'justice too long delayed is justice denied'.
> Martin Luther King Jr, 'Letter from Birmingham Jail' (April 1963)

On 6 March 1957 at midnight, Ghana's national flag was raised, replacing the Union Jack and marking the establishment of the Republic of Ghana and its independence from the United Kingdom. Among the dignitaries in attendance was Martin Luther King Jr, fresh from the success of the Montgomery County bus boycotts in the American South and invited to attend by Kwame Nkrumah. In a sermon at the Dexter Avenue Baptist Church the following month, King drew parallels between the civil rights movement in America and the push for independence in Ghana, using the story of Exodus as both metaphor and model for freedom struggles. Often linking civil rights and freedom movements across the globe, from Ghana and India to the American South, King was convinced 'that the black struggle in the Jim Crow South had much to contribute to and learn from movements for independence abroad'.[1] Of the particular events of that midnight ceremony in Ghana, King remembered the crowds teeming with people who 'had waited for this hour and this moment for years' – a sight that brought the American civil rights activist to tears.[2] Before ending the sermon, King appealed to the congregation, asking them not to

> go out this morning with any illusions . . . If we wait for it to work itself out, it will never be worked out. Freedom only comes through persistent revolt,

---

[1] Baldwin, 'General Introduction', xx.
[2] King, *In a Single Garment of Destiny*, 64.

through persistent agitation, through persistently rising up against the system of evil.³

From civil rights movements within countries to anticolonial nationalist movements across the globe, agitation for change has often been linked with refusals to wait. In *Why We Can't Wait*, which draws from and expands upon the 'Letter from Birmingham Jail' that serves as the epigraph to this Introduction, King argues that the United States 'had come to count on [the Negro] as a creature who could quietly endure, silently suffer and patiently wait'.⁴ The Revolution gained momentum, King writes, as African Americans were motivated by 'the decolonization and liberation of nations in Africa and Asia since World War II'.⁵ As King sat in attendance at that midnight ceremony in Ghana, the first African country south of the Sahara to achieve independence from European colonial rule, he heard Kwame Nkrumah declare, 'We are not waiting; we shall no more go back to sleep. Today, from now on, there is a new African in the world and that new African is ready to fight his own battle'.⁶ Although there are limits to the comparisons that can be drawn between the United States and Ghana, King felt that 'the parallels between colonialism in the Third World and racial oppression in the United States converge on the roles of violence and temporality'.⁷ Waiting, as both Nkrumah and King observed, expresses an oppressive temporal modality that must be rejected in the struggle for freedom and independence.

Rather than disappear in the post-independence era, however, the temporal dimensions of waiting continue to be evoked, revised, critiqued and reconfigured in postcolonial fiction. This book argues that 'waiting' is an essential concept in the theorisation of postcolonial temporalities, and charts a genealogy of the temporal dimensions of waiting from the colonial-era *Heart of Darkness* to the 2014 novel *The Radiance of Tomorrow* by Sierra Leonean author Ishmael Beah. Other studies have characterised postcolonial time as the temporal experience wherein 'colonial experience appears, simultaneously, to be consigned to the past *and*, precisely due to the modalities with which its "overcoming" comes

---

³ Ibid., 67.
⁴ King, *Why We Can't Wait*, 2.
⁵ Ibid., 9.
⁶ Nkrumah, *I Speak of Freedom*, 106–7.
⁷ Hanchard, 'Afro-Modernity: Temporality, Politics, and the African Diaspora', 295.

about, to be installed at the centre of contemporary social experience'.[8] While postcolonial accounts of time and temporality certainly respond to the lasting effects of the colonial experience, throughout this book I demonstrate that postcolonial novels draw on manifold temporalities that exist in relation to, as well as independently of, colonial regimes of time. I aim to show that waiting is at the centre of colonial regimes of time, but rather than a wholesale rejection of waiting at the end of formal colonial rule, postcolonial novels reframe waiting as a multivalent temporality that can register the tensions of multiple temporal modalities that give shape to the postcolonial world: allowing for palimpsests of temporalities, layering time's various frames, and permitting a fuller exploration of the way temporal discourses are used to liberate, oppress and defer.

For the purposes of this study, postcolonial fiction is not distinguished by the period in which it is produced, but rather by its preoccupations; postcolonial fiction is concerned with critically reflecting, confronting and challenging the enduring experiences of colonialism, decolonisation and neocolonialism. By loosening the strictures of periodisation, we can better appreciate how a postcolonial consciousness emerges in the margins of Joseph Conrad's *Heart of Darkness*, or how white South African writers, J. M. Coetzee and Nadine Gordimer, writing during apartheid, generate 'postcolonial' futures in a country both unshackled from European control and yet tyrannically controlled by a white minority. From their various positions, the authors of postcolonial fiction both await a postcolonial future and attempt to write it into being. Though casting a critical eye on colonial relationships, struggles for self-determination, and the challenges of postcolonial governments, many of the novels that this book examines are equally concerned with making manifest a more equitable, more just and more *postcolonial* future. Postcolonial fiction, Elleke Boehmer notes,

> gives structure to, as well as being structured by, history . . . The space-time framework and patterns of causality in a narrative work not only to impart coherence to a fragmented history, but also help organize and clarify foundational moments in the anti-imperial movement.[9]

The relationship between historical and fictional narrative is reciprocal; postcolonial fiction is part of the reconstruction of postcolonial

---

[8] Mezzadra and Rahola, 'The Postcolonial Condition: A Few Notes on the Quality of Historical Time in the Global Present'.
[9] Boehmer, *Colonial and Postcolonial Literature*, 198.

history – with all of its vertiginous layers – even as it provides some structure to an already fragmented history.

An understanding of waiting that draws on its multiple etymological valences can usefully revise the static connotations of the term and provide a temporal framework that captures its passive and active registers. The *Oxford English Dictionary* indicates that to wait can entail delay, deferral and submissiveness, from which we derive the sense of waiting as waiting upon others as a servant, or 'to continue in expectation of' or even 'to remain for a time without something expected or promised'.[10] But older meanings of waiting suggest strategy and scheming, as in the sense 'to lie in wait for', 'to keep hostile watch' and 'to take precautions'. Waiting as a temporal state or condition emphasises the present moment, but waiting in the sense of 'look[ing] forward to some future event', from which we derive the word 'await', registers waiting's orientation towards the future. Waiting can and has been used to defer justice and to distort a lived sense of historicity for colonial subjects, but it can also, I suggest, be actively engaged as a strategy that resists the imperatives of colonial time, formulating a sense of temporality poised between and in active relation to the past and future. I am especially interested in the counterintuitive dimensions of waiting, where waiting is at turns active, agentive, contemplative and strategic. The texts under examination in this book demonstrate that waiting is neither wholly repressive, as configured by Nkrumah and King above, nor fully liberating, but rather is a temporality that can register a spectrum of passive and active modalities.

In the years since King and Nkrumah articulated their rejection of waiting, Black studies scholarship on time and temporality has demanded that we attend to the imbrication of time, justice and power. Daylanne English, for example, notes that 'time, justice, and the written word are deeply intertwined',[11] and that the 'temporal-political thematic – of the past inhabiting the present, and of a troubled present leading into an imagined better future – occurs throughout the African American literary tradition and across genres'.[12] English calls for an expansive account of time and Black writing, and she argues that 'a focus on time serves to overcome what [Bonnie J.] Barthold terms the "fragmentation" of traditional literary scholarship that, in her view, all too often separates African from Caribbean from American, past from present, and form

---

[10] *Oxford English Dictionary*, 'Wait, v. 1'.
[11] English, *Each Hour Redeem*, 1.
[12] Ibid., 160.

from content'.¹³ *Postcolonial Fiction and Colonial Time: Waiting for Now* contributes to this agenda, strengthening links between Black diasporic thought and postcolonial studies and increasing the dialogue between two fields that have much (more) to say to one another.¹⁴

Both postcolonial studies and Black studies exhibit a 'temporal turn', though a preoccupation with the temporal has been an integral part of both fields for decades. In addition to Saidiya Hartman's groundbreaking work on the time of slavery, which seeks to 'illumine the disparate temporalities of unfreedom',¹⁵ Katherine McKittrick, Christina Sharpe, Matthew Omelsky and Julius B. Fleming have grappled with what Sharpe calls the 'unresolved unfolding' of slavery, such that the 'past that is not past reappears, always, to rupture the present'.¹⁶ As Fleming notes in his study of black patience and the Free Southern Theater, 'time has operated as a historical weapon of antiblack violence', and that the 'radical grammar of the present – of the here and now – was pivotal to black people's efforts to exist and imagine otherwise'.¹⁷ Fleming charts how the temporalities of waiting characterised the timespace conditions of Atlantic slavery, from the confines of the slave ship's hold to the 'historical use of "the wait" as a mechanism for deferring and denying black freedom' in the present, or the now.¹⁸ On the other hand, waiting or endurance might yet be harnessed to instigate political change. Katherine McKittrick argues that endurance, epitomised in a black graveyard in Quebec, Canada, is a model for 'reject[ing] the preordained colonial outcome of waiting', and can help us to 'imagine the ways in which black Canada can, and does, anticipate a different multicultural future'.¹⁹ In a similar vein, Gregory Laski interrogates the possibilities that might emerge from stagnation (or in the language operative in this book, 'waiting'). Laski tracks the 'democratic possibilities that might emerge in moments of temporal stasis', noting that African American authors 'challenge the notion that "time never stands still in politics," and the attendant sense that stasis is not a mode in time,

---

¹³ Ibid., 158.
¹⁴ In addition to the scholars and works I discuss briefly below, see also Anthony Reed, *Freedom Time* (2014), Calvin Warren, 'Black Time: Slavery, Metaphysics, and the Logic of Wellness', Charles Mills, 'White Time: The Chronic Injustice of Ideal Theory' and Michelle Wright, *Physics of Blackness* (2015).
¹⁵ Hartman, 'The Time of Slavery', 762–3.
¹⁶ Sharpe, *In the Wake*, 13–14, 9.
¹⁷ Fleming, 'Transforming Geographies of Black Time: How the Free Southern Theater Used the Plantation for Civil Rights Activism', 587–8.
¹⁸ Ibid., 599.
¹⁹ McKittrick, 'Wait Canada Anticipate Black', 245.

much less a politically viable one'.[20] My approach to the temporalities of waiting as refracted in postcolonial fiction is to strike a balance between rejection and embrace; each chapter in *Postcolonial Fiction and Colonial Time* attends to the contingencies of waiting, noting the context, positionalities, historical setting and interconnected colonial discourses of time and idleness that impact the potential for waiting to catalyse change and anticipate a more just future.

Indebted to these studies that challenge us to radically rethink temporality, waiting and stasis, I situate the temporalities of waiting within postcolonial approaches to time – especially the critiques of Western time and history that have always been under the discipline's purview, but which have become more salient and urgent in light of the emergent field of critical time studies. In his 2014 *Omens of Adversity*, a study of temporality and the 1983 Grenada Revolution, David Scott observes that the accumulating scholarship on justice, memory, trauma and time suggest that 'a new time-consciousness is emerging everywhere in contemporary theory'.[21] More recently, the contributors to *South African Writing in Transition* advocate for several concepts, including waiting, 'that might help illuminate not only South African culture and its trajectories, but potentially also the uncertain and uneven temporalities of the world at large'.[22] Within postcolonial studies, and South African literature in particular, David Attwell perceives, 'The axis has been shifting . . . from an emphasis on how to write about sameness and difference, to writing about *temporality*, which is to say, writing about one's place in history or one's place in the present and future'.[23] This 'temporal turn' reinvigorates diverse areas of scholarship, from globalisation studies to American studies and theories of nations and territoriality.[24] In part, the increased attention to time responds to the intense focus on space previously; Bob Jessop argues that for globalisation studies,

---

[20] Laski, *Untimely Democracy*, 16.
[21] D. Scott, *Omens of Adversity*, 1.
[22] Barnard and van der Vlies, 'Introduction', 2–3.
[23] Attwell, *Rewriting Modernity*, 8.
[24] Similarly, Ulrich Beck and Daniel Levy observe that 'the spatially rooted understanding of social theory is being challenged by a "temporal turn"' more broadly, which has implications for reading national collectivities. 'Cosmopolitanized Nations: Re-Imagining Collectivity in World Risk Society', 6. See also Jeffrey Insko's 'Prospects for the Present', which summarises that the temporal turn in American Studies has produced 'some of the most compelling Americanist scholarship of the twenty-first century', in part by 'address[ing] the formations, reformations, and promises of the present, the *now* and the *not yet*'. 'Prospects for the Present', 836.

'the spatial turn . . . has been overdone and a temporal (re)turn is overdue'.[25] *Postcolonial Fiction and Colonial Time* shares with Pheng Cheah's recent account of world literature an emphasis on the temporal over the spatial. A 'more rigorous normative account of the world', he argues, 'should focus on its temporal dimensions'.[26] Cheah is critical of postcolonial studies' tendency to posit the possibility of a clean break with Western capitalist modernity in its pursuit of 'multiple temporalities'.[27] Instead, Cheah refuses to posit heterotemporalities as external to globalisation, and argues that multitemporality is 'the intensification of an already existing heterogeneity'.[28] In my assessment of waiting, the multiple tempos, rhythms and disruptions to dominant temporal modes depicted in the literary works allows me to identify multiple temporalities activated within a given timescape without valorising temporal difference as signifying a utopian rupture with either Western capitalist modernity – as Cheah fears[29] – or with colonial regimes of time. While South African literary studies has been the locus for much of the current scholarship on waiting and fiction, this book demonstrates that across various histories of colonisation, the temporalities of waiting materialise as central, to trope on David Scott, to postcolonial time-consciousness more broadly – though certainly shaped by the specific experiences and unique circumstances of diverse geographies and times.

Postcolonial Fiction and Colonial Time contributes to the temporal turn in critical theory and in literary studies by bringing together critical time studies and postcolonial studies to interrogate the temporal dimensions of waiting across the long twentieth century. Critical time studies – defined by Paul Huebener as 'a process of inquiry that advances thoughtful re-evaluations of the social politics of time through the examination of temporal assumptions and the fostering of critical temporal literacy' – has produced innovative approaches to the social politics and cultural practices of time in fields from sociology to anthropology, political studies to philosophy.[30] Throughout, the temporality of waiting has emerged as a modality of temporal experience that increasingly characterises the lived experiences of ethnographic subjects and the temporal politics of literary narratives alike. Indeed, Harold Schweizer's observation in 2008

---

[25] Jessop, 'Time and Space in the Globalization of Capital and Their Implications for State Power', 97.
[26] Cheah, *What Is a World?*, 191.
[27] Ibid., 12.
[28] Ibid., 207.
[29] Ibid., 17.
[30] Huebener, *Timing Canada*, 14.

that waiting is undertheorised – his first chapter asserts that 'waiting is a temporal region hardly mapped and badly documented' – is now a dated assessment.[31] Many ethnographic studies focused on the Global South note how the banality of waiting characterises everyday life, but also how ritual can transform waiting into 'a goal-oriented, meaningful practice, lessening its burden'.[32] Unemployed, educated young men are particularly well represented in this literature. 'Gymmers', in Ato Quayson's study of Oxford Street in Accra, handle un- or under-employment by turning to formal and makeshift gyms to spend their time. The economic conditions that compel the gymmer to wait yield what Quayson calls a 'phenomenology of waiting'.[33] He writes:

> The choice is not between work and rest, or work and boredom, but between active and inactive understandings of the agency that is required to survive the incoherences [sic] generated by economic informality. This view requires the interpretation of free time as at once a set of urban practices *and* a peculiar phenomenology that is experienced *as an obligation to do something* as a way of combating the vagaries of free time.[34]

Waiting can be understood here as an urban practice that yields a particular orientation to time and temporality, encouraging the subject to act ('to do something') even as she waits.[35] I would add that waiting can also function as an indirect form of social critique aimed at the institutional or systemic inequalities that force free time on the gymmer and permit leisure time for the employed. Gymmers navigate their free time by using the gym as an 'orientation toward change and self-transformation', where the time of waiting becomes a time of negotiation.[36]

---

[31] Schweizer, *On Waiting*, 1.

[32] Masquelier, 'Teatime: Boredom and the Temporalities of Young Men in Niger', 472.

[33] Quayson, *Oxford Street, Accra*, 245–6.

[34] Ibid., 246.

[35] See also Abdoumaliq Simone's 'Waiting in African Cities', which notes that waiting is becoming 'a modality of living in cities that needs to be enacted in new ways as a site of possibility'. 'Waiting in African Cities', 97.

[36] Quayson, *Oxford Street, Accra*, 210. Other important work on the temporalities of waiting include Craig Jeffrey's *Timepass: Youth, Class, and the Politics of Waiting in India*, June Hee Kwon's 'The Work of Waiting: Love and Money in Korean Chinese Transnational Migration', Morton Andersen's 'Time-Use, Activism and the Making of Future', and Alcinda Manuel Honwana's 2012 *The Time of Youth: Work, Social Change, and Politics in Africa*. Honwana uses the term 'waithood' (first coined in studies on youth in the Middle East and North Africa) to describe a 'prolonged adolescence of an involuntary delay in reaching

Significantly, Quayson remarks that the choice is not between 'work and rest, or work and boredom'. Rather the 'phenomenology of waiting' is intertwined certainly with feelings like boredom,[37] but that the *work* of waiting exceeds the indexing of affect. Nevertheless, as I discuss further in the section on the temporal dimensions of waiting below, waiting is associated with disappointment, boredom, expectation and hope. Saikat Majumdar has already argued for the significance of boredom – 'an affective marker of exclusion from the most thriving narratives of modernity and capitalism in the present world' – across global Anglophone literature of the former British Empire.[38] Several important studies of time and stasis in South African fiction have approached the reading of literary texts through an emphasis on affect, especially the work of Andrew van der Vlies, Katherine Hallemeier and Derek Hook. Hook, for example, characterises post-apartheid temporality as one of 'petrification'.[39] Drawing on Vincent Crapanzano's anthropological study of waiting in apartheid South Africa – which I discuss in detail in Chapter 2 – Hook finds that waiting 'span[s] an array of experiential phenomena' and is a 'complex temporality' that encapsulates both expectant longing and fearful dread.[40] When expectant longing is unfulfilled, however, the temporality of waiting marks disappointment and disillusionment. Van der Vlies notes that disappointment is both a 'structuring affect' and 'temporal condition' in South African fiction.[41] In his view, the entanglement of affect and literary studies has enabled 'us to understand as political those feelings . . . that might otherwise seem merely personal or private . . . [T]hese feelings index a potential to *reinvigorate* the political'.[42] Taken together, Quayson, Hook and van der Vlies gesture towards the possible reinvigoration of the politics of waiting, which tends to be associated with impasse, stasis, passivity or disempowerment only.

---

adulthood'. She argues that waithood is in fact a 'dynamic' period, where youths 'invent new forms of being and interacting with society'. Honwana, *The Time of Youth*, 4.

[37] I am reminded here of Walter Benjamin's rendering of boredom: 'We are bored when we don't know what we are waiting for'. Benjamin and Tiedemann, *The Arcades Project*, 105.

[38] Majumdar, *Prose of the World*, 23–4.

[39] Hook, 'Petrified Life', 7.

[40] Ibid., 8–9.

[41] Van der Vlies, *Present Imperfect: Contemporary South African Writing*, 2.

[42] Ibid., 4.

What it feels like to wait can reveal much about the temporal dimensions of power. As Sara Ahmed observes,

> Emotions tell us a lot about time; emotions are the very 'flesh' of time ... The time of emotion is not always about the past, and how it sticks. Emotions open up futures, in the ways they involve different orientations to others.[43]

As I will show across the chapters that follow, rarely do characters wait for a singular event or outcome; rather, the temporalities of their waiting open up several different, possible futures that become more legible in suspended time. By building directly and indirectly from the work on affect and temporality, this book demonstrates that the discourses, sensations, emotions and experiences of waiting are martialled in literary texts towards a better understanding of power and the weaponisation of time – and also towards positing temporal orientations and modalities in opposition.

Though my central interest is in the representations of time and waiting in postcolonial fiction, I do not organise my argument strictly chronologically; rather, this book is organised by the themes, politics and temporal dimensions of waiting that particular novels share or respond to. Each chapter situates the authors and texts under discussion in their historical moments in order not to lose sight of the variability of 'postcoloniality'. In order to situate 'waiting' in the larger context of colonial discourse, the remainder of this Introduction provides an overview of postcolonial studies' engagement with colonial time and describes how colonial time regimes mapped temporal difference onto perceived racial and cultural difference. Drawing on Dipesh Chakrabarty's *Provincializing Europe*, I then discuss anticolonial nationalist rejections of the 'waiting room' model of history, and how the rhetoric of waiting lingered in development discourses after colonies achieved political independence. Before concluding with chapter summaries, I offer a robust description of waiting's temporal dimensions, creating a framework through which to read waiting as a cultural practice, as well as an essential analytical concept to scrutinise structures of power.

Colonial Time and Postcolonial Studies

Time has always been a central concern and battleground for scholarship grappling with the legacies of colonialism. In its earliest stages,

---

[43] Ahmed, *The Cultural Politics of Emotion*, 202.

postcolonial criticism aimed to uncover the violence of Eurocentric notions of history and difference, as well as the relationship between colonial power and knowledge. 'If the discourse of postcolonial criticism evinces a concern with problematizing the issue of time', Keya Ganguly observes, 'this is in turn shaped by questions of historicity, modernity, and temporality that constitute the broader horizon of present approaches to knowledge'.[44] A hallmark of postcolonial approaches, Stuart Hall notes, has been 'the proliferation of histories and temporalities, the intrusion of difference and specificity into the generalizing and Eurocentric post-Enlightenment grand narratives'.[45] Edward Said's *Orientalism*, which argues that the West's relationship with its Orient other is unevenly structured and 'based on the Orient's special place in European Western experience',[46] and V. Y. Mudimbe's *The Invention of Africa*, which focuses on the West's representation of African philosophy as well as African responses, are two emblematic studies of early postcolonial critiques and their engagements with colonial time.

In addition to its place as foundational text for postcolonial studies, Said's *Orientalism* is also significant for its description of Orientalist interpretations of time. Orientalist discourse views the Orient as 'fixed in time and place for the West' so that encounters with the Orient can be framed as predictable and knowable; implicit here is a sense of progression through time where the West is further ahead and the Orient is further behind.[47] This temporal difference contains two opposing positions: (1) the view that if the Orient is to exist coevally with the West, it is the West's obligation to usher the Orient into the present through integration into the world economy and history, and (2) given the West's advanced position, the Orient will always be 'not yet' ready for integration on equal footing. In the Orientalist project of dominating, knowing and restructuring the world, seemingly contradictory narratives coexist, employed depending on their usefulness to colonial expansion and its attendant colonial discourse. Mudimbe's *The Invention of Africa* addresses similar distortions by Western and colonial discourses for African areas of knowledge and cultural production, including philosophy, history and art. Unlike Said, Mudimbe is additionally concerned with how contemporary Afrocentric perspectives depend on a 'Western epistemological order'.[48] In both Africanist

---

[44] Ganguly, 'Temporality and Postcolonial Critique', 163.
[45] Hall, 'When Was "the Post-Colonial"? Thinking at the Limit', 248.
[46] Said, *Orientalism*, 1.
[47] Ibid., 108.
[48] Mudimbe, *The Invention of Africa*, x.

and Orientalist discourses, colonists and colonialists 'tended to organize and transform non-European areas into fundamentally European constructs'.[49] In Africa and elsewhere, the 'colonializing structure' has produced a 'dichotomizing system' whose 'paradigmatic oppositions' include 'traditional versus modern; oral versus written and printed' among others.[50] Mudimbe's later *The Idea of Africa* continues in this vein, and asserts that 'Africa (as well as Asia and Europe) is represented in Western scholarship by "fantasies" and "constructs" made up by scholars and writers since Greek times', and these constructions have 'simplified cultural complexities'.[51]

Both Mudimbe and Said respond to a theorisation of time and history grounded in Western epistemological practices and assumptions, which became integral to philosophical and political motives, and later justifications, for colonial expansion. Many Enlightenment thinkers, from Kant and Rousseau to Mill and Hegel, opined about the place of Africa and other non-European locales in world history.[52] The association of Africa with timelessness was especially pernicious and prevalent across the European continent and scholarly disciplines. Joseph K. Adjaye's introduction to *Time in the Black Experience* provides an overview of this widespread practice, citing British physician Thomas Hodgkin's conclusion that in Africa '"there was no account of Time; no Arts; no Letters; no Society"' and French philosopher Lucien Lévy's assertion that '"[t]o the primitive time is not, as it is to us, a kind of intellectualized intuition, an 'order of succession'"'.[53] Adjaye then concludes, 'For much of the first half of the twentieth century, therefore, theories and conceptions of time in Africa merely articulated popular European misconceptions and prejudices'.[54] Integral to these prejudices are assumptions about European temporal attentiveness and authority that imagined Europe 'as a time-conscious civilisation in opposition to a time-less Other', producing claims to 'universal definitions of time,

---

[49] Ibid., 1.
[50] Ibid., 4.
[51] Mudimbe, *The Idea of Africa*, xv.
[52] Although Said's *Orientalism* is concerned with the East/West axis, several of his examples typify the tendency to substitute one 'Other' for another. Take, for example, this excerpt Said pulls from England's representative in Egypt, Lord Cromer's essays: '"in dealing with Indians or Egyptians, or Shilluks, or Zulus . . . . each special issue should be decided mainly with reference to what, by the light of Western knowledge and experience tempered by local considerations, we conscientiously think is best for the subject race"'. Said, *Orientalism*, 37.
[53] Adjaye, 'Time in Africa and Its Diaspora: An Introduction', 3.
[54] Ibid., 3.

regularity, order; hence also to definitions of knowledge, religion, [and] science'.⁵⁵

At the centre of the colonial discourse that developed across the European continent in tandem with these prejudices is a will to remove colonial others from the universal narrative of history, a temporal distancing that erases precolonial history and understands the colonial other's present in terms of the Western subject's past. Hegel's account of world history, for example, combines the East and Africa together in one world (the 'Oriental') in opposition to the Greek, Roman and Germanic.⁵⁶ For Hegel, the latter is the highest stage of modernity, and these stages 'not only succeed one another and advance through time, but they are also organized geographically from east to west'.⁵⁷ As implemented by colonial regimes, colonial time 'place[s] temporal boundaries between an "advancing" people and a "static" people, locating the latter out of time'.⁵⁸ This temporal regime tends towards total incorporation through the imposition of one time and one History, a 'colonization of time' that Walter Mignolo calls 'a spectacular case of a global design'.⁵⁹ The reverberations are still felt in postcolonial writing around the globe; the Martinican writer and critic Édouard Glissant observes that Amerindian peoples were relegated to a 'prehistorical' position in relation to Europeans, and because 'the Caribbean notion of time was fixed in the void of an imposed nonhistory, the writer must contribute to reconstituting its tormented chronology'.⁶⁰ In its attempt to describe and contest the legacies of colonialism, postcolonial writers have necessarily engaged with the imbrication of power, knowledge, history and time as central problematics of colonial discourse.⁶¹

---

[55] Nanni, *The Colonisation of Time*, 2.
[56] Agacinski, *Time Passing*, 3.
[57] Ibid., 3.
[58] Bruyneel, *The Third Space of Sovereignty*, 2.
[59] Mignolo, *Local Histories/Global Designs*, xiii.
[60] Glissant, *Caribbean Discourse*, 64–5.
[61] Paul Gilroy's *Black Atlantic* challenges the diametrical opposition of Hegel's philosophy and black resistance and creativity. In Gilroy's view, 'Hegel provides the terms for "a firm rebuke to the mesmeric idea of history as progress" and "an opportunity to re-periodise and reaccentuate accounts of the dialectic of Enlightenment"' (quoted in Fischer, *Modernity Disavowed*, 25). It is not my intention to ignore these recent reinterpretations of Enlightenment philosophy, but rather to track how these theorisations dovetailed with and fostered colonial discourse, and especially how postcolonial writers and thinkers have responded to this intellectual history.

From the 'post' prefix in its name, to its description of the violence of colonial discourse's temporalities, postcolonial studies as a discipline has always acknowledged and contended with time as part of its critique. As Gayatri Spivak puts it in *A Critique of Postcolonial Reason*, 'the epistemic story of imperialism is the story of a series of interruptions, a repeated tearing of time that cannot be sutured'.[62] One way more recent work in postcolonial studies has addressed the concerns is to examine more carefully and critically what we might take to be 'colonial time', acknowledging that linear, developmentalist time is belied by lags, delays and disruptive competing temporalities. Adam Barrows usefully describes the process of synchronising the world to one standard time at the Prime Meridian Conference, which pitted a universal, standard time against dissenting local conceptions of time that revolved around agriculture, religion and other cultural practices.[63] Signs of struggle over the imposition of standard time not only gesture towards competing temporalities, but also caution against a too easy conception of colonial time as a monolithic concept.[64] In a similar vein, On Barak's *On Time* shows how '"Western time" [came] to be associated with standard clock time and "Egyptian time" with a substandard approximation', and he finds that Egypt's modernising classes in the early twentieth century tended to characterise 'the slowing down of colonial modernity as Egyptian and its acceleration as Western'.[65] Thus, 'colonial time' is not only not homogeneous, but is also marked equally by sensations of delay and waiting, as well as acceleration and speed.

By colonial time, then, I refer to colonial discourse's production of an ostensibly homogenising and universalising temporality, indebted to the Enlightenment, that underpinned European colonial expansion during high imperialism and remains influential for imperial ideologies of control. Colonial time is, like 'modern historical time ... organized around a notion of discrete but continuous, modular change, and in particular, modular change as a linear, diachronically stretched-out *succession* of cumulative instants, an endless chain of displacements of before and after'.[66]

---

[62] Spivak, *A Critique of Postcolonial Reason*, 208.
[63] Barrows, *The Cosmic Time of Empire*, 43.
[64] Vanessa Ogle also describes these temporal tensions; the movement for 'universal time' at Greenwich in fact 'made contemporaries realize not how similar but how heterogeneous the world was – to the degree of being incomparable'. The practice of 'plotting the histories of nations and peoples onto a grid of universal, evolutionary time' was integral to managing this difference. Ogle, *The Global Transformation of Time 1870–1950*, 6–7.
[65] Barak, *On Time: Technology and Temporality in Modern Egypt*, 1–2.
[66] D. Scott, *Omens of Adversity*, 5.

It is true that postcolonial critiques of time have often been 'premised on a simplified and even monolithic understanding of Western modernity as an ideology of "linear progress", the consequence of which is a binary conception of time'.[67] By noting the perceived linearity of historical and colonial time, I refer both to how colonial writers and politicians characterised history as linear progress, as well as to how early postcolonial studies tended to reproduce this notion with the shorthand 'homogeneous, empty time'.[68] Focusing on the temporalities of waiting in fiction across the twentieth century to the present, I aim to work across the colonial/postcolonial temporal divide that assumes an 'underlying structure . . . of segmented absolute time'.[69] Instead, waiting reveals what Russell West-Pavlov describes as 'a plurality of heterogeneous temporalities',[70] which I further explore in Chapter 4's delineation of postcolonial timescapes. Throughout this book, attention to heterogeneity is especially important given colonies' divergent trajectories after independence, and varying experiences with white minority rule.

By colonial regimes of time, I emphasise the power of this temporal organisation to regulate and influence interactions and behaviours at all levels of society. I view colonial regimes of time to be a subset of cultural time regimes, which 'refer to a temporal ordering and orientation that is deeply entrenched in the culture and provides a basis for implicit values, patterns of thought and the logic of action'.[71] As cultural artefacts, novels participate in the reflection and production of cultural time regimes, and an analysis of fiction can in turn illuminate the text's temporal politics and values – which may be at odds with the prevailing organisation of time and society outside of the text. Across this book's chapters, I demonstrate that the narratives of imaginative literature are also productive sites to illuminate how colonial time both operates and

---

[67] Helgesson, 'Radicalizing Temporal Difference: Anthropology, Postcolonial Theory, and Literary Time', 546.
[68] The phrase 'homogeneous, empty time' originally comes from Walter Benjamin's 'Theses on the Philosophy of History'. Benjamin, *Illuminations*, 261. Even when postcolonial studies has 'deconstruct[ed] the "time of history" as specifically "Western' time," these insights have not been incorporated into new practices by historians or philosophers of history, whose works 'are still generally based on an absolute, homogeneous and empty time'. Bevernage and Lorenz, 'Breaking up Time – Negotiating the Borders between Present, Past and Future. An Introduction', 9, 13.
[69] West-Pavlov, *Temporalities*, 166.
[70] Ibid., 166.
[71] Assmann, 'Transformations of the Modern Time Regime', 42.

is resisted. Importantly, colonial regimes of time are 'fractured, uneven, and co-constituted by tension', and, as a result, 'colonial time nurtures the conditions for its own subversion'.[72]

Waiting, as it manifests in postcolonial fiction, evinces what Achille Mbembe calls the 'time of entanglement': 'an interlocking of presents, pasts, and futures that retain their depths of other presents, pasts, and futures', constituted by 'disturbances . . . not necessarily resulting in chaos and anarchy', and 'harbor[ing] the possibility of a variety of trajectories neither convergent nor divergent but interlocked, paradoxical'.[73] Entanglement, moreover, usefully 'offers an alternative to historical linearity' because the concept encapsulates 'the heterogeneous forms of modernity' in diverse settings, each with unique configurations of 'neoliberal, nationalist logics' and 'differentiated cultural ones'.[74] The term colonial regime of time is meant to capture the ideological and epistemic consequences of the imposition of colonial time (and its associated assumptions about history and modernity), as well as its material and political consequences. Formulated this way, colonial regimes of time include the temporal entanglements emerging from colonial encounters, including what Michael Hanchard terms 'racial time'. Racial time refers to 'the inequalities of temporality that result from power relations between racially dominant and subordinate groups', and 'produce[s] unequal temporal access to institutions, goods, service, resources, power, and knowledge, which members of both groups recognize'.[75] Crucially, Hanchard identifies 'waiting' as the first conceptual facet of racial time: 'Members of subordinate groups objectively perceive the material consequences of social inequality, as they are literally made to wait for goods and services that are delivered first to members of the dominant group'.[76] 'The end of waiting', Hanchard concludes, 'meant the beginning of a more autonomous existence'.[77] It is not surprising, then, that refusing to wait became central to anticolonial movements across the world.

---

[72] Ibid., 1–2.
[73] Mbembe, *On the Postcolony*, 16.
[74] Moore, *Vulnerability and Security in Human Rights Literature and Visual Culture*, 33.
[75] Hanchard, 'Afro-Modernity: Temporality, Politics, and the African Diaspora', 280.
[76] Ibid., 284.
[77] Ibid., 259.

Theorising Waiting after Independence

In response to colonial regimes of time and history, which situated colonised subjects in prehistorical or ahistorical stages of history in comparison with their European others, anticolonial nationalist movements insisted with urgency that they ought not to wait any longer for self-rule. Dipesh Chakrabarty writes in *Provincializing Europe* that the classical liberalism deriving from John Stuart Mill's writings utilised a historicist sense of time – the historical time of development and civilisation – to argue that 'Indians or Africans were *not yet* civilized enough to rule themselves'.[78] This 'historicist consciousness', Chakrabarty summarises, was 'a recommendation to the colonized to wait. Acquiring a historical consciousness . . . was also to learn this art of waiting. This waiting was the realizing of the "not yet" for historicism'.[79] Anticolonial nationalisms in India rejected this 'waiting room' of history both by insisting on home rule now and by integrating the peasant as a citizen and 'full participant in the political life of the nation'.[80] Whereas the European narrative of modernity mandated that the 'primitive' colonial subject must wait to progress through stages of civilisation before integrating into world history as a modern political subject, the anticolonial response was predicated on an interruption of this historical chronology. In his gloss of twentieth-century anticolonial movements, Chakrabarty contrasts the 'not yet' of European discourse with the 'now' of anticolonial nationalism. While useful as a general heuristic, this opposition overlooks the persistent prevalence of waiting in anticolonial democratic movements and fiction around independence and after. In Chakrabarty's account, waiting is wholly negative and a process of deferral that reproduces a Eurocentric view of history by relegating (pre)colonial histories to a primitive past that the West has already experienced and surpassed. This waiting ends only when the steps of progress and development (a narrative written in the West's image) are followed. Yet the insistence on acceleration common to decolonisation discourse recapitulated to a model of Western modernisation,[81] what Chakrabarty characterises as

---

[78] Chakrabarty, *Provincializing Europe*, 8.
[79] Ibid., 8.
[80] Ibid., 9.
[81] By way of example, Richard Wright's *Black Power* recounts an exchange he had with a Ghanaian clerk on the eve of Ghana's independence: '"You American chaps are three hundred years ahead of these Africans. It'll take a long time for them to catch up with you. I think that they are trying to go too fast, don't *you*?"' Quoted

an 'uncritical emphasis on modernization'.[82] Implicating both waiting and refusing to wait, this discourse of modernisation abandons waiting as a temporality that could provide meaningful political resistance.

But waiting might also benefit from a reconsideration of its complexity as a concept that could create room to manoeuvre. The political possibilities of waiting are present in some of the earliest postcolonial writings, such as Homi Bhabha's description of the time lag produced through the temporality of waiting. Bhabha's 1991 reading of Frantz Fanon in '"Race," Time and the Revision of Modernity' describes this relationship between belatedness and postcolonial critiques of time. Bhabha writes that in addition to rejecting the belatedness of colonial regimes of time that place 'the Black man [in] . . . the past of which the white man is the future',[83] Fanon 'speaks from the signifying time-lag of cultural difference' that can posit 'another time, another space'.[84] Here, we see important precursors to Pheng Cheah's work; Bhahba asserts that through the time-lag, modernity contains within itself the conditions of contradiction: 'the project of modernity is itself rendered so contradictory and unresolved through the insertion of the "time-lag" in which colonial and postcolonial moments emerge as sign and history'.[85] In stressing the '*problem of the ambivalent temporality of modernity* that is often over looked in the more "spatial" traditions of some aspects of postmodern theory',[86] Bhabha, like Cheah after him, privileges time and sees his work correcting the dominant focus on space in postmodern, postcolonial, and world literature studies. Kara Keeling's own reading of Fanon shares with Bhabha an insistence that the temporal is integral to Fanon's *Black Skin, White Masks*; she observes that, 'metaphorically speaking, the black's cage is itself temporal: the past traumas of colonization and slavery continue to affect and shape the present at the expense of the black's future liberation'.[87] Drawing on David Marriott's reading of Fanon, Keeling usefully points out that Fanon described himself as '"one who waits"'.[88] Waiting is experienced as enduring in an interval;

---

in Hanchard, 'Afro-Modernity: Temporality, Politics, and the African Diaspora', 291.

[82] Chakrabarty, 'The Legacies of Bandung: Decolonization and the Politics of Culture', 53.
[83] Bhabha, '"Race", Time and the Revision of Modernity', 195.
[84] Ibid., 194.
[85] Ibid., 195.
[86] Ibid., 196.
[87] Keeling, *The Witch's Flight*, 35.
[88] Ibid., 36.

the 'time Fanon posits in the interval', Keeling argues, 'is open'.[89] Taken together, Bhabha, Fanon, Keeling and Chakrabarty make clear that the condition of waiting and the production of time lags illuminate structures of power that mediate the expectation of eventual fulfilment, or the arrival of that for which one waits – and also foster new temporal modalities that can help us to imagine Fanon's 'another time, another space'.[90]

The Temporal Dimensions of Waiting

Fictional representations of the temporal dimensions of waiting are not disconnected from lived experiences of time; in both cases, waiting is expressed through narrative. Philosopher David Carr argues that narrative plays an essential structuring role in our experience of time and historicity. Carr demonstrates that the past, present and future are not clearly demarcated and exclusive temporal conditions. Carr's term 'field of occurrence' helps to situate the 'present' within the horizons of past and future together.[91] Additionally, the future is connected directly with the present insofar as actions now are intended make manifest a particular future, which makes the future 'something *to be brought about by* the action in which I am engaged . . . it *is* what I am doing'.[92] The retention-protension mechanism that stretches back in time and reaches forward to the future in order to structure experience 'constitutes a *closure* which articulates time by separating the given temporal configuration (action or event) from what goes before and after'.[93] Narratives that play with time in the representation of history or characters' experiences do not automatically forfeit claims to depicting various realities; fiction's proleptic and analeptic narrative devices are, in a sense, faithful to the way people structure their experience of time and history. Whether narrative hopelessly distorts or is faithful to experience is at

---

[89] Ibid., 38.
[90] Many of the theorists on time, history and affect that have influenced my reading of waiting are indebted to Walter Benjamin's conceptualization of time and history. In 'Theses on the Philosophy of History', Benjamin 'posits the subversive significance of conceptualizing a "present which is not a transition, but in which time stands still and has come to a stop"'. Quoted in Laski, *Untimely Democracy*, 15. I want to note here Benjamin's direct influence on my interlocutors and his indirect influence on this book as well.
[91] Carr, *Time, Narrative, and History*, 23.
[92] Ibid., 34.
[93] Ibid., 41.

the centre of disagreement between early theorists like Frank Kermode and Paul Ricoeur and later philosophers like Carr. Kermode argues that time is perceived through a sense of duration 'only when it is organized', and this organisation is imposed by the perceiver as 'fictions' necessary to impose a sense of ending, organisation, and form on time.[94] Writing decades later, Carr revises Kermode, pointing out that there is a mistake in calling the organisation of time 'fictional' and opposing it to 'mere sequence'.[95] By foregrounding narrative, fiction is uniquely situated to engage with imagination and 'reality'. Even when characters and plot are total products of the imagination, narrative's temporal sequencing and attendant tensions between stability and insufficiency, success and failure, reveal much about the world in which we live as well as the ways in which we might change it.

In order to evaluate and schematise the active and passive dimensions of waiting, we must first give an account of how individuals conceive of and orient themselves in time more generally. Differences between how time is measured and experienced highlight the distinction between time and temporality, terms that philosopher David Couzens Hoy carefully separates. An analysis of the nature of time would present 'a complex array of issues about the status of what could be called "scientific" or "objective" or "universal" time, that is to say, the "time of the universe."'[96] Temporality, on the other hand, is 'time insofar as it manifests itself in human existence.'[97] That is not to say that temporality is less real, or merely subjective. As Hoy clarifies, temporality 'seems equally objective and subjective', because the sensation that time is passing 'faster or slower is subjective, yet nevertheless it is generally acknowledged that the flow is objectively happening'.[98] As we will see in the fictional case studies analysed in the subsequent chapters, a temporality of waiting can be exacerbated by the friction of time passing differentially for the waiting subject and external markers of time, such as clocks and calendars. The temporality of waiting is shaped by the sensations and impressions of time passing, as well as the subjective experience of being oriented in time.

This insistence that temporality is not any less real than time is particularly important for analysing the temporality of waiting in postcolonial contexts. As studies of time and colonial power have revealed,

---

[94] Kermode, *The Sense of an Ending*, 45.
[95] Carr, *Time, Narrative, and History*, 25.
[96] Hoy, *The Time of Our Lives*, xii.
[97] Ibid., xiii.
[98] Ibid., xv.

the powerful discourse of mathematical and scientific time as objective and universal encouraged the degradation of other ways of marking and experiencing time. After Greenwich Mean Time was established, demarcating time zones as resonating from the European centre, 'social temporality' – that is, time

> embedded . . . within a social community, produced by and inseparable from a grid of contextually determined variables . . . [was] degraded to a second-order reality, while the abstract, neutral, universal constant of Greenwich-based time [was] projected as an immutable law, a truth of Nature discovered by science and independent of various judgments, needs, and activities of the communities forced to restructure themselves according to its image and dictates.[99]

Attending to the temporality of waiting as it is expressed in postcolonial fiction cannot undo this epistemic violence; nevertheless, I aim to recuperate the value of temporality as a means of structuring social relationships and reality alike.

Though the temporal dimensions of waiting may be mobilised to create strategic delay through effecting belatedness, waiting as it is commonly understood instantiates a power differential that places the waiting subject in a position of deference. Thus, while a notion of waiting as a productive suspension of linear time opens up the narrative of historicism and gestures towards how events might have happened otherwise, waiting's temporal dimensions may also oppressively defer or postpone. In this configuration, waiting is a temporal relation associated with 'boredom or "discontent" in the sense used by Hegel . . . a dissatisfaction with the present that implies the negation of the present and the propensity to work towards its supersession'.[100] This dimension of waiting privileges the future in such a way that not only diminishes the present and past, but also sets the present in opposition as an obstacle to be overcome as quickly as possible. In this way, the passage of time is more acute and frustrating for the waiting subject, for whom time moves too slowly.[101] Waiting, then, affects one's sense of duration through the lack of desired event or activity; time passes at a loss, yielding a sense of time that is antagonistic and paralysing for someone who feels helpless to actualise the desired future.

As Harold Schweizer describes in his book, *On Waiting*, those who wait 'find themselves in an exemplary existential predicament, having

---

[99] Barrows, *The Cosmic Time of Empire*, 30.
[100] Bourdieu, *Pascalian Meditations*, 209.
[101] Ibid., 224.

time without wanting it'.[102] Waiting has a positive polarity when experienced as an expectant state of anticipation or longing, but a negative polarity when experienced as awaiting something dreaded or uncertain.[103] One way to catalogue the state of waiting in relation to these temporal variables and constraints is illustrated in Table I.1 below.

Table I.1 is not an exhaustive representation of all the possible ways that one may wait. At the same time, the table usefully underscores the fact that the experience of waiting exists on a spectrum influenced by the interaction of a multitude of variables, including whether outcomes are apprehended as predictable and whether the duration of the wait is believed to be temporary or permanent. The table yields one further insight about the experience of waiting and time; waiting as described in both (1) and (4) may manifest in practice as 'patience', where the waiting is endured more easily because of the combinations of desire and certitude, dread and uncertainty. In both (2) and (3), the waiting may produce 'impatience', where waiting is experienced as prolonging unnecessarily what is certain to occur but undesired, or what is desired but may not necessarily come to pass. The repetition of the word 'may' in the preceding analyses of the table is suggestive of other variables that can affect the experience of waiting. For example, a waiting subject may be more willing or able to wait for longer durations if certain that a desirable event will occur, but this schema does not take into account whether she can, literally, afford to wait.

If we return briefly to the figures of Quayson's gymmers, we can see how waiting might express dejection or disillusionment with current political or economic conditions, but it might also be the operative temporality to produce a politically charged refusal to work in an economy that withholds security and stability. Kathi Weeks posits that refusing to work, as both 'analysis and strategy', critiques 'the organization and social value of work' and thus 'can make time and open spaces – both physical and conceptual – within which to construct alternatives'.[104] Javier Auyero's *Patients of the State*, a study of waiting in Argentina, reveals that waiting works in both capacities, on the part of ordinary citizens as well as the Argentinian state. On the one hand, Auyero understands 'acts of waiting . . . as *temporal processes in and through which political subordination is reproduced*', as Argentinians are reminded of their disempowerment and begin to view waiting as their eternal

---

[102] Schweizer, *On Waiting*, 2.
[103] Hook, 'Indefinite Delay: On (Post)Apartheid Temporality', 54.
[104] Weeks, *The Problem with Work*, 99–100.

Table I.1: Temporal Variables and Constraints of Waiting

	Shorter Duration	Longer Duration
1. Excitement/ anticipation with belief of certain outcome	Easier to wait; waiting is mitigated by hope and belief that the duration of the wait will be temporary or short	Easier to wait; longer duration is offset by certainty; more likely to invest in waiting
2. Dread, with belief of certain outcome	Waiting is anxious, but shorter wait allows for the 'known' future to manifest and be dealt with faster	Waiting is more anxious; duration heightens anxiety and makes waiting more difficult
3. Excitement and/or anticipation with uncertainty about outcome	Waiting for a short time is welcomed; ending waiting is desirable; waiting is not valued	Potential for anticipation to be reduced by the duration of the wait; it is not clear that the waiting will pay off
4. Dread, with uncertainty about outcome	While waiting is anxious, the end of waiting is not necessarily desired because waiting could postpone the undesired outcome	Waiting is anxious, but slightly desirable; the longer the wait, the greater the impression that the undesired outcome might not occur

temporal condition.[105] Through queues, wait lists and unpredictable bureaucracy, their subordinate positions are reinforced through the 'uncertainty and the arbitrariness that is already present in poor people's daily lives'.[106] The queue, or waiting line, is an exemplary site to observe the complicated power dynamics intertwined in the temporal experience of waiting. The more powerful one is, for example, the less likely one is to wait; the powerful who 'have the resources to refuse to wait . . . can often afford to go elsewhere for faster service or cause others, such as servants or employees, to wait in their places'.[107] Additionally, servers can become more powerful to the extent that clients wait for them.[108] As a corollary, one 'can maintain and dramatize his worth by purposely causing another to wait'.[109] At the same time, Auyero recognises that

---

[105] Auyero, *Patients of the State*, 2.
[106] Ibid., 20.
[107] Schwartz, 'Waiting, Exchange, and Power: The Distribution of Time in Social Systems', 849.
[108] Ibid., 857.
[109] Ibid., 859.

waiting is not simply a description of the powerful leveraging their dominance over the powerless, nor is it merely 'a negative practice that tells people it is not yet their turn'.[110] Auyero asserts that waiting 'ceases to be "dead time"', and 'reveals acts of cognition that are, simultaneously, acts of recognition of the established political order'.[111] While state policies and a larger geopolitical and economic context certainly produce the temporal experience of waiting, this waiting can be a transformative experience through which the waiting subject gains a deeper understanding of the mechanisms of power and the inequities built into the prevailing political order.

The temporality of waiting is thus intimately tied to power: the power to fulfil and satisfy, the power to negotiate, and the power to withhold. 'Waiting', Pierre Bourdieu writes in *Pascalian Meditations*,

> is one of the privileged ways of experiencing the effect of power, and the link between time and power . . . both on the side of the powerful (adjourning, deferring, delaying, raising false hopes, or, conversely, rushing, taking by surprise) and on the side of the 'patient', as they say in the medical universe, one of the sites par excellence of anxious, powerless waiting.[112]

Bourdieu points to how the temporality of waiting is fundamentally a shared temporality between people who wait as well as the thing, event, person or abstract future they wait for. To study waiting is to study the construction, manipulation and effects of power, making the ubiquity of waiting in postcolonial fiction especially significant. But where I depart from Bourdieu's theorisation of waiting is his assertion that waiting 'implies submission' and that a person can 'be made to wait, hope, etc . . . only to the extent that he is invested' in that which he desires.[113] Indeed, the critical attention that temporalities of waiting as cultural practices have begun to receive indicate that waiting indexes power differentials with more nuance than the powerful/powerless schema Bourdieu references. A panoply of variables condition the experience of waiting, including certainty, anxiety, hope, fear, duration, class, gender and education among others. Given these variables, we can conclude with Auyero that 'waiting is stratified, and there are variations in waiting time that are socially patterned and responsive to power differentials'.[114] While the recent proliferation of ethnographic research on

---

[110] Auyero, *Patients of the State*, 8.
[111] Ibid., 9.
[112] Bourdieu, *Pascalian Meditations*, 228.
[113] Ibid., 228, 231.
[114] Auyero, *Patients of the State*, 27.

waiting and the Global South might suggest that 'waiting' is a newly legible, temporal experience, the fictional texts under review in this book affirm that 'waiting' has a much longer history as part of colonial and postcolonial discourses alike.

Waiting for 'Now': Chapter Summaries

The rest of this study examines the temporal dimensions of waiting in postcolonial fiction, assessing how waiting engages and conflicts with, as well as responds to, colonial regimes of time, and interacts with the rhetoric of anticolonial nationalist movements, colonial discourses of idleness, widespread disillusionment after independence, and the temporalities of reconciliation undergirding Truth and Reconciliation Commissions. Temporalities of waiting refract power dynamics – they do not simply reflect them. Waiting, I contend, is a temporality of tension and struggle, not simply dispossession. In Chapter 1, I establish that waiting is both characteristic of colonial time regimes' exertion of power and control, and in Chapter 2 I identify waiting as a temporality that indexes the contradictions and inherent weaknesses of colonial power. In later postcolonial works, the dimensions of waiting expand; beginning with Chapter 3, I show how waiting enacts resistance when mobilised as part of a programme of delay or the politics of slowness. In Chapter 4, I demonstrate that recalcitrant waiting may also figure as trenchant political critique, against the disillusionment politics of postcolonial nation-states. An extension of critique and resistance, Chapter 5 suggests that the temporalities of waiting, through quietude and reflection, produce time to heal communities through resistance to premature closure. While these various dimensions of waiting may certainly appear in a range of contexts, times and places, the temporalities of waiting as I theorise them in this book emerge out of and in tandem with colonial violence. Waiting here is a particular temporality exhibited within postcolonial texts in dialogue with colonial regimes of time (along with, as we will see in Chapter 1, other ways of marking and living time). Waiting is not dead time but rather, as it emerges in postcolonial fiction and in the chapters that follow, a rich, creative temporal modality that embeds both duress and resilience.

Postcolonial novels, I argue, exceptionally foreground time, history and narrative practices. As Elleke Boehmer argues,

> the postcolonial novel, play, or poem might be understood as itself an alternative mode of seizing hold upon the now, upon the right to define *this moment*,

although a seizing-hold that, importantly, does not involve a negation of the future.[115]

It is not simply that the novels are 'of' their time, or rewrite histories of colonial violence, but also that they are a form of temporal projection that can 'restore temporal depth, a sense of the deep layering or thickness of history ... by narrating simply yet powerfully what it is to project and seize hold in these ways'.[116] I have chosen novels to ground this study because I have found, following Edward Said, the novel to be 'immensely important in the formation of imperial attitudes, references, and experiences'.[117] The novel too has occupied a special place in relation to the imagination of nations and communities; in different ways, both the newspaper and the novel, Benedict Anderson famously argues, 'provided the technical means for "re-presenting" the kind of imagined community that is the nation'.[118] Though Anderson is primarily concerned with how the novel form consolidated communities through a sense of simultaneity and horizontal comradeship, the postcolonial novels discussed in the following chapters illuminate the corollary power to exclude. Given, too, that the 'birth of the novel coincided with the European colonial project', and that I aim to expose the temporal dimensions of waiting across the colonial and postcolonial divide, postcolonial novels are an apposite form to begin this examination.[119] I anticipate that further research on other forms, with their own characteristic narrative strategies – short stories, poems, film, drama – could be fruitfully explored through the analytic of 'waiting' as well.

By pulling together texts from diverse times and places, I contend that texts may speak from their particular histories and locations, but they also speak to the larger world. The implications of tracking waiting in subsequent postcolonial novels are threefold. First, this thematic concept revises dominant narratives of anticolonial nationalism – movements that are characterised by 'refusals to wait' – by opening up alternative and competing temporalities for both the characters and the nation they inhabit. Second, the methodology of pairing novels from different geographical locations, authors and times reveals unexpected correspondences across postcolonial novels through their shared investments in

---

[115] Boehmer, 'Postcolonial Writing and Terror', 148.
[116] Ibid., 149.
[117] Said, *Culture and Imperialism*, xii.
[118] Anderson, *Imagined Communities*, 24.
[119] Azim, *The Colonial Rise of the Novel*, 30.

waiting as a temporal mode, yet their contrasts underscore the ways that specific historical and cultural contexts condition the experience of waiting. As the anthropologist Julie Peteet argues, comparison 'opens . . . new ways of conceptualizing and critiquing standard formulations of exceptionalism'. [120] Peteet acknowledges the real differences between the histories, geographies and peoples of the two places under comparison; however, her point is that a comparative framework can accommodate 'both specificity and uniqueness', and that 'pinpointing difference does not invalidate comparison as a method of inquiry'.[121] In short, comparison highlights contrasts (exemplified in Chapters 2 and 4), shows surprising similarities (Chapter 1 and 5), enables extension (Chapter 3), expands generic categories within postcolonial literary studies beyond national settings (Chapter 4), and de-centres certain national literary traditions from their staid positions within postcolonial scholarship. Here, I have in mind interventions offered across the book's chapters: the prominence of South African literature for affect studies and TRCs; the Ghanaian writer Ayi Kwei Armah's role as quintessential 'disillusionment' fiction writer; Anita Desai's *Cry, the Peacock* as a domestic (rather than politically engaged) psychological thriller; or *Heart of Darkness* as simply interested in representing the denial of coevalness between Marlow and his African counterparts through tropes of prehistoric time. The comparative model might, to some readers, inadvertently suggest a polarity of waiting as either oppressive or liberating; what we will see through juxtaposition is that the political possibilities of waiting – from disempowerment to active resistance – exist not only on a continuum, but also simultaneously and affected by the variables described in Table I.1.

In other words, the methodology is part of the book's argument: that these texts which heretofore have not been brought into direct conversation with one another, in dialogue and contrast yield a finer understanding of waiting in postcolonial fiction, its dimensions and implications. Departing from Saikat Majumdar's important study on boredom in

---

[120] Peteet, 'The Work of Comparison: Israel/Palestine and Apartheid', 249.
[121] Ibid., 254. On this point, Natalie Melas's justification for comparative methods in *All the Difference in the World: Postcoloniality and the Ends of Comparison* (2007) has influenced this project here as well. Like *Postcolonial Fiction and Colonial Time*, the texts Melas selects 'hail from diverse traditions', motivated by her desire 'to bring them into relation over a ground of comparison that is in common but not unified' (43).

Anglophone novels,[122] I argue that waiting emerges in texts in ways that exceed boredom; this is what a comparative study, motivated by the various ways that waiting appears in postcolonial fiction, can uniquely offer. In turn, the work of comparison inadvertently bolsters the utility of the postcolonial framework itself amid challenges by other organising categories, such as the 'global Anglophone' or 'transnational'. While many of the literary texts under investigation in this book are Anglophone, I have intentionally included several works in translation (*El reino de este mundo* and *L'Aventure ambiguë*) as well as others whose contexts and settings interact with empires that range from the Belgian, the French and the Tukulor/Toucouleur, and regimes of white supremacy like South Africa's Apartheid government. These diverse geographies have unique colonial histories to be sure, and can be loosely captured by the rubric 'postcolonial', but importantly and again in contrast to Majumdar's study, this book is not restricted to the former colonies of the British Empire. Moreover, the diachronic approach of juxtaposing novels across colonial/postcolonial divides offers the opportunity to imagine or to identify new temporal horizons, wherein neither the 'colonial' nor the 'postcolonial' emerges as unproblematically linear conceptions. Third and finally, examining waiting as manifested in these novels illuminates the contradictory temporalities that underlie narratives of progress, modernisation, and development. Contrary to the widespread association of waiting with passivity or powerlessness, waiting can become an active strategy of resistance in the face of pressures to develop and to modernise in the West's image.

South African literature and cultural studies has proven to be an important location for the articulation of the temporality of waiting. This accounts for the prominence of South African texts in this book, but the comparative methodology I use allows me to widen the scope of 'waiting' beyond this national context and, in the process, see the temporalities of waiting in South African fiction anew through a comparative lens. The increased critical attention to waiting in African studies more broadly – across literature, history, anthropology, and cultural studies – also influences my selection of texts and the book's partial focus on the African continent. For example, in my juxtaposition of a South African novel and a Sierra Leonean novel in Chapter 5, I intend to show their distinctive engagements with strategies of waiting during processes of reconciliation. Despite settings on the African continent, I want to suggest that a 'global' or 'postcolonial' analysis can emerge

---

[122] Majumdar, *Prose of the World*.

through the juxtaposition of two African novels just as it might between a South African and Caribbean text, or an Indian and Ghanaian one.[123]

Chapter 1 anchors my discussion of waiting and colonial time in two novels: Joseph Conrad's 1899 *Heart of Darkness* and Cheikh Hamidou Kane's 1962 novel *Ambiguous Adventure* (*L'Aventure ambiguë*). I turn to *Heart of Darkness* first in order to locate the temporality of waiting in the colonial context, creating a genealogy for 'waiting' that extends from the turn of the twentieth-century to the present day. Given its canonical status in world literature, Conrad's novel has been fertile ground for discussions of European imperialism, racism, and representations of history and time. The novel is also remarkable for its early mobilisation of waiting to register the ambivalences of temporal difference and conflict that, in my view, become implicit in critiques of colonialism and later postcolonial theory. *Heart of Darkness* foregrounds the complex relationship between waiting and dominant and alternative temporalities, which are not necessarily in strict opposition. *Ambiguous Adventure*, on the other hand, is a disaffected bildungsroman, set in Senegal after World War II and as French colonial rule is beginning to set. *Ambiguous Adventure* reverses the Conradian journey to the heart of Africa, as the protagonist Samba travels from Senegal to Paris, where he experiences acute alienation from the traditions and religion of his childhood. My interest in putting these two novels into dialogue relies less on the ways that *Ambiguous Adventure* reverses the colonial gaze, but rather in how the novel complicates our discussions of colonial time. I aim to theorise a more expansive view of the social life of time and 'colonial' time specifically in Kane's *Ambiguous Adventure* by examining the various syncopations and dissonances produced by Islamic temporalities, modernisation discourses, and precolonial cosmologies, which I contend are all activated in the novel's timescape.

Chapter 2 then pairs two novels with intertextual relationships to *Heart of Darkness*: V.S. Naipaul's 1979 *A Bend in the River* and Nadine Gordimer's 1981 *July's People*, and argues that these authors' constructions of 'waiting rooms of history' in the interior of Africa are designed to achieve very different ends. I re-evaluate the 'waiting rooms of history' model and its relationship to independence by drawing on

---

[123] In the background here is Stephen Clingman's reading of transnational fiction, which locates the transnational first in the form of a text, which in turn informs the content to produce a transnational 'way of being and seeing'. In this way, novels typically characterized by their nationalist concerns evince transnational characteristics: Nadine Gordimer's *July's People* as well as Salman Rushdie's *Midnight's Children*. Clingman, *The Grammar of Identity*, 10.

the work of Uday Mehta. I then turn to Naipaul's fiction, and assess his rendering of the eponymous bend in the river as a waiting room for Salim and other African citizens of Indian descent where, notwithstanding political independence, 'not yet' will never become 'now'. With reference to Vincent Crapanzano's *Waiting: The Whites of South Africa*, I conclude that Gordimer's novel depicts a different kind of 'waiting room', where the spatiotemporal experience of moving to July's Village disrupts Maureen's relationship to time and its lived patterns. The temporal modality of waiting encourages Maureen to re-evaluate herself in relation to others (her own family, as well as July's), and her final refusal to wait embraces the uncertainty of her position in the new dispensation to come.

The midpoint of the book shifts to consider the subversive potential of inhabiting temporalities of waiting intentionally. Chapter 3 analyses the Cuban writer Alejo Carpentier's 1949 novel depicting the Haitian Revolution, *The Kingdom of This World* (*El reino de este mundo*), and argues for the importance of maroons to the narrative's theme and structure. Maroons were escaped slaves who fled to the hills, and I argue the maroon's separateness or withdrawal – the insistence on spatial difference – produces a sense of time and history antagonistic to the colonial state. I then read South African author J.M. Coetzee's 1983 novel *Life & Times of Michael K* through the lens of marronage, identifying idleness as a strategy of resistance. The lens of marronage permits a reading of their protagonists' flight, labour, and 'idleness' as newly legible dimensions of resistive waiting.

Chapter 4 studies the temporal dimensions of waiting in postcolonial novels of disillusionment. Drawing on the concept of timescapes as a way to capture the interplay between different temporalities and temporal modes in the text, I read Ayi Kwei Armah's 1970 novel *Fragments* and Anita Desai's 1963 novel *Cry, the Peacock* for their representations of waiting in relation to patience and urgency. While any explicit discussion of gender has been absent from timescape scholarship, the novels themselves emphasise their imbrication – especially in regard to representing patience and urgency – which have been traditionally coded as feminine and masculine respectively. Because I am interested in the genre of disillusionment novels in this chapter – a term that emerges from studies of African fiction – I pair *Fragments*, a novel that is uncontroversially 'disillusioned', with *Cry, the Peacock* in order to apply pressure to the concept. Whereas African fiction transitions from utopian nationalist texts to disillusioned ones during the 1960s and 1970s, in the Indian literary tradition, the trauma of Partition effectively inaugurated disenchantment concurrently with independence. The reinscription of masculine national identity in these postcolonial settings after independence creates additional tensions for the women in the novels, and their embodied dramatisations of patience and urgency disrupt the dominant narrative of disillusionment and its attendant, underlying association of waiting with passivity and femininity.

Chapter 5 examines Njabulo Ndebele's 2003 *The Cry of Winnie Mandela* and Ishmael Beah's 2014 *Radiance of Tomorrow* in order to assess what I call 'strategic waiting' as a temporal modality that can be productively inhabited in service of reconciliation. The novels, set in South Africa and Sierra Leone respectively, were published after Truth and Reconciliation Commissions (TRCs) in both countries reported their findings. Although neither novel suggests that waiting should be inhabited indefinitely, both depict important community-building work being accomplished while characters wait. Ndebele's novel is structured like a waiting room, where ordinary women discuss their personal histories of waiting until they are ready to embark together on a journey out of the unspecified present moment and into the future. Likewise, the elders of *Radiance of Tomorrow* wait as they rebuild, and waiting produces time to heal even as it facilitates reconciliation through small, deliberate silences.

Beah's *Radiance of Tomorrow* extends the study of waiting and postcolonial fiction to the twenty-first century and the challenges that confront a world that is still decolonising. In the conclusion, I reflect on the significance of waiting in the post-9/11 world, such as in the rhetoric of pre-emptive military strikes that frame national security in terms of refusing to wait. Those in power have certainly leveraged waiting as a temporality of oppression and deferral, but as I will demonstrate throughout this study, waiting can also be actively engaged to disrupt the imperatives of colonial regimes of time. By arguing for the centrality of waiting to the experience of postcoloniality, this book challenges the dominant narrative of the twentieth century as a time only of acceleration. Waiting, I argue, is not only prevalent in the discourses of colonial administration and anticolonial nationalisms, but also deployed in strategic and political expressions of resistance and remains central to the formation of geopolitical realities. In this way, *Postcolonial Fiction and Colonial Time* expands that scope of what waiting signifies in postcolonial fiction, including its power to signal unwillingness to cede the premises of colonial regimes of time (with their 'wait your turn' administrative logic), its positioning of colonial subjects as either timeless or pre-modern, and its temporal violence of imposing regimes not only of measuring but also of valuing time. The disciplining power of waiting was intended to transform colonial subjects into (eventual, though postponed indefinitely) 'modern' subjects, yet in practice waiting signified far in excess of its meaning in colonial regimes of time. It is this excess that this book aims to describe and account.

In tracking the ambivalence of the temporality of waiting in fiction across the postcolonial world, *Postcolonial Fiction and Colonial Time* offers correctives to postcolonial theories of time that focus narrowly on the implications of the 'post', or the endurance of the past in the colonial aftermath. The temporalities of waiting as elucidated here accentuate the richness of the present as well, particularly the overlaying of past hopes, present historicising, and future aspirations and desires that are embedded in portrayals of postcolonial waiting. The dimensions of waiting elucidated in this book reinvigorate waiting as a modality that can be in turns debilitating, depressing, strategic, calculating and meditative. My intention is not to valorise waiting, nor to celebrate it prescriptively as a practice. The book's title evokes the tensions of waiting's temporal dimensions, especially in the context of postcolonial contestations over time, power and self-determination. On the one hand, given the appearance of belatedness or deferral, especially with regard to under- or unemployment in the global economy, waiting subjects are still waiting for 'now' – when preoccupations with an imagined future become a reality in the present. On the other hand, waiting for now also captures the strategic use of waiting as a temporal modality inhabited for the time being, and the dimensions of being in the midst of time; that is, a sense of waiting for now, but not for always.[124]

---

[124] As the rest of the book will demonstrate, this 'now' is not reducible to the present. Here, Andrew van der Vlies's reading of Benjamin's sense of the now re-inflects the 'now' with its radical potential: 'Now-time . . . is for Benjamin consequently *not* the present . . . The historical materialist "stops telling" the sequence of events like a rosary and is committed instead to revivifying the utopian possibilities of the past from a point in the present structured by disappointment and anticipation.' *Present Imperfect: Contemporary South African Writing*, 7.

Chapter 1

Waiting at the Heart of Colonial Time Regimes

> The *Nellie*, a cruising yawl, swung to her anchor without a flutter of the sails, and was at rest. The flood had made, the wind was nearly calm, and being bound down the river, the only thing for it was to come to and wait for the turn of the tide.
>
> Joseph Conrad, Heart of Darkness (1899)

Heart of Darkness opens with an image of stillness: The *Nellie* is anchored, the sails are stationary, and the crew mirrors the ship's immobility as they rest at ease on the deck. Barges are 'drifting up with the tide', but despite this ostensible movement, the narrator remarks that the 'tanned sails . . . stand still' – unsurprising given that the air, 'condensed into a mournful gloom', is 'brooding motionless' over the city of London.[1] Caught in this stillness, the narrator remarks, the only option is to wait for the tide to turn.

Heart of Darkness thus begins by evoking waiting, and this waiting is the impetus for Marlow's tale, which comprises the rest of the text. The framing narrator explicitly makes the connection between storytelling and waiting. After Marlow remarks, '"The conquest of the earth, which mostly means the taking it away from those who have a different complexion or slightly flatter noses than ourselves, is not a pretty thing when you look into it too much"', the narrator observes, 'We looked on, waiting patiently – there was nothing else to do till the end of the flood.'[2] The period of waiting is a time of forced contemplation for Marlow and his listeners as Marlow's recollections oblige them to look into the darkness of colonial conquest and exploitation. The waiting begins while '[t]he day was ending in a serenity of still and exquisite brilliance',[3]

---

[1] Conrad, *Heart of Darkness and Other Tales*, 99.
[2] Ibid., 103.
[3] Ibid., 100.

at twilight – a time of day that will becoming increasingly important over the course of this chapter. During the wait, as light and dark intermingle into an inseparable gloom, Marlow reflects on the 'very old times, when the Romans first came here, nineteen hundred years ago – the other day', strikingly evoking a paradoxically elongated and compressed sense of time.[4] The suspension of day and night, mirroring the suspension of the tide and the suspension of time during their waiting, prompts Marlow to reflect that with a long view of time and history, it seems as though the 'darkness was here yesterday'.[5]

While the repetition of various words – darkness, whiteness, haze, light, voice, ivory – in the novel has not gone unnoticed, the repetition and significance of 'waiting' throughout the text has.[6] When critics have turned their attention to issues of time and representation in Conrad's fiction, they have emphasised Conrad's historical context, pointing to new theories about time and experience circulating at the turn of the twentieth century and contrasting human-centred temporality with 'objective' and mechanical time. J. A. Bernstein's 2012 article in *The Conradian*, for example, pairs Conrad with the philosophy of J. M. E. McTaggart, whose 1908 article 'The Unreality of Time' argued that time is ideal rather than a physical fact of the universe. McTaggart demonstrated that a paradox exists between what he designates as the A and B series of time, corresponding respectively to the perspective of a fixed observer and an absolute series of events arranged for all.[7] Bernstein concludes that Conrad 'wrestles with the questions of temporality by conferring an uncertain status on his narrative', allowing 'the reader to share . . . in the very dilemmas of chronologic uncertainty – a theme that very much reflects the debates of Conrad's day'.[8] John G. Peters broadens the discussions of Conrad and time, surveying Conrad's oeuvre and arguing that his characters in general 'experience difficulties precisely when they forget or fail to realize that mechanical time is merely a convenience, not an absolute measurement of time'.[9] In all of these accounts, the narrative

---

[4] Ibid., 101.
[5] Ibid., 101.
[6] F. R. Leavis famously faults the novel for being 'marred' by repeated 'adjectival insistence', *The Great Tradition*, 174.
[7] Bernstein, '"No audible tick": Conrad, McTaggart, and the Revolt against Time', 32–3.
[8] Ibid., 44. *The Secret Agent* is the focus of the Conrad portion of Bernstein's discussion; the novel is perhaps Conrad's most explicit in its attention to time and politics, as the plot concerns an attempt to blow up the Greenwich Observatory.
[9] Peters, 'Joseph Conrad's "Sudden Holes" in Time: The Epistemology of Temporality', 436.

time evoked in Conrad's work is opposed to mathematical or physical time.[10]

But, as I argue in this chapter, *Heart of Darkness* expresses a temporality of waiting that blurs such strict distinctions between human-centred and mathematical, linear time. As we will see, waiting is Marlow's dominant temporal experience in the interior of Africa. In their descriptions of waiting, Conrad's characters refer implicitly to a sense of time passing or moving forward independently of their own temporal experiences, but the frequent references to waiting emphasise the effect of time on the characters and their subsequent shaping of the past and future in an uncertain and ominous present. Throughout Marlow's framed narrative, his experience as well as those of his African counterparts in the Congo are described in terms of waiting. The text's use of what Ian Watt famously called 'delayed decoding' in Marlow's storytelling – combining 'the forward temporal progression of the mind, as it receives messages from the outside world, with the much slower reflexive process of making out their meaning'[11] – in effect reproduces for the reader the sensations of waiting Marlow experienced in the Congo. Though waiting is instrumental to the function of colonial time regimes, the temporalities of waiting in *Heart of Darkness* also produce temporal ambiguities and unruliness with the potential to undermine the hegemony of colonial time regimes themselves.

The second half of this chapter discusses Chiekh Hamidou Kane's 1962 novel *Ambiguous Adventure* (*L'Aventure ambiguë*), to which I dedicate more space, given that it is under-studied in comparison with *Heart of Darkness*. The two novels share a journey between the African continent and Europe, a protagonist in search of himself, and the unruly temporalities of waiting that trouble *Ambiguous Adventure*'s ostensible *bildungsroman* form. Whereas Samba initially begins to come of age at the Golden Hearth, the Koranic school, his studies are concluded prematurely and he is sent to the foreign school, and eventually to Europe. Both texts mobilise motifs of lightness and darkness, and while *Ambiguous Adventure* has often been read as a novel that straddles tradition and modernity, I argue that, just as *Heart of Darkness* subtly evokes a *longue durée* of time and history, so too does *Ambiguous Adventure*, and this

---

[10] This opposition in Conrad scholarship can be traced back to J. M. Kertzer's 1979 'Joseph Conrad and the Metaphysics of Time', which traces a temporal spectrum in Conrad's work that ranges from, 'on the one hand, the temporal, coherent, full, and meaningful; and on the other hand, the timeless, empty, and archaic'. Kertzer, 316.

[11] Watt, *Conrad in the Nineteenth Century*, 175.

long view decentres the strict focus on European colonisation that has dominated prior readings of the text. Fernand Braudel's *longue durée* deemphasised 'events' in favour of a 'wide-scale view of environmental, socioeconomic, and cultural forces combining to define the history of a region and its relationship to other regions'.[12] Waiting, too, might appear emptied of events, yet the Introduction to this book already shows its potential richness as a temporality of negotiation. More than just an expansion of already existing temporal periods, the *longue durée* is 'a scale of history with its own rhythm that intermingled and combined with the short and medium term'.[13]

This chapter aims to articulate the richness and depth of colonial time regimes through a *longue durée* view; the novels present a view of colonial regimes of time that is complex, heterogeneous, and marked by both waiting, acceleration and delays. As I argued in the Introduction, recent scholarship on time and empire certainly acknowledges the heterogeneity of temporalities in colonised spaces. Despite these insights, colonial and independence-era narratives are often read in terms of their investments in either 'modern' or 'traditional' temporalities, where colonial time stands in for European time-consciousness foreign to equally homogeneous ways of life prior to colonisation. A *longue durée* view, one that is trans-temporal, transnational and attentive to relationships that change over time, can upset 'the story of modernity as an invention of the West'[14] and pushes the boundaries of 'existing analytic categories of space (region, nation, empire) and time (periods, centuries, decades)'.[15] This chapter, through the juxtaposition of *Heart of Darkness* with *Ambiguous Adventure* and with a focus on the temporalities of waiting in colonial regimes of time in the *longue durée*, offers a new way of understanding the temporal politics of the texts and their respective historical moments.

Waiting in Conrad's Congo

The association of the centre of Africa with the temporality of waiting in *Heart of Darkness* begins subtly, in a waiting room within the Company offices. Two women knitting with black wool greet Marlow before he is ushered into the waiting room, whose wall is decorated with the colonial

---

[12] Friedman, *Planetary Modernisms*, 94.
[13] Sawyer, 'Time after Time: Narratives of the Longue Durée in the Anthropocene', 7.
[14] Friedman, *Planetary Modernisms*, 98.
[15] Gillman, 'Oceans of Longues Durées', 329.

map of Africa. Here, while waiting for his examination, he remarks that he will travel to the yellow area, 'Dead in the center', where the Congo River slithered 'fascinating – deadly – like a snake'.[16] Marlow's examination takes all of forty-five seconds, and again Marlow is escorted back into the same waiting room, where he begins 'to feel slightly uneasy' and blames 'something ominous in the atmosphere'.[17] In the midst of this apprehension, Marlow's gaze returns to the knitting women, whom he imagines to be 'guarding the door of Darkness.'[18] Marlow perceives the door of darkness and the door to the waiting room to be one and the same. The waiting room, whose temporality is embedded in its name, functions as a mediating space between lightness and darkness, and Marlow's unemployment and enlistment in the Company. Marlow passes through the waiting room twice, on his way in and out of the interior Company office, and it is only after he has signed the papers that the waiting room takes on an ominous and fateful aura. On the first walk through the waiting room, Marlow follows one of the knitting women, who he notes continues to knit her black wool as she walks. After the second walk through the waiting room, Marlow enters the outer room and insistently remarks on the blackness of the wool, which now becomes increasingly associated with death and foreboding – an association the text continues to make as Marlow travels further into the interior of Africa. Here, Marlow hastens to get away from the women who are now knitting 'black wool feverishly', as if 'knitting black wool as for a warm pall', and he remarks one more time for good measure, 'Old knitter of black wool'. These last three instances of 'black wool' occur in quick succession over the course of a short paragraph, the pace mimicking the speed with which Marlow seeks his exit. The open-endedness of waiting on the first pass through the room is upended by a sense of inescapable doom encapsulated in the motto '*Morituri te salutant*' that concludes the paragraph: 'Those who are about to die salute you'.[19]

In addition to imagery of sepulchres and funerals, darkness and death, the temporality of waiting contributes to the foreboding mood of *Heart of Darkness*. Throughout the trip up the Congo River, Marlow continues to associate waiting with frustration and hopelessness. Marlow's arrival at the Central station and encounter with the brick-maker serves

---

[16] Conrad, *Heart of Darkness and Other Tales*, 106.
[17] Ibid., 106.
[18] Ibid., 107.
[19] Ibid., 107.

as a representative scene, linking waiting with futile absurdity. Marlow relates:

> The business entrusted to this fellow was the making of bricks – so I had been informed; but there wasn't a fragment of a brick anywhere in the station, and he had been there more than a year – waiting. It seems he could not make bricks without something, I don't know what – straw maybe . . . However, they were all waiting – all the sixteen or twenty pilgrims of them – for something; and upon my word it did not seem an uncongenial occupation, from the way they took it, though the only thing that ever came to them was disease – as far as I could see.[20]

Here, waiting is the operational temporality in the interior; the brickmaker stands in for the experience of the employees generally, who are united in their waiting. With over a year passing without a sign that the straw will be delivered, the waiting has become indeterminate and unrelenting. Instead of signalling a future-oriented temporality, waiting here emphasises an unending present, especially as the waiting itself becomes their primary occupation. Marlow indicates that the waiting is more empty habit than genuine hope, observing that instead of the delivery of straw, the only surety is disease.

The brick-maker scene, combined with later episodes of Marlow travelling up the Congo River, emphasise the potential danger of waiting in the interior. Just eight miles from Kurtz's inner station, Marlow and his crew are forced to wait for a debilitating fog to lift.[21] The men pass the night in anxious concern that the boat, now vulnerable in the fog, will be attacked. When the fog does lift and the steamer presses on, Marlow's crew is assaulted with arrows. An end to waiting does not guarantee increased security and stability either, as Company employees are also thwarted in their impatient efforts. Marlow, for example, must wait months for rivets in order to repair the steamer at the Central station, but his waiting is a direct result of the Company manager's impatience. After revealing that the steamer had sunk two days prior, the manager explains that Marlow 'had been very long on the road. He could not wait. Had to start without me. The up-river stations had to be relieved. There had been so many delays already that he did not know who was dead and who was alive, and how they got on – and so on, and so on.'[22] Waiting, structured as a series of delays, is exacerbated by the European Company employees who succumb to their impatience. Later, the Company condemns Kurtz's

---

[20] Ibid., 121.
[21] Ibid., 137.
[22] Ibid., 119.

impatient, destructive and violent methods. The manager concludes, '"But there is no disguising the fact, Mr. Kurtz has done more harm than good to the Company. He did not see the time was not ripe for vigorous action. Cautiously, cautiously – that's my principle. We must be cautious yet. The district is closed to us for a time."'[23] Marlow then assesses, 'My hour of favour was over; I found myself lumped along with Kurtz as a partisan of methods for which the time was not ripe.'[24]

The Company's sense of its own strategies rests on a sense of the not-yet that is indebted to colonial regimes of time. As I outlined in the Introduction to this book, by colonial time, I refer to colonial discourse's production of an ostensibly homogenising and universalising temporality that underpinned European colonial expansion during high imperialism. Colonial time shares with 'modern historical time' the 'notion of discrete but continuous, modular change, and in particular, modular change as a linear, diachronically stretched-out succession of cumulative instants, an endless chain of displacements of before and after'.[25] Affecting the past, present and future, colonial time exhibits 'the merger of time, distance, and difference', which 'objectifie[s] the concept of tradition and thus reproduced notions of modernity through the binary of civilized and uncivilized'.[26] Whereas in some contexts, as Chakrabarty's argument in *Provincializing Europe* demonstrates, the not-yet is used as a political strategy to postpone rights for colonised subjects, here the waiting serves the Company's interests by championing patience. The Company believes it can embrace patient and cautious action because its eventual domination of the district is inevitable and all-but guaranteed by the ideologies of progress, development and civilisation that undergird colonial time. At the same time, Marlow's frustration with the series of delays that occur on the trip undercuts the Company's position on patience. The seemingly contradictory ways that the narrative evokes waiting suggests contradictions at the heart of empire and colonial regimes of time.

Thus, even as colonial regimes of time insist on inevitable forward movement and linear chronology, they are belied by delays and disruptions. The homogenising and universalising tendencies characteristic of colonial time regimes are undercut by the differences, drags and delays that they seek to subsume. Many of the images that evoke this forward march of progressive time carry a double valence in *Heart of Darkness*.

---

[23] Ibid., 161–62.
[24] Ibid., 162.
[25] D. Scott, *Omens of Adversity*, 5.
[26] Adib and Emiljanowicz, 'Colonial Time in Tension: Decolonizing Temporal Imaginaries', 3.

For example, the decrepit and abandoned boiler and railway truck that Marlow observes at the outer station, signs of European technological prowess, suggest the misguided vanity of imperialist narratives of progress. On the other hand, these images might also suggest, for other readers, Africa's primitivism and unsuitability for the 'gifts' of European civilisation. The ambiguity of the text's language and its complicated form and frame narrative have encouraged vigorous debate, providing support for a variety of stances on the novel's representation of Africa. Patrick Brantlinger's 1985 article took a moderate approach, arguing that the novel 'offers a powerful critique of at least certain manifestations of imperialism and racism, at the same time that it presents that critique in ways which can only be characterized as both imperialist and racist'.[27] To borrow Brantlinger's language, my reading of time in *Heart of Darkness* finds that the novel forwards a critique of the narratives of time that underwrite European imperialism, but that this very critique evokes, in some ways, colonial regimes of time.

Waiting engages with this doubling, working alternatingly between trafficking in colonial regimes of time that render Africans temporally removed from their European counterparts, and gesturing towards alternative temporalities that expose the contradictions and heterogeneities inherent in colonial constructions of time. We might read this doubleness as embodying the 'time-lag of cultural difference' that Homi Bhabha describes, which serves to 'destroy the binary structure of identity and difference' and operates 'as a structure for the representation of subaltern and postcolonial agency'.[28] Attention to the temporal dimensions of waiting in the text revive the novel's complicated relationship with colonial regimes of time. The text suggests that waiting is a modality that inscribes these temporal tensions, resisting the aspiring total dominance of colonial regimes of time. The resistive potential of waiting surfaces in Marlow's remarks about the colonial enterprise in the Congo. After discovering that his steamer is sunk at the Central station, Marlow ascribes 'waiting' to the environment itself:

> All this talk seemed to be so futile . . . and then I saw this station, these men strolling aimlessly about in the sunshine of the yard . . . And outside, the silent wilderness surrounding this cleared speck on the earth struck me as something great and invincible, like evil or truth, waiting patiently for the passing away of this fantastic invasion . . . It had been hopeless from the very first.[29]

---

[27] Brantlinger, '"Heart of Darkness": Anti-Imperialism, Racism, or Impressionism?', 364.
[28] Bhabha, '"Race", Time and the Revision of Modernity', 194.
[29] Conrad, *Heart of Darkness and Other Tales*, 23.

Several elements are noteworthy here. First, the passage exemplifies a trend that continues throughout *Heart of Darkness*, associating waiting with futility, at least from Marlow's Eurocentric perspective. Significantly, however, the language of the passage allows for an alternative reading of waiting as a resistive modality for colonial Others just beyond the limits of Marlow's comprehension and understanding. With a *longue durée* or alternative view of history, the colonial episode appears as a 'fantastic invasion' which too might pass. Waiting, here, is a mode of survival, where the Congo and its people may be poised for an opportunity to transform waiting into action, or a perspective informed by deep time, waiting to outlive this epoch.

The significance of this passage is underscored by the repetition of 'fantastic invasion' two subsequent times in the text. The second occurrence concludes the episode where Marlow eavesdrops on the nephew and uncle at the Central station. The two discuss the series of delays in reaching Kurtz, and exhibit beliefs in line with the Company's alleged civilising mission: '"Each station should be like a beacon on the road towards better things, a centre for trade of course, but also for humanizing, improving, instructing."'[30] The uncle assures his nephew of his inevitable promotion with a sweeping gesture of his hand towards the wilderness and an admonition to '"trust to this – I say, trust to this."'[31] Despite their conviction, Marlow frames their conversation with the observation, 'The high stillness confronted these two fantastic figures with its ominous patience, waiting for the passing away of a fantastic invasion.'[32] The third occurrence is after Marlow has discerned that the round knobs on sticks outside Kurtz's hut are not ornaments, but rather impaled human heads serving as symbols of madness and despotism. Marlow breaks narrative chronology and draws from conclusions reached after his return to Europe, explaining that Kurtz's methods were a result of the wilderness, which 'had found him out early, and had taken on him a terrible vengeance for the fantastic invasion'.[33] The phrase 'fantastic invasion' occurs once in each of *Heart of Darkness*'s three parts, and the concept of waiting transitions from passive observance and perseverance to active assault on Marlow's sensibilities. The association of the 'fantastic invasion' with waiting drops out of the third occurrence, when the wilderness is most assertive and combative. This shift suggests to me that the 'waiting out' of empire here is not without end, though

---

[30] Ibid., 130.
[31] Ibid., 131.
[32] Ibid., 131.
[33] Ibid., 157.

Conrad is certainly limited in imagining the forms this resistance might take. In its third iteration, what Conrad offers here is less a valorisation of waiting as passive endurance of colonial rule with the aim of outlasting the 'fantastic invasion', and more a site of temporal contradiction. The 'ominous patience' that Marlow notes attends the waiting in the Congo signals an active waiting that he deems threatening to the colonial invasion. If this waiting were simply fatalistic or capitulatory to the colonial status quo, I submit that Marlow would not find it so ominous; instead, this ominous patience suggests that the colonial invasion will not end on its own terms nor in its own time.

Waiting is a way that Marlow registers both the frustrations of colonial incursion into the Congo – waiting for rivets, for straw to make bricks, for 'something' unnamed, for repairs to be completed – and the encounter with colonial Others. Conrad's novel is a model of how waiting can function in fictional narratives to express temporal tensions between colonial discourses and alternative modalities of time. *Heart of Darkness* is a landmark text for emerging critiques of colonial and imperial exploitation at the turn of the twentieth century, and the divide among scholars of the work on the issue of its racism and representation of the Congo ensures that the novel is continually revisited within postcolonial studies in general. While the representation of Africans may traffic in developmentalist and evolutionary time centred in Europe, Conrad's deliberate obscuring of linear time in the novel has political import. Although there is no 'outside' to European time here,[34] waiting registers that time regime's contradictions, paradoxes, and potential alternative conceptualisations that exist beyond Marlow's (and Conrad's) comprehension. These contradictions, however, can prove devastating when transcribed onto the level of the individual; in the following section, we will see how *Ambiguous Adventure* illustrates the formidable effects of colonial time's contradictions through their impact on its protagonist, Samba Diallo.

Ambiguities of 'Colonial' Time

While *Heart of Darkness* remains a mainstay of colonial and postcolonial literatures alike, Kane's *Ambiguous Adventure* has not had the same fortune. Though incorporated into the African Writers series in the 1970s, the novel has received far less critical attention than Kane's contemporaries writing in English, which include the Nigerian Chinua

---

[34] Said, *Culture and Imperialism*, 24.

Achebe, the Kenyan Ngũgĩ wa Thiong'o, and the Ghanaian Ayi Kwei Armah. Kane wrote *Ambiguous Adventure* during the twilight of French colonial rule in the 1950s, and the novel was subsequently published in French in 1962. The novel, author and main character straddle the postcolonial divide; in the novel, Samba Diallo is first educated in a Koranic school called the Glowing Hearth, but before his education there is complete, his aunt sends him to the foreign French school to learn '"the art of conquering without being in the right."'[35] Kane, likewise, attended a Koranic school in Louga before attending the '*école étrangère*', and while the break between the two schools is violent and abrupt for Samba Diallo in the novel, Kane attended both simultaneously at first.[36] Samba's journey roughly tracks Kane's own – to Paris, to study philosophy, among other disciplines – until Kane returned to Senegal in 1958, just two years before Senegal's independence from France.[37] While some scholars, such as John Conteh-Morgan, situate the novel in its most immediate context – 'the wake of the French colonial conquest of Senegal'[38] – and others, such as Ahmed Bangura, assert that pre-Islamic culture is utterly absent from the text,[39] I focus on Samba and his aunt, The Most Royal Lady, and suggest that the novel demands a *longue durée* sense of history and time to make sense of the conflicts Samba internalises.

Where waiting in *Heart of Darkness* gestures towards a *longue durée* sense of time and history, in *Ambiguous Adventure*, this perspective is more explicit, pointing to histories of trade, cultural exchange, empire and resistance that not only reach back centuries, but also remain activated in the present. More than 1,000 years ago, inhabitants of present-day Senegal encountered Islam through the trans-Saharan trade.[40] Prior to French colonisation, the region was variously conquered and controlled by the Wolof empire, and the later Islamic Tukulor empire. Given its position on the Western coast of Africa, Senegal was also one of the

---

[35] Kane, *Ambiguous Adventure*, 37.
[36] Little, 'Autofiction and Cheikh Hamidou Kane's "L'aventure Ambigue"', 81.
[37] Ibid., 82. Little concludes that Kane 'both is and is not the character he has created, making him a repository for cultural aspirations that continue way beyond the text'. Ibid., 88.
[38] Conteh-Morgan, 'Beyond Race: Class Conflict and Tragic Vision in an African Novel', 18. See also Samba Gadjigo's 'Literature and History: The Case of Cheikh Hamidou Kane's *Ambiguous Adventure*', which responds to Conteh-Morgan's limited historical view. My own reading will discuss and build on Gadjigo's rejoinder.
[39] Bangura, *Islam and the West African Novel*, 109.
[40] Gellar, *Senegal*, 1.

first regions 'to develop direct commercial ties with Europe, more than five centuries ago, and to send large numbers of slaves to the Americas'.[41] From 1673 to 1677, Muslim clerics organised resistance to the slave-trading aristocracy; the French intervened by supplying weapons to the aristocracy to thwart the revolt.[42] During the colonial period, however, Muslim brotherhoods actively spread Sufi Islam across the region and 'organiz[ed] the faithful',[43] occupying a vexed position between colonial administrators and local inhabitants of the Senegal River region. Kenneth Harrow notes that '[i]n the Futa Toro of northern Senegal, home to Kane's Diallobé people [in *Ambiguous Adventure*]', there was 'a pattern of steady resistance on the part of the marabouts in the struggle against the French'.[44] The world that Samba Diallo inhabits evinces palimpsests of prior empires, residues of a multiplicity of religious practices even in the majority-Muslim context of his village. Resistance to French colonisation is located in characters associated with both African animist religious practice, and Islamic practices alike.

It is tempting to read resistance, especially in independence-era texts, only in terms of oppositions between colonised and coloniser, which is a dichotomy that also animates colonial discourses of time and culture. Colonial regimes of time work to erase or suppress precolonial histories, alternative temporalities and temporal practices, though *Ambiguous Adventure* exhibits both accommodation and resistance to colonial time. It is true that even postcolonial critiques of time have often been 'premised on a simplified and even monolithic understanding of Western modernity as an ideology of "linear progress," the consequence of which is a binary conception of time'.[45] *Ambiguous Adventure* confronts this binary conception of time and dichotomous thinking directly, staging and deconstructing this sense of time through its representations of various 'twos': the novel is structured in two parts, with the country of the Diallobé and Paris, France at opposite poles; Samba and his father, whose shared love of Continental philosophy produces a Socratic dialogue on work and faith; and the Koranic school is pitted against the foreign school. Master Thierno, the religious centre of the novel, debates the decision to send Samba to the foreign school, wondering whether

---

[41] Ibid., 1.
[42] Ibid., 5.
[43] Ibid., 111.
[44] Harrow, *Faces of Islam in African Literature*, 285.
[45] Helgesson, 'Radicalizing Temporal Difference: Anthropology, Postcolonial Theory, and Literary Time', 546.

the students can 'learn this without forgetting that'.[46] For many critics, *Ambiguous Adventure* appears to pit 'tradition', embodied by Thierno's Sufi mysticism, against 'colonial modernity', embodied by the foreign school. Joyce Block Lazarus characterises the depiction this way: 'Kane contrasts the modern Western world, with its scientific and technical achievements, with Islamic Africa, with its spirituality and harmony with nature.'[47] Yet Lazarus's own reading of Thierno, who she describes as straddling 'the mystical and the pragmatic', along with her characterisation of Samba's father and aunt as 'fusions of Western and Islamic traditions'[48] belies the strict demarcation suggested by the separation of 'modern West' and 'Islamic Africa'. Further, as Mark Rifkin argues, labelling any and all non-Western cultural practices as 'traditional casts them as residual of some other, older time instead of characterizing them as participating in a present whose frame of reference differs from that of the chrononormativities of settler governance'.[49] This habit in literary and cultural studies mirrors the same problematic practice of the denial of coevalness in anthropology that Johannes Fabian identified in the 1980s.[50]

To understand how 'modernity' signifies in *Ambiguous Adventure*, David Wehrs's discussion of Islamic modernists and Islamic fundamentalists is instructive.

> The crucial difference between the modernists and the fundamentalists lies in their notions of reason. Modernists embrace critical rationality . . . as integral to the Qur'anic imperative to pursue knowledge . . . By contrast, the fundamentalists define reason as 'obedience to God', so that 'requiring proofs before submitting to God is unbelief'.[51]

As Samba wrestles with different philosophical points of view – he goes to Paris in fact to study philosophy – we might read this struggle, as Wehrs does, as giving novelistic 'articulation to themes and traditions deeply embedded in Islamic philosophy and practice, themes and traditions that potentially enjoin opposition *not just* to secular Western modernity but also the qualities in West African polytheism'.[52] Wehrs reminds us not only of the multiplicities of modernity, which are erased

---

[46] Kane, *Ambiguous Adventure*, 34.
[47] J. B. Lazarus, 'Islam and the West in the Fiction of Cheikh Hamidou Kane', 179.
[48] Ibid., 182–3.
[49] Rifkin, *Beyond Settler Time*, 44.
[50] Fabian, *Time and the Other*.
[51] Wehrs, *Islam, Ethics, Revolt*, 55.
[52] Ibid., 64, emphasis mine.

by collapsing 'modernity' with the 'West', but also of the role of pre-Islamic practices and traditions lying beneath the surface of the texts.

Yet other readers are not as keen to attend to the pre-Islamic presence in the novel. Ahmed Bangura, for example, argues that 'there is no place in [*Ambiguous Adventure*] for a pre-Islamic worldview' because 'Islam has simply obliterated all traces of the millennial Diallobé culture before it.'[53] In my own view, not only is a pre-Islamic worldview identifiable in the text, but also it contributes to the complex timescape that Samba attempts to navigate. The Most Royal Lady, Samba's formidable aunt, is described as being 'sixty years old, and she would have been taken for scarcely forty'.[54] If the setting is roughly contemporaneous with the novel's production, then The Most Royal Lady would have been born sometime between 1880 and 1890 – the height of European imperial violence in Africa. This history is written onto her body; her face is 'like a living page from the history of the Diallobé country. Everything that the country treasured of epic tradition could be read there'.[55] Wehrs argues that this passage's allusion to the epic tradition suggests that The Most Royal Lady has 'an intense connection with her people's pre-Islamic, epic-heroic past', and that 'the novel presents French conquest as an apparently recent trauma'.[56] I agree that The Most Royal Lady represents the strongest link to a pre-Islamic past, and I want to build from Wehrs's suggestion that French conquest is 'apparently recent'. In evoking a pre-Islamic past – one that extends more than a millennia ago – The Most Royal Lady is the locus for a *longue durée* historical consciousness, one that views the French colonial conquest as a recent, short and, to recall the language of *Heart of Darkness*, 'fantastic' episode. While The Most Royal Lady embodies this *longue durée* view, she is not its only marker. We can note the impact of histories of conquest and exchange in the political, cultural, economic, historical and religious setting that grounds Samba's childhood.

In this way, *Ambiguous Adventure* orients us away from a narrow focus on European colonisation; a *longue durée* framework makes this expansive account of coloniality more visible. In literary studies, a *longue durée* approach integrates the 'longer, wider "connected histories" ... to deepen our understanding of politics and literature' by giving 'wider attention to the global genesis of modernization',[57] thus challenging the association of

---

[53] Bangura, *Islam and the West African Novel*, 109.
[54] Kane, *Ambiguous Adventure*, 20.
[55] Ibid., 20.
[56] Wehrs, *Islam, Ethics, Revolt*, 59.
[57] Doyle, 'Inter-Imperiality and Literary Studies in the Longer *Durée*', 337.

modernity with European colonisation. Laura Doyle brings together this *longue durée* approach and postcolonial studies to create what she calls an inter-imperial mode of analysis, which 'focuses on the geopolitical field created by multiple empires across hemispheres and periods' to 'explor[e] how each of these registers the embedded legacies of successive empires *and* the pressures created by contemporaneous empires'.[58] I want to suggest that this inter-imperial mode of analysis is precisely what is missing in prior studies of *Ambiguous Adventure*. The novel foregrounds Western and Islamic modernities, and through The Most Royal Lady's evocation of a pre-Islamic past, reminds us that more than a century before French colonialism, Samba Diallo's people were conquered by the Tukulors, who suppressed animist practices and religions. Following Pheng Cheah, I do not find that a 'clean break from global processes'[59] is necessary to locate heterotemporality; through a *longue durée* framework, we can observe new and different temporal positionalities emerging prior, alongside, and out of Senegal's position in the world system over the last 500 years. In *Ambiguous Adventure*, what some read as a conflict between a homogeneous West and an equally homogeneous Islamic Africa, should instead be read as a conflict embedded in the specific imperial histories of northern Senegal, where African animism, Sufi Islam and French colonial worldviews interact and intersect.

This sense of time and history upsets a neat demarcation between colonial and postcolonial Senegal, a view that, once again, The Most Royal Lady espouses. Chapter 5 in Part One begins with the omniscient narrator recounting the defeat of the Diallobé, a conflict that stands in for the whole of Africa:

> The country of the Diallobé was not the only one which had been awakened by a great clamor early one day. The entire black continent had had its moment of clamor. Strange dawn! . . . Those who had no history were encountering those who carried the world on their shoulders.[60]

We should note the tongue-in-cheek tone of Kane here, in his characterisation of the Diallobé as without history, especially because Diallobé history has already been recounted by The Most Royal Lady in the previous chapter. She articulates the colonial encounter thus:

> A hundred years ago our grandfather, along with all the inhabitants of this countryside, was awakened one morning by an uproar arising from

---

[58] Ibid., 337.
[59] Cheah, *What Is a World?*, 17.
[60] Kane, *Ambiguous Adventure*, 48.

the river . . . Our grandfather, and the élite of the country with him, was defeated . . . Furthermore, the conflict has not yet ceased.⁶¹

Indeed, the conflict has continued with the word rather than the cannon, and Samba Diallo, her nephew, is the latest battleground. Though ostensibly following Samba Diallo's childhood, adolescence, and – caught between French education and the religion he has lost – suspended transition to adulthood, the language in these passages, associating the colonial encounter with morning, point us to a different temporal landscape. While the French empire is associated with a tragic dawn or morning, the Diallobé people in the novel dwell on the possibilities and ambiguities of twilight.

Waiting for the Twilight of Empire

Although the events depicted in *Ambiguous Adventure* span Samba's childhood and early adulthood, the consistent references to dawn and twilight throughout the text associate its action with the compressed time of a single day rather than simply with a tragically short lifetime. *Ambiguous Adventure* exhibits several characteristics of the *bildungsroman*, a form with its own attendant temporalities that underpin the education, formation and development of its subject. Combined with the *longue durée* historical view in part espoused by The Most Royal Lady, I propose that the deceptively straightforward story of Samba's estrangement is characterised by various temporal syncopations and disjunctions that illuminate the machinations of colonial time regimes.

If we understand *Ambiguous Adventure* as a 'coming of age novel',⁶² then we might, as Wehrs does, observe the 'techniques of the *Bildungsroman*' in Kane's use of 'pivotal dialogical exchanges, by making the events in Samba's story mostly speech acts, [and] by allowing multiple characters to articulate distinctive, philosophically rich worldviews'.⁶³ The novel opens with Samba at Master Thierno's Koranic school, and the first major conflict in the novel concerns the choice to send him to the foreign school, thereby aborting Samba's religious education. Whereas a classical *bildungsroman* would follow the protagonist's successful initiation into society, here, we have a 'horrific parody' of

---

⁶¹ Ibid., 37.
⁶² Wehrs, *Islam, Ethics, Revolt*, 51.
⁶³ Ibid., 72.

'the tale of initiation'.⁶⁴ In this way, Kane joins other postcolonial writers by modifying the form of the *bildungsroman* to emphasise the difficulty of 'formation' or development in fraught post/colonial contexts. In Caribbean literature, this modified genre has been characterised as a 'sad initiation', where '[t]he story of development has been placed in the service of portraying a protagonist's understanding of the pressures of colonial, sexist and racial realities', concluding with the 'fragmentation of identity or a neurotic self-image rather than towards wholeness, thus narrating an anti-bildung'.⁶⁵ According to Ralph Austen, these departures from the classical form of development are vehicles to analyse the genre's ideological constructions of self and society. While he does not discuss *Ambiguous Adventure*, he does note several important characteristics of the African *bildungsroman* that differentiate it from the classical form, and which are resonant with Samba's coming-of-age story: an emphasis on the collective over the individual, a vexed relationship to autodidactic or colonial education, and the suspension of the protagonist's development between youth and adulthood.⁶⁶ These characteristics in *Ambiguous Adventure* lead Wangari wa Nyatetũ-Waigwa to conclude that Kane's novel is a 'liminal novel', because Samba is 'still in the middle of the quest, still moving towards what supposedly constitutes the final stage in that quest or having consciously suspended the adoption of a final stance'.⁶⁷ Twilight embodies that liminal space and time; Kane links Samba's development to twilight, an ambiguous time suspended between night and day. Whereas Samba initially associates twilight with religious ecstasy, throughout the novel twilight increasingly becomes the setting for his doubts and alienation.

The contrast between Samba's prayer in Jean's company and Samba's death at the hands of The Fool offer a tale of two twilights – in the first, Samba's religious belief is intact and twilight reflects the beauty of God's creation, but in the second twilight is the backdrop for doubt and Samba's alienation. The first scene, which takes place in Part 1 before Samba has left the Glowing Hearth, but is recounted by the narrator afterwards, depicts Samba discoursing with Jean Lacroix, the son of a

---

⁶⁴ Masterton, 'Islamic Mystical Readings of Cheikh Hamidou Kane's Ambiguous Adventure', 41.
⁶⁵ Ilmonen, 'Talking Back to the Bildungsroman: Caribbean Literature and the Dis/Location of the Genre', 62.
⁶⁶ Austen, 'Struggling with the African Bildungsroman', 216, 219, 222.
⁶⁷ Nyatetũ-Waigwa, *The Liminal Novel*, 3.

French administrator. A review of the scene illuminates Kane's insistence on the temporal setting of twilight:

> While they were talking twilight had fallen . . . The sun had disappeared, but already in the east the moon had risen, and it, too, shed a light. One could see that the ambient light was made up of the paling rose from the sun, the milky whiteness from the moon, and also the peaceful penumbra of a night which was felt to be imminent.[68]

This description of twilight undoes a strict distinction between night and day, as both the sun and the moon shed light. Both Samba and Jean continue to comment on the significance of twilight. Samba comments to Jean, '"It is twilight, and I must pray"', while Jean observes that 'Nothing in [Samba] was alive except this voice, speaking in the twilight a language which Jean did not understand.'[69] Samba reflects later that 'this twilight that was so beautiful' accounts for the 'sudden exaltation while he was praying'.[70]

At this point, regardless of the manifold political, religious and cultural contexts that the above *longue durée* approach revealed through The Most Royal Lady, here Samba subscribes to a worldview wholly shaped by Master Thierno's teachings. We might view Samba and later scholars of the novel alike reproducing a problematic schema of irreconcilable difference – between the Koranic school and the foreign school, 'tradition' and 'modernity', and the Glowing Hearth and Paris. Though Samba expresses his childhood worldview as one unified and unencumbered by either pre-Islamic or foreign influences, The Most Royal Lady and Samba's father (referred to as the Knight, who also works as an administrator for the French) should undercut the reader's confidence in Samba's own assessment. As the novel progresses, twilight reveals Samba's growing estrangement. A philosophical discussion with his father about the West, God and materialism ends abruptly with the Knight's observation, '"But now it is the hour of twilight. Let us pray."'[71] Though Samba does finish the prayer, he becomes increasingly preoccupied with reconciling 'the discipline of faith and the discipline of work'.[72] This distraction becomes exacerbated in France, and a letter from home upsets Samba such that he forgets his evening prayer.[73] The twilight's

---

[68] Kane, *Ambiguous Adventure*, 59.
[69] Ibid., 59–60.
[70] Ibid., 63.
[71] Ibid., 102.
[72] Ibid., 104.
[73] Ibid., 126.

transition from beautiful ambiguity to menacing, tragic estrangement occurs after Samba's return to the country of the Diallobé, and after his studies in France have similarly ended prematurely. The Fool – friend of Master Thierno and strident opponent of the engagement with the West – demands that Samba accompany him to pray at Master Thierno's grave. Samba and the Fool walk to the cemetery, and the Fool notes, '"The shadows are falling. See, it is twilight. Let us pray."'[74] As Samba wrestles internally with questions of belief, he finds himself uttering, 'No – I do not agree' aloud, which The Fool interprets as an unequivocal renunciation of faith, and strikes him down. Thus, while the story of the Diallobé opens with a '[s]trange dawn' of French colonisation, Samba's life concludes in twilight, a time of 'temporal ambiguity' that Obioma Nnaemeka views as 'reflect[ing] the philosophical, ideological, social and locational ambiguities that pervade the novel'.[75]

The importance of twilight is additionally stressed by Paul Lacroix, Jean's father and a French colonial administrator, when he expresses uneasiness as the sun sets. The narrator comments, 'Paul Lacroix stood waiting. Waiting for what? The whole town was waiting too, in the same dismayed expectation.'[76] As the sun sinks below the horizon, he thinks, '"I really believe that this is the moment. The world is about to come to an end. The moment is fragile. It may break. Then, time will be blocked off. No!"' Turning to the Knight, Lacroix asks, '"Does this twilight not trouble you? Myself, I am upset by it. At this moment it seems to me that we are closer to the end of the world than we are to nightfall."'[77] Following this conversation is a discussion about the universe's order, and apocalyptic time. The timing of this conversation, in terms of Senegal's history, is important; in some ways, Lacroix is facing the twilight of formal French colonisation. He reassures himself that at least 'the West' (his words) 'conquer[s] a little more of truth each day, thanks to science. We do not wait.'[78] The Knight is deeply suspicious of this association of progress and acceleration with truth. He observes, 'In truth, it is not acceleration which the world needs', and he laments, 'Those who, even down to his own family, who were racing headlong into the future, if they could only understand that their course was a

---

[74] Ibid., 173.
[75] Nnaemeka, 'Exile(s), Choice, and the Burden of Memory in Cheikh Hamidou Kane's Ambiguous Adventure', 229.
[76] Kane, *Ambiguous Adventure*, 74.
[77] Ibid., 75.
[78] Ibid., 76.

suicide, their sun a mirage!'[79] The Knight repeats to himself the rhetorical question, 'To have this, must one renounce that?'[80] Where Lacroix places his faith in progress and the succession of time, the Knight rejects succession in favour of simultaneity. His complaint contains within it a vision of the world where one can have, at the same time, both this and that. As the sun sets, the Knight predicts, 'We have not had the same past, you and ourselves, but we shall have, strictly, the same future. The era of separate destinies has run its course.'[81] The temporality of waiting and suspension, mirrored in the twilight that suspends day and night, indexes the anxiety of the French and the hope of the Diallobé as they await the future.

What is the significance of mapping this 'liminal novel' onto the temporality of the day? For Fernand Braudel, who popularised the *longue durée* perspective in the mid-twentieth century, '[t]he time of today is composed simultaneously of the time of yesterday, of the day before yesterday, and of bygone days'.[82] If we follow Frederic Jameson,[83] we might conclude that the novel works allegorically, where Samba stands in for Senegal, and his suspended transition to adulthood anticipates the postcolonial disillusionment that would follow political independence. Indeed, Simon Gikandi observes that the 'disillusioned African assimilados' in Kane's novels 'often posit themselves as symbolic figures, illustrative of what colonialism has done to a whole generation of Africans'.[84] Yet this reading, limited to a 'whole generation', does not capture the generational time evoked by the novel's characters who reach back far earlier than the narrative present. One instance is the already discussed characterisation of The Most Royal Lady, whose face reflects the long history of the Diallobé and who gives voice to the experiences of the colonial invasion that occurred before Samba's lifetime. Another example can be found in the practice of reciting the Koran, the central focus of Samba's education at the Golden Hearth and a tradition that connects Samba to his forebears. During the Night of the Koran, Samba reflects that he 'was repeating for his father what the Knight himself had repeated for his own father, what from generation to generation through centuries the sons of the Diallobé had repeated for their fathers'.[85]

---

[79] Ibid., 68.
[80] Ibid., 76.
[81] Ibid., 79.
[82] Braudel, 'History and the Social Science: The Longue Durée', 254.
[83] Jameson, 'Third-World Literature in the Era of Multinational Capitalism'.
[84] Gikandi, *Reading the African Novel*, 43.
[85] Kane, *Ambiguous Adventure*, 71–2.

Both the histories that The Most Royal Lady relates and the Night of the Koran episode reorient Samba in generational time, which is produced through oral recitation. The significance of the oral practices is revealed near the novel's close, when Adèle asks Samba, '"Tell me how they conquered you, personally"', and Samba responds, '"Perhaps it was with their alphabet. With it, they struck the first hard blow at the country of the Diallobé."'[86] The threat that the foreign school embodies, then, is not simply one of cultural estrangement,[87] but one that fundamentally threatens Samba's connection to the generational time that provides continuity. In sum, the generational time that orients the Diallobé in the present syncopates with the narrative's other organising temporalities, such as the span of a day, and colonial regimes of time that aim to suppress precolonial histories.

Given the myriad temporalities that shape *Ambiguous Adventure* – which a reading attuned only to the juxtaposition of so-called 'traditional' and 'modern' sensibilities would miss – we can now return to how Samba and The Most Royal Lady produce temporal unruliness in the novel that undermines the efficacy of colonial time regimes to control the representation of time. Though it is tempting to read Samba as merely torn between two cultures, The Most Royal Lady observes that Samba himself is not synchronous with his contemporaries. In contrast to Demba, who has succeeded Master Thierno at the Golden Hearth, Samba, she thinks, 'should have been born as the contemporary of his ancestors'.[88] Likewise, in the suspension of Samba's development, the novel produces an indefinite caesura where the classical *bildungsroman* depicts its protagonist's harmonisation of self and society. The temporal unruliness of the text is not limited to its manipulation of the genre, but also includes its evocation of a precolonial, pre-Islamic past disavowed by the elite of the Diallobé and the French administrators alike. In this way, the immediate episode of the French colonisation of the Diallobé might instead be viewed as one day that has been preceded, and will continue to be succeeded, by many others.

The Knight, and indeed the novel, place their hope for this shared future in Samba Diallo. But as I have suggested with my reading of The Most Royal Lady, Samba's sense of time and history is influenced by his exposure to Western philosophy, Islam and the epic-heroic tradition that harkens back to a pre-European and pre-Islamic past. Modifying Wai

---

[86] Ibid., 159.
[87] See Caplan, 'Nos Ancêtres, Les Diallobés: Cheikh Hamidou Kane's Ambiguous Adventure and the Paradoxes of Islamic Negritude', 941.
[88] Kane, *Ambiguous Adventure*, 121.

Chee Dimock, Laura Doyle muses that the aesthetics of 'epic, cyclical, or ancient time' in postcolonial texts might point us to 'deep inter-imperial time', instead of the 'mythic, nostalgic, or magical' label that scholars tend to give them.[89] When I conceptualise the *longue durée* in tandem with *Ambiguous Adventure*, I do not have in mind a facile sense of linear history that simply extends longer than European colonisation. Rather, the temporal disjunction that we see in the novel, I contend, indexes a dynamic, inter-imperial positionality amid contemporary discourses of modernity, tradition, European culture and language, assimilation and estrangement.

An advantage of inter-imperial analysis, I contend, is its ability to capture both successive as well as simultaneous colonial entanglements. Mobilising Laura Doyle's inter-imperial model of analysis, I suggest that we read both Samba Diallo and The Most Royal Lady for their respective inter-imperial positionalities. Colonial and imperial engagements are violent, 'transformative engagements' that 'involve change and adaptation, willing and unwilling'.[90] The Most Royal Lady acknowledges that her decision to address the Diallobé and advocate for sending their children to the foreign school is against their traditions, but that 'more and more we shall have to do things which we hate doing, and which do not accord with our customs'.[91] The *longue durée*, inter-imperial approach positions French colonisation as one conquest among others, and this sense of history provides additional sources of resistance and alternative worldviews that are unable to be reduced to simplistic West/Africa, or Christian/Islam dichotomies. This in turn opens up 'colonial time' to consider the tempos of Islamic practice, and the role of Sufi Islam in particular in the social life of time in newly postcolonial Senegal. In a book that appears to stage conflicts between various twos – between 'this' and 'that', between the French and the Diallobé – twilight remains an ambiguous signifier whose importance coheres in the comingling of night and day. Though Samba's individual story is a tragic one, a larger tragic arc is produced by the reflections and revelations the characters have at twilight; tragically, the characters are so preoccupied with the oppositions between tradition and 'modernity', this and that, that they are unable to dwell in the ambiguity of twilight as a potentially rich third space – a space and time of possibility. As Obioma Nnaemeka argues, twilight throughout the novel is 'devastatingly disorienting for those seeking the truth as assurances and definite answers', a 'cosmic drama

---

[89] Doyle, 'Inter-Imperiality and Literary Studies in the Longer Durée', 343.
[90] Ibid., 337.
[91] Kane, *Ambiguous Adventure*, 45.

of temporal ambivalence', which 'mark[s] impossibility and possibilities' alike.[92] Twilight and the temporality of waiting, as it intersects with the machinations of and resistance to colonial time regimes, share characteristics of ambiguity, and as such are rich sites of possibility.

Journeying to the Heart of Empire

From Europe to Africa, and from Africa to Europe, Marlow and Samba's respective return journeys seem, at first blush, to emphasise the jarring disorientation of traversing colonial spaces – and yet, as the above focus on the temporality of waiting and twilight reveals, the novels are equally invested in how the journeys are shaped by the politics of colonial regimes of time. In Marc Caplan's assessment, *Ambiguous Adventure* (not unlike *Heart of Darkness*) associates 'tradition . . . with night, infirmity, asceticism, and death' and 'modernity and Paris, the City of Light . . . with daytime, material plenty, and technology'.[93] But a careful reading of *Ambiguous Adventure* using a *longue durée* approach challenges any simplistic reading of 'modernity' and 'tradition' as homogeneous polarities, or as Europe as the centre of light in contrast to African darkness. Rather than pitting traditional temporalities against modern ones, the ambiguity of time in *Ambiguous Adventure* embeds a long history of imperial conquest and resistance that the novel indexes through its pairing of the imagery of twilight with the temporality of waiting. Just as in *Heart of Darkness* Marlow perceives the continent of Africa as waiting for the fantastic invasion to be over, in *Ambiguous Adventure* the temporal markers of the day imply that the 'dawn' of the French colonial conquest is quickly approaching its own twilight, and another dawn will approach soon enough. Together, the novels demonstrate that the temporality of waiting is central to the way colonial time regimes work, as well as, potentially, to the way the regimes might be subverted, such as in the Knight's commitment to a coeval, shared future.

To be sure, the tempos and rhythms associated with Samba's religious practice do not constitute a monolithic 'Islamic time'. Nevertheless, Samba's estrangement from the Diallobé is marked in the text by the syncopation of the times of prayer and his observance of them. The Diallobé's social and cultural time is not tied to immutable tradition,

---

[92] Nnaemeka, 'Exile(s), Choice, and the Burden of Memory in Cheikh Hamidou Kane's Ambiguous Adventure', 230.
[93] Caplan, 'Nos Ancêtres, Les Diallobés: Cheikh Hamidou Kane's Ambiguous Adventure and the Paradoxes of Islamic Negritude', 950.

but rather is dynamic and accommodating to the exigencies of the times. Not only does The Most Royal Lady note that customs may have to change to ensure the Diallobé's survival, but also Demba's first order of business as Master Thierno's successor is to 'change the schedules at the Hearth. In this way, all the parents who might so desire would be able to send their sons to the foreign school.'[94] Additionally, the *longue durée* view of time and history in Kane's novel affirms the role of pre-Islamic cultures in shaping the Diallobé's present, reminding us that the form that Islam takes is affected by the history of Tukulor conquest, trade across the African continent, French colonisation, and local movements towards decolonisation. As Shahzad Bashir writes in 'On Islamic Time: Rethinking Chronology in the Historiography of Muslim Societies', modern studies of Islamic history and time tend to problematically reify an orientalist 'chronographic tradition' that produces Islam as 'a timeless entity', and 'cast[s] Islamic perspectives produced outside the Middle East as being forever derivative on the one hand and encumbered with accretions from "other" cultures on the other'.[95] Attention to the multiplicity of temporalities and temporal practices in *Ambiguous Adventure*, then, offers not only a rejoinder to views of colonial time that erase Islamic temporalities, but also produces a rich sense of Islamic temporalities as practiced and lived – not ahistorical or timeless.

In my pairing of *Heart of Darkness* and *Ambiguous Adventure*, I have been less interested in the latter writing back to the former than in their juxtaposition to create an expansive account of colonial time regimes as depicted in colonial and postcolonial texts. If *Heart of Darkness* reveals that waiting is central to colonial regimes of time, *Ambiguous Adventure* adds that, nevertheless, the temporalities of waiting may signify in excess of their use by colonial administrators to delay and to defer as a method of exercising power over colonial subjects. For example, both Marlow and Paul Lacroix exhibit extreme unease and anxiety as they wait for the fog to lift or for twilight to conclude respectively; the Knight's subsequent condemnation of acceleration in *Ambiguous Adventure* might then be interpreted as an affirmation of the politics of slowness to challenge the temporal politics of the colonial administration. The embrace of waiting here is not a capitulation to colonial power; rather, we might view the politics of slowness as one form of disruption and temporal unruliness (and which will we examine further in Chapter 3, where my interest is more explicitly in the resistive potential of waiting). Primarily,

---

[94] Kane, *Ambiguous Adventure*, 122.
[95] Bashir, 'On Islamic Time', 521, 524, 529.

the above analysis of time in Conrad's and Kane's novels confirms not only that 'waiting' appears across the colonial/postcolonial divide, but also that it embeds the tensions constitutive of colonial regimes of time more generally. The comparison of these texts shows that the temporal politics of each novel – despite how differently each author positions their text vis-à-vis decolonisation – are surprisingly similar. Postcolonial studies in general has not adequately contended with the role of Islam in shaping culture and history, as well as temporal experience. I offer this reading of *Heart of Darkness* and *Ambiguous Adventure* as a first step towards theorising the manifold ambiguity of colonial regimes of time. The following chapter shifts from waiting times to waiting spaces, and the pernicious discourses of colonial time that position formerly colonised or marginalised groups in the waiting room of history.

Chapter 2

Projects and Promissory Notes: The Waiting Rooms of V. S. Naipaul and Nadine Gordimer

> As a response to the temporizing and the various conditionalities with which empires typically opposed the demand for national freedom, it is ironic that newly independent nations, such as India, should themselves have made the assertion of freedom conditional on achievements which could at best only be prospective . . . [T]he terms in which new states conceived of freedom, once independence was secured, made its affirmation a most capacious *project* and a *promissory note* that was issued not just to all members of the nation itself, but to the world at large . . . The nation and its freedom, following independence, was a project for the future.
>
> Uday Mehta, 'Indian Constitutionalism: The Articulation of a Political Vision' (2007)

After signing his enlistment papers with the Company, Marlow in *Heart of Darkness* exits the waiting room with a sense of ominous foreboding – at least that is how he recollects the event as part of the larger narrative of his Congo journey. From that point forward, the narrative proceeds inexorably towards Marlow's encounter with Kurtz in the interior of the 'Dark Continent', where time seems to move backward to the 'prehistoric ages'. It is not just the African environment that contributes to Marlow's impression, but also his appraisal of the Africans themselves, which Conrad marks in Marlow's speech parenthetically:

> (I don't think a single one of them had any clear idea of time, as we at the end of countless ages have. They still belonged to the beginnings of time – had no inherited experience to teach them, as it were).[1]

While Conrad, through Marlow and the frame narrator, does not draw out the implications of this timelessness with respect to waiting, throughout *Heart of Darkness*, Marlow's anxious waiting contrasts sharply with his African others. Without a 'clear idea of time', without a sense of the

---

[1] Conrad, *Heart of Darkness and Other Tales*, 139.

present retreating into the past, and without a sense of progression into the future, the Africans appear not to experience waiting the way that Marlow does. As Chinua Achebe pointed out in 1976, this depiction 'was and is the dominant image of Africa in the Western imagination and Conrad merely brought the peculiar gifts of his own mind to bear on it'.[2]

Writers of fiction from around the world have subsequently engaged with Conrad's legacy and influence in a myriad of productive and revealing ways. The previous chapter showed, in part, how *Ambiguous Adventure* reworks motifs of lightness and darkness into the promising ambiguity of twilight, therein revising the Manichean dichotomies that underwrite colonial regimes of time. This chapter pairs two novels with more direct intertextual relationships to *Heart of Darkness*: V. S. Naipaul's 1979 *A Bend in the River* and Nadine Gordimer's 1981 *July's People*.[3] In addition to their intertextual triangulation with *Heart of Darkness*, the novels share the striking final image of their protagonists escaping existences of anxious waiting for imminent revolutions or civil wars to commence. Their refusals to wait, however, are imbued with diametrically opposed attitudes towards the future. This chapter advances a claim that, building from the previous chapter, will be a touchstone throughout the book: that the temporality of waiting and the 'waiting room' model of historicism persisted even as formal declarations of independence occurred across the globe, or as struggles against colonial or white minority rule intensified. The arguments in this chapter focus on the waiting-room model of history, as described by Dipesh Chakrabarty, and how Naipaul's and Gordimer's fictional works invite renewed engagement with his conceptual framework. Both novels literalise the spatiotemporal metaphor of history's waiting room through their characters' movements to specific locations tied to the temporal experience of waiting, where characters reflect on their understandings of history and time, and their roles in the emerging future. Whether looking back on independence, as Naipaul's novel does, or imagining the moment of imminent revolutionary change, as in Gordimer's novel, both narratives ruminate on the significance and possibilities of political

---

[2] Achebe, 'An Image of Africa: Racism in Conrad's Heart of Darkness', 15.

[3] While comparisons to *Heart of Darkness* have become commonplace in Naipaul scholarship, only Byron Caminero-Santangelo explicitly links *July's People* to Conrad's fiction. Caminero-Santangelo contends that *July's People* illuminates 'the disruptive potential in colonial discourse', and how the protagonists' journeys force their focalizing characters to confront colonial structures of power. *African Fiction and Joseph Conrad: Reading Postcolonial Intertextuality*, 27, 90.

transition in African countries in the postcolonial period. These authors' constructions of 'waiting rooms of history' in the interior of Africa achieve very different ends; for Naipaul, the waiting room of history is both the default and requisite temporal model for the formerly colonised Africans of the unnamed country in *A Bend in the River*. For Gordimer's Maureen, her perception of July's village as a kind of waiting room pushes her to confront the apartheid regimes of temporality that have structured the economic, social, and political relationships between her family and July's. Her refusal to wait any longer signifies a rejection of that apartheid temporality, whereas Salim's refusal to wait in *A Bend in the River* ultimately signifies acquiescence to the waiting rooms of history, to which certain occupants of the globalised, postcolonial world will always be relegated. Naipaul's nihilism, as so many critics have characterised his racist pessimism, results from taking the 'refusal to wait' and inverting its revolutionary potential. Because the precolonial past lies in wait to reclaim the present in *A Bend in the River*, the future is already foreclosed. His narrative suggests that the formerly colonised are still waiting, and always will be.

Chakrabarty's *Provincializing Europe* usefully chronicles the imbrication of historicism and colonialism, noting that historicism 'posited historical time as a measure of the cultural distance (at least in institutional development) that was assumed to exist between the West and the non-West. In the colonies, it legitimated the idea of civilization.'[4] This model of history and political modernity encouraged a view, at least from the colonising powers' perspectives, that colonised peoples were not yet ready for self-rule and political independence.[5] Although Chakrabarty's area of interest is primarily India, he notes that this historicist perspective 'consigned Indians, Africans, and other "rude" nations to an imaginary waiting room of history. In doing so, it converted history itself into a version of this waiting room.'[6] Europe was destined to 'arrive earlier' than its colonised counterparts, but ultimately the path to modernity was expected to be the same. The 'arrival' of colonial others into European modernity, however, was never guaranteed; indeed, colonial regimes of time tended to postpone this potential future indefinitely. Historicism's powerful narrative also gave anticolonial nationalist movements their shape, as anticolonial nationalist movements insisted on the 'now' (rather than the delay tactics of 'not yet'). Chakrabarty observes that nationalist struggles in India, for example, asserted that

---

[4] Chakrabarty, *Provincializing Europe*, 7.
[5] Ibid., 8.
[6] Ibid., 8.

the peasant was already 'a full participant in the political life of the nation', meeting the requirements of citizenship 'long before he or she could be formally educated into the doctrinal or conceptual aspects of citizenship'.[7] While this nationalist claim appears to trouble the teleological, stagist progression of time and history underpinning the 'waiting room of history model' (and indeed Chakrabarty cites this strategy as a 'practical, if not theoretical, rejection' of historicism), this acceleration does not, in the end, undo historicism's temporal assumptions.

On this point, Uday Mehta's chapter on Indian independence and political visions is instructive. In Mehta's view, countries such as India reinstated the 'waiting room' of history after independence by 'mak[ing] the assertion of freedom conditional on achievements [such as national unity, social uplift, and recognition] which could at best only be prospective'.[8] Here, independence and freedom are delinked, where freedom became 'a most capricious *project* and a *promissory note*', effectively deferring a complete realisation of national freedom as a 'project for the future'.[9] His analysis invites a reconsideration of the temporalities underpinning this conceptualisation of Indian national independence. Mehta suggests that Indian independence 'was marked not so much by metaphors of novelty and revolutionary rupture, but rather, by those of transference and continuity'.[10] The re-entrenchment of the waiting room model of history, I contend, fostered this temporal continuity, even as advocates for independence stressed acceleration and jumping ahead. In Meera Ashar's view, anticolonial nationalist movements in India 'did not really challenge or reject the colonial "not yet"; at least not in principle. Instead, they claimed their freedom as a compensation for the years of tyranny and domination during colonization.'[11] Put another way, some advocates for Indian independence insisted that the requisite time had already passed, not that the need to wait itself was unnecessary.

What, then, would characterise a revolutionary temporality, one that would more directly reject this waiting room model? Drawing from Mehta, I suggest that revolutionary temporalities involve 'radical disjunction and rupture with the past'.[12] For Mehta, India's revolutionary moment occurred when the constitution was ratified, because ratification

---

[7] Ibid., 10.
[8] Mehta, 'Indian Constitutionalism: The Articulation of a Political Vision', 16–17.
[9] Ibid., 17.
[10] Ibid., 19.
[11] Ashar, 'Decolonizing What? Categories, Concepts and the Enduring "Not Yet"', 261.
[12] Mehta, 'Indian Constitutionalism: The Articulation of a Political Vision', 21.

'ruptures the particular relationship with time and history ... the Indian constitution does not so much emerge from history as it emerges in opposition to history and with a firm view of the future.'[13] Ironically, Naipaul would agree with Mehta that political independence alone does not signify a meaningful rupture of colonial regimes of time and history; however, Naipaul stops short of affirming a revolutionary temporality that could dismantle the waiting room of history model.[14] In Naipaul's essentialist logic, those who occupy waiting spaces become waiting people, destined to wait even after they relocate to Western countries. In contrast, Gordimer's novel reworks the concepts of both history and time, therein affirming the temporal disjunction necessary for revolutionary change.

Conrad's Heir: Naipaul's African Fiction

When the Swedish Academy awarded Naipaul the 2001 Nobel Prize in Literature, the announcement heralded Naipaul as 'Conrad's heir' – a comparison proudly printed on the back cover of the Vintage International edition of *A Bend in the River*, and one courted by Naipaul in his fiction and non-fiction alike. In 'Conrad's Darkness and Mine', originally published in the *New York Review of Books* in 1974, Naipaul reflects on parallels between Conrad's world and his own. In an oft-quoted remark, Naipaul proclaims that Conrad, 'sixty years before, in a time of a great peace – had been everywhere before me', documenting 'a vision of the world's half-made societies as places which continuously made and unmade themselves'.[15] Naipaul elaborates on this affinity with Conrad and his world, noting, 'Conrad's value to me is that he is someone who sixty to seventy years ago meditated on my world, a world

---

[13] Ibid., 24.

[14] In his review of Chakrabarty's *Provincializing Europe* titled 'In the Waiting-Room of History', writer Amit Chaudhuri allots two paragraphs to suggest a link between Naipaul and this historical model. He writes, 'The non-West – the waiting room – is therefore doomed either never to be quite modern, to be, in Naipaul's phrase, "half-made"; or to possess only a semblance of modernity.' He continues, with reference to *The Mimic Men*, *A Bend in the River*, and 'In a Free State', to assert that Naipaul 'is a writer who seems to have subscribed quite deeply to the sort of historicism that Chakrabarty describes ... In fiction, the greatest explorers of this Millian terrain have been Naipaul and Naipaul's master, Conrad.'

[15] Naipaul, *Literary Occasions*, 170.

I recognize today.'¹⁶ Of course, between Conrad's era and Naipaul's own, significant changes occurred within Africa as well as across the globe, including several world wars, the onset of the Cold War and decolonisation and national independence movements. When Naipaul begins to set his fiction in Africa in the 1970s, then, he not only ignores the radical aspects of Conrad's formulation of time, but also glosses over the entire independence period when he draws on this temporal framework of changelessness, circular creation and destruction.

Naipaul's 1971 short story 'In a Free State' and 1979 novel *A Bend in the River* bookend the 1970s, and share a vision, through the eyes of outsiders, of postcolonial African countries fractured by the capricious desires of dictators. 'In a Free State', the longest of the four pieces collected in the volume of the same name, follows Bobby and Linda as they travel outwards from the capital city of an unnamed country, concluding at a checkpoint where Bobby is beaten by army soldiers. The encounter is initiated with Bobby's question about curfew, pointing to his watch. After Bobby declines to hand over the watch, the soldiers assault him; while he initially resists, he ultimately submits to the punishment. Upon returning to the car, Linda remarks emptily, '"Your watch is broken."'¹⁷ This is the second time Bobby's watch has been 'broken' within the narrative; the first occasion is referenced earlier in the car ride, when he recalls the failed treatment to 'cure' his homosexuality. After accidentally stepping on his watch, he decided not to fix it until he was cured. He confides to Linda, '"Walking around with a smashed watch . . . how quickly you can adapt to having your whole life written off. At first I used to say, 'I'm going to get better next week.' Then it was next month. Then it was next year."'¹⁸ The echoes of the broken watch connect the attempt to 'cure' Bobby's homosexuality to his attempt to serve the new government; neither the treatment nor the offer of service is successful, and his humility in serving the postcolonial country is met with his humiliation. Bobby is no longer able to measure the movement of time, which destroys his confidence in time moving forward altogether as well as his aspiration for the future.

Several developments in the narrative of 'In a Free State' are important for how Naipaul will return to them in *A Bend in the River*. First, both texts use 'outsiders' as dominant focalising perspectives. A homosexual Englishman, Bobby is doubly displaced, from his native England as well as from the unnamed former colony where the narrative's action

---

¹⁶ Ibid., 173.
¹⁷ Ibid., 241.
¹⁸ Ibid., 162.

is set, whereas Salim in *A Bend in the River* feels increasingly isolated by his Indian lineage as enthusiasm for Black Nationalism increases in the country. Additionally, the image of the broken watch in 'In a Free State' suggests that the forward march of time is suspended. The narrative mourns the inapplicability of mathematical time to measure the passing of moments, and presents no other mechanism or perspective to offer an alternative symbol to affirm a future – for Bobby, or for the Africans now in charge. Likewise, *A Bend in the River* presents a bleak picture for the future of independent African nations. As Naipaul infamously proclaimed in an interview with Elizabeth Hardwick, prompted by the subject of *A Bend in the River*, 'Africa has no future'.[19] Naipaul's novella and his novel alike depict protagonists with no choice but to escape African locales, where time is endlessly circular and violence hopelessly repetitive.

Naipaul's view of African temporalities is informed by his sympathies with colonial regimes of time, which share Western historicism's teleological assumption that every society ought to tend towards modern nation-states modelled in the West's image. In Naipaul's fiction, the inability to replicate this model reflects poorly on the countries and their inhabitants rather than calling into question the model itself. With reference to Naipaul's entire oeuvre, Fawzia Mustafa finds that Naipaul's 'implication within colonialist discursive practice' is partly due to his 'obsessive privileging of the Word and Book and the "coherence" and "order" leading to "knowledge" they represent'.[20] Naipaul's rendering of time and history in the African interior in *A Bend in the River* is compatible with the characteristics of colonialist discursive practice that Mustafa identifies; Naipaul underscores differences between his ethnically Indian protagonist Salim and his black African neighbours in terms of the latter's association with chaos, irrationality, inscrutability and timelessness. Indeed, Mustafa identifies echoes of Hegel in *A Bend in the River*'s endorsement of trampling the past, citing Hegel's proclamation that '"Africa proper, as far as History goes back, has remained . . . shut up . . . the land of childhood, which lying beyond the day of self-conscious history, is enveloped in the dark mantle of Night."'[21]

The opening pages of *A Bend in the River* establish the novel's complicated relationship to Western historical time, which anchors Salim's sense of his family's history on the continent. At the same time, Naipaul introduces the *longue durée* history of Arab and European interactions

---

[19] Jussawalla, *Conversations with V. S. Naipaul*, 47.
[20] Mustafa, *V. S. Naipaul*, 27.
[21] Hegel, quoted in ibid., 148.

to frame Salim's historical consciousness. As Bruce King points out, this history decentres European colonialism, in a way, by situating the continent within 'a long history of contacts with the outside world'.[22] Though the *longue durée* is evoked by Conrad's description of the centre of Africa waiting for the fantastic invasion to pass, as I argued in the previous chapter, this historical context is not given specificity in *Heart of Darkness*. Instead, Marlow reserves a detailed elaboration of a historical perspective only for England – a history of barbarity and conquest stretching from Roman times to Marlow's contemporary, turn-of-the-century moment. Where Conrad limits his focus to Europe's interactions with its southern continental neighbour, Naipaul places the eastern coast of the continent at the centre, at least initially, identifying it as 'an Arab-Indian-Persian-Portuguese place, and we who lived there were really people of the Indian Ocean'.[23] This ostensible affirmation of Afro-Indian interculturation, however, is undercut by Salim's observation that the east coast was then 'not truly African'.[24] This pattern of essentialism continues throughout the novel; among Salim's observations is that black Africa is 'True Africa', Zabeth is a 'good and direct businesswoman . . . unusually for an African', and that 'there is a simple democracy about Africa: everyone is a villager'.[25]

Salim's view of Africa as timeless and unchanging is consistent with his other generalised essentialisms about Africa and its inhabitants. 'The world is what it is',[26] Salim remarks twice in a tautology that, in the context of Salim's observations about Africa more generally, underscores Africa's fundamental characteristics and its propensity for chaos and disorder. Naipaul's description of the 'timeless ways of village and river'[27] is reminiscent of Conrad's Marlow likening his trip to 'travelling back to the earliest beginnings of the world'.[28] As a location of timelessness, the bend in the river becomes increasingly associated with the temporality of waiting, and functions as a 'waiting room' – not only for Salim, but also as a microcosm intended to encapsulate the dynamics of an entire continent. The shop that Salim buys at the bend in the river was originally owned by Nazruddin, a family friend who is admired for his instinct to pull his investments from African countries before political crises disrupt

---

[22] King, *V. S. Naipaul*, 121.
[23] Naipaul, *A Bend in the River*, 10.
[24] Ibid., 10.
[25] Ibid., 10, 6, 48.
[26] Ibid., 3, 15.
[27] Ibid., 36.
[28] Conrad, *Heart of Darkness and Other Tales*, 131.

trade. After Salim's relocation, he is joined by his family's servant Ali, renamed Metty (from the French *métis*) by the locals in response to his mixed-race ancestry. Other characters who converge at the bend in the river include Ferdinand, a trader's son who studies at the *lycée* and has the novel's final word on the future of their country; Indar, Salim's Indian childhood friend who goes to London for school and returns for a time to the country to teach; and Raymond, the 'Big Man's white man' and historian who aborts his own attempts to write the country's history. While Salim is initially hopeful that he can start over in the town at the bend in the river, he is disappointed in the violence he sees as both recurrent and inevitable.

In this way, Naipaul depicts time differently here than in 'In a Free State', but though time appears recurrent and circular in *A Bend in the River* rather than broken, both texts evince a future already foreclosed. Structurally, the novel is divided into four parts, beginning with 'The Second Rebellion'. The title implies the event of a first rebellion, and the fourth section, 'Battle', gestures towards a continuation of the pattern of conflict. Salim characterises the country in terms of endless conflict; when an uprising on the coast results in the murder of Arabs, he remarks, 'But what had happened was not new. People who had grown feeble had been physically destroyed. That, in Africa, was not new; it was the oldest law of the land.'[29] In the return to chaos and barbarism, Naipaul collapses the country's past and future in 'a hopeless, repetitious circling or returning from the prehistoric bush to another bush, where there is no democracy, but only the rise and fall of Kurtz-like dictators.'[30] The futility that Bobby senses in 'In a Free State' is here more directly mapped onto the African inhabitants, who are depicted as 'agents of their own cyclical destruction . . . because they are locked into a hermetic system of self-destruction.'[31]

The narrative increasingly links Salim's waiting to despair because the temporality of cyclical violence disturbs his confidence in progress in Africa. The text's condemnation of Africa for the inability to nurture progress is significant; Salim's valuation of development and Western cultural values remains unshaken throughout the text, and his decision to leave the country at the end is the logical outcome of the twinned beliefs in Western progress and African devolution. Given the inherent, unharnessed rage and irrational violence that Naipaul attributes to the

---

[29] Naipaul, *A Bend in the River*, 29.
[30] Nakai, 'Journey to the Heart of Darkness: Naipaul's "Conradian Atavism" Reconsidered', 10.
[31] Nixon, *London Calling*, 92.

Africans within *A Bend in the River*, Joseph Walunywa concludes that 'the prevailing idea that underlies the book is the problematic notion that Africa has no hope in terms of its future economic development precisely because Africans are inherently incapable of resolving the crises that bedevil their environment.'[32] Within this context, waiting takes on a contingent form; Salim is doomed to wait for the future he desires only to the extent that he remains at the bend in the river. The gap between the present and the future can only be bridged, Walunywa notes, by a spatial 'relocation to globally powerful nations'.[33] As we will see below, with respect to Indar's travels specifically, this relocation does not guarantee an escape from the temporality of aimless waiting. Nevertheless, it is here that we can see most clearly the text's formulation of the bend in the river as a waiting room, whose occupants include those inhabitants of the formerly colonised world who were not, and are still not yet, ready for independence.

As narrator and protagonist, Salim conveys this 'not yet' following independence in two ways. One way is the commentary he provides on independence and its significance directly. Rather than representing a decisive break with colonial rule, independence, for Salim, is synonymous with 'troubles'. His arrival at the bend in the river coincides with the de-escalation of post-independence violence. Finding other traders and foreigners who 'had been there right through the troubles', Salim 'waited with them. The peace held. People began coming back to the town . . . And slowly business started up again.'[34] The new beginning is short-lived, however, and Naipaul depicts the African country going back to its 'old ways' and drifting further back to a prehistoric, precolonial past. Salim laments,

> You could imagine the land being made part of the present: that was how the Big Man put it later, offering us a vision of a two-hundred mile 'industrial park' along the river . . . In daylight, though, you could believe in that vision of the future. You could imagine the land being made ordinary, fit for men like yourself, as small parts of it had been made ordinary for a short while before independence – the very parts that were now in ruins.[35]

Drawing on *Heart of Darkness*'s tropes of darkness and light, Naipaul here contends that the lightness of colonial rule is finally extinguished

---

[32] Walunywa, 'The "Non-Native Native" in V. S. Naipaul's A Bend in the River', 4–5.
[33] Ibid., 2.
[34] Naipaul, *A Bend in the River*, 5.
[35] Ibid., 8–9.

after independence. The old colonial town lies in ruins, formulating the colonial period as an irregularity in a longer African history.

The second way that Naipaul formulates the bend in the river as another 'waiting room of history' after political independence is through characters with explicit ties to Western historical traditions. These characters, which include the academic historian Raymond as well as Father Huismans, are rejected by their local African communities. Their associations with waiting and history contribute to the narrative's overall rendering of spatial distance between Europe and Africa into temporal distance, and suggest that it is impossible to envision a future in Africa any different from the cycles of violence Salim identifies as constituting its past. While Peggy Nightingale views these characters as evidence that Naipaul 'seems close to recanting his faith in the study of history',[36] I contend that his commentary here directly targets Africa, Africans and African history, creating distinctions from Europe, Europeans and European history. This binary is ultimately employed to underscore Salim's alienation as an Indian-African, and the experiences of other Indian-Africans abroad suggests that his exit from Africa will not necessarily create an exit from the so-called waiting rooms of history.[37]

The Belgian Father Huismans and the white academic Raymond offer different commentaries on the status of 'history' at the bend in the river, yet neither proves to be a lasting presence in the African interior; the former is killed mysteriously, while the latter flees Africa abruptly. Salim observes, 'All that I know of our history and the history of the Indian Ocean I have got from books written by Europeans', and Raymond is one such European academic.[38] Indar introduces Salim to Raymond, who resides at the new Domain polytechnic school and is known as the 'Big Man's white man' for his early mentorship of the current African president. But as the Big Man consolidates his power, Raymond's utility for the Big Man's administration begins to fade. His wife Yvette gives Salim insight into Raymond's struggles with the history book: '"He's working on this book, and has been for some years now. The government were

---

[36] Nightingale, *Journey through Darkness*, 210.
[37] I employ the term 'Indian-African' to draw attention, through the hyphen, to the split identity Salim exhibits. Other scholars have chosen Arab-African, Muslim Indian, or even simply 'Indian' as a descriptor; given Salim's complicated relationship to national belonging – a difficulty that Indar shares as he attempts to get a job as an Indian embassy and is rejected: '"How can we have a man of divided loyalties?"' (Naipaul, *A Bend in the River*, 149) – I have used 'Indian-African' to capture this tension.
[38] Naipaul, *A Bend in the River*, 11.

going to publish it, but now apparently there are difficulties.'"[39] Salim notes that the difficulties were not specified, but that 'Raymond had temporarily put aside his history to work on a selection of the President's speeches.'[40]

Raymond's inability to write the history of the country confirms the narrative's larger suggestion: that such a history cannot be written in Raymond's forms. Elsewhere, Naipaul has been candid about his views on writing the history of his native West Indies. In *The Middle Passage*, he asks rhetorically, 'How can the history of this West Indian futility be written? What tone shall the historian adopt?' and answers summarily, 'The history of the islands can never be satisfactorily told . . . History is built around achievement and creation; and nothing was created in the West Indies.'[41] While his focus here is on the Caribbean, evidence of Naipaul similarly assessing the African continent is clear in 'In a Free State' and *A Bend in the River*, for which Naipaul drew inspiration from locales as diverse as Uganda, Zaire and Trinidad. Naipaul, Timothy Weiss writes, gives the impression that

> all of these places are images of a single, fictional state . . . This vision of a Fourth World derives in part from European colonial discourse about sub-Saharan Africa, especially from Conrad's stories set in "half-made societies" forever making and unmaking themselves.[42]

Since Raymond has already written the nation's colonial history, the suggestion here is that nothing further – or new – can be produced. Instead of advancing through an unfolding future, the country in *A Bend in the River* is poised only to restage its turbulent past. In Raymond's waiting for the Big Man to ask for his assistance, and waiting for inspiration for a new history book, the text situates this ostensibly 'transitional' moment between rebellions as yet another waiting room of history.

As long as Raymond remains at the bend in the river and in a subservient position to the Big Man, he too feels entrapped by the temporality of waiting. For most of his stay at the Domain, Raymond resists the lull of waiting and ignores insinuations that he grows irrelevant to the Big Man. Raymond praises the Big Man in the face of criticisms from the Youth Guard, and Salim interprets his defensiveness on the Big Man's behalf as a sign that he 'was still waiting, then' while he 'might have nowhere else

---

[39] Ibid., 172.
[40] Ibid., 173.
[41] Naipaul, *The Middle Passage*, 29.
[42] Weiss, *On the Margins*, 167.

to go'.[43] Nevertheless, by the time Raymond gives up on the Big Man and departs the country, Salim has framed Raymond's stay at the Domain as a time of powerless waiting: 'At some moment he seemed to have decided that he wasn't going to be called back to the President's favour, and he had stopped waiting, stopped reading the signs.'[44] Significantly, Raymond's resignation coincides with Salim's impression that Raymond 'was reading old things he had written'. The past continues to be a refuge for Raymond, but he has given up on fashioning new narratives for the present. Instead, Raymond's tragic alignment with the country's past – which does not fit the vision that the Big Man seeks to promote – reduces Raymond to a state of impotent waiting.[45] The text does not directly depict Raymond and Yvette's departure from the country, and Salim hears about it second-hand. The bend in the river is destined to be a place of indefinite waiting, but given Raymond's ability to claim ties to elsewhere – he and his wife have ties to Europe, as well as the United States – he is able to end his waiting and exit the country.

Father Huismans embodies another kind of historical project, but his murder in the narrative suggests that, similarly, Naipaul does not endorse his approach. Huismans's unwavering belief in Africa's greatness depends on a static, romanticised view of Africa encapsulated in the artefacts he collects. Weiss argues that 'Father Huismans represents a certain Western viewpoint that looks at Africa as a museum (or wildlife reserve) rather than as a changing, human world of cultures in conflict and collision.'[46] In a conversation with Father Huismans, Salim learns that Huismans 'saw himself as part of an immense flow of history'.[47] As a result, he views the recent uprisings and 'troubles' with more tranquility than Salim can muster, because

> [f]or him the destruction of the European town, the town that his countrymen had built, was only a temporary setback. Such things happened when something big and new was being set up, when the course of history was being altered.[48]

Huismans's admiration for Africa is coupled with a seemingly paradoxical regard '[f]or everything connected with the European colonization,

---

[43] Naipaul, *A Bend in the River*, 196.
[44] Ibid., 214.
[45] The association of impotency with Raymond works on two levels; not only is he unable to produce new histories, but also his wife Yvette has an affair with Salim.
[46] Weiss, *On the Margins*, 187.
[47] Naipaul, *A Bend in the River*, 63.
[48] Ibid., 63.

the opening up of the river'.⁴⁹ Salim explains that Father Huismans can maintain this position because he is able to see 'beyond' the bitterness of colonisation.

While the tensions between Huismans's complicated views on history and Africa might be resolved through this *longue durée* historical view, where Africa's 'primitive' greatness is eventually grafted on to colonial modernisation as 'something big and new', I want to suggest that Huismans's murder early in the text signals that, in Naipaul's Africa, the two views are incompatible. When Huismans abruptly dies at the conclusion of the novel's first part, Salim notes that his body, 'mutilated, his head cut off and spiked', had been sent down river in a dugout intentionally to send a message.⁵⁰ Ferdinand speculates that Huismans's African obsessions were anachronistic in the postcolonial context. He asserts, '"It is a thing of Europeans, a museum. Here it is going against the god of Africans. We have masks in our houses and we know what they are there for. We don't have to go to Huismans's museum."'⁵¹ Ferdinand's language here carefully identifies the masks' usefulness in the present ('what they are there for'), in contrast to the museum's practice of ossifying cultural artefacts as relics. Weiss's reading of Huismans referenced above is closely aligned with Ferdinand's view. But Salim himself suggests another reading of this scene, one more consistent with the narrative's larger commentary on time in the interior of Africa. Whereas Huismans insists on something big and new manifesting at the bend in the river soon, Salim cynically sees hopeless repetition. A character with such an optimistic – and Salim suggests, also misguided – view cannot last long in *A Bend in the River*.

Far from representing critiques of European historicising, Huismans and Raymond are removed by Naipaul from their places at the bend in the river precisely because the historical perspectives they espouse are incompatible, from the narrative's point of view, with the repetitious circularity of African history and time. Naipaul underscores this association through the imagery of the Big Man's new Domain buildings, designed to propel the country and its people into postcolonial modernity. The Domain was built both on African bush and on the ruins of the old European settlement, with the aim of 'creating modern Africa'.⁵² Naipaul 'divide[s] Africa into Old and New', with the former 'receiving somewhat more favorable treatment than the New' because – and here,

---

⁴⁹ Ibid., 64.
⁵⁰ Ibid., 82.
⁵¹ Ibid., 83.
⁵² Ibid., 100.

Kenneth Harrow exaggeratedly mimics the narrative's position – it is the 'natural home of the blacks'.[53] Despite becoming the site of a university and research centre, Salim observes, 'The Domain had been built fast, and in the sun and the rain decay also came fast.'[54] The modernity supposedly embodied in the new buildings 'is therefore represented as shallow and superficial – a mere graft' that also implies '[t]he incongruity of imported European notions of progress'.[55] The characterisation of the Domain as being built too quickly situates independence as occurring too quickly as well; the Africans, Naipaul proposes, perhaps should have waited longer (or indefinitely) for self-rule.

In this way, Naipaul constructs a 'waiting room of history' for the entire country's population, affirming utter incommensurability between the time of European modernity and progress and the time of postcolonial Africa. Through images of the new Domain, erected and now rotting with equal speed, and the figures of Raymond and Huismans, *A Bend in the River* depicts an Africa that will never catch up with its Western others, so refusing to wait and fomenting further revolutions alike will ultimately change nothing. In the following section, which concludes my reading of *A Bend in the River*, I analyse the specific experiences of waiting described by Salim and his friend Indar. These two characters further develop Naipaul's pessimistic vision of African futures as a continuation of waiting rooms of history. Not only is the country destined to repeat the rebellions and conflicts of the past, but for Indian-Africans who attempt to escape abroad, their waiting will also follow them wherever they go.

'I will wait for the rest of my life': Indian-Africans Abroad

Although scholars often interpret Salim as Naipaul's mouthpiece, espousing the values of and his identification with Western neocolonialism, Salim's relationship to colonial time is complicated by his Indian ethnicity and a worry that, no matter how much he tries, he is fated to exist with a sense of belatedness. Together, Salim and Indar indicate that from the novel's perspective, Indian-Africans are doubly removed from history; even though they appear more cognisant of the need to record history, their ethnic backgrounds in the context of Black Nationalism leave them feeling written out of it. Salim is particularly concerned

---

[53] Harrow, 'An African Reading of Naipaul's "A Bend in the River"', 238.
[54] Naipaul, *A Bend in the River*, 102.
[55] Hayward, *The Enigma of V. S. Naipaul*, 174.

that 'as a community we [Indian-Africans] had fallen behind', and that 'Europeans were better equipped to cope with changes' associated with independence, opting 'to get out, or to fight, or to meet the Africans halfway' while the Indians on the coast 'continued to live as we had always done, blindly'.[56] The ethnically Indian community in Africa, Salim submits, suffers feelings of belatedness even at independence because they are not temporally integrated with their black African neighbours. As Bruce King observes, this positioning of Hindu Indians as outsiders at the moment of postcolonial independence is consistent with Naipaul's view of decolonisation in his native Trinidad as well, where the 'rhetoric of decolonization was filled with black nationalism, pan-Africanism, Judeo-Christian notions of black racial deliverance and Marxist models of single party states', situating the Hindu Indian as an 'outsider, the marginal, the opposition to those who felt destined to inherit the apparatus of the state at independence'.[57] Even if independence marked a revolutionary temporal rupture that rejected the waiting room of history for black Africans – and the narrative undermines this assumption through its emphasis on waiting and cyclical violence – Naipaul suggests that ethnic minorities in Africa and Indian-Africans in particular were not necessarily included in this future imagined community.

At the same time, Salim notes that the temporal experiences of Indian-Africans on the African coast are not homogeneous. Reminiscing on his youth, Salim remembers that Indar's departure to go to England to study exacerbated his feeling of falling behind. Salim reflects, 'He had always made me feel so backward', in part because of Indar's family's greater financial investments and subsequently higher standard of living, their enjoyment of physical exercise as leisure activities, marked them 'as "modern" people' for Salim.[58] Renouncing jealousy, Salim nevertheless admits to feeling 'the unhappiness of a man who felt left behind, unprepared for what was coming'.[59] When Indar returns to the country as a visiting lecturer in the Domain, he alone reflects the passage of the years, his London clothes symbolising the distance if not the time travelled. Self-deprecatingly, Salim remarks, 'And I – well, I was in my shop, with the red dirt road and the market square outside. I had waited so long, endured so much, changed; yet to him I hadn't changed at all.'[60] When Indar finds Salim in the same state of waiting for the future that he was

---

[56] Naipaul, *A Bend in the River*, 16–17.
[57] King, *V. S. Naipaul*, 11.
[58] Naipaul, *A Bend in the River*, 109.
[59] Ibid., 110.
[60] Ibid., 110.

in eight years ago, he perceives that time has passed differentially for the two childhood friends.

Naipaul explicitly contrasts Indar's distinct relationship with the past with Salim's future-oriented present; Indar's view of the past is more aggressive, and he advocates several times, '"We can trample the past."'[61] Though the novel is primarily focalised from Salim's perspective, the voices of other characters interrupt several times with long digressions, flashbacks or sustained reflections. Indar takes over in the second section, 'The New Domain', and he advises, '"We have to learn to trample on the past, Salim . . . It isn't easy to turn your back on the past. It isn't something you can decide to do just like that. It is something you have to arm yourself for, or grief will ambush and destroy you."'[62] Indar intends his strategy of trampling on the past to contrast starkly with Salim's waiting at the bend in the river, but the language of waiting in fact creates continuity between their temporal experiences. The fifteen pages that comprise chapter nine in 'The New Domain' are told exclusively from Indar's perspective, and it is remarkable how often waiting punctuates his story of purported forward movement. Indar's initial excitement over acquiring a university degree is tempered by his unsavoury realisation that he had been naïve in believing '"that after my time in the university some wonderful life would be waiting for me"'.[63] His pursuit of a diplomatic position with the Indian embassy yields more waiting, before the embassy dismisses him with the charge of having 'divided loyalties' between the India of his heritage and the Africa of his birth.[64] At this point, Indar's association of the life and job 'out there' in the world just waiting for him transfers from Europe to Africa as he remembers '"our stretch of the African coast . . . I felt I had known that life, and that it was waiting for me again somewhere."'[65] At the conclusion of Indar's retrospective narrative, he quickly qualifies the dream of a future waiting in Africa: '"It was fantasy, of course."'

Indar's exit from the story, aboard a steamer that prefigures Salim's eventual escape, reinforces rather than resists the state of waiting. Indar is the novel's most mobile character, traversing the unnamed African country, England, Africa again, America, and beyond. There is no sense of Indar's restlessness receding as he seeks out a future to match his desires. Flustered, Indar is last depicted making his way to a private

---

[61] Ibid., 136.
[62] Ibid., 141.
[63] Ibid., 142.
[64] Ibid., 149.
[65] Ibid., 150–51.

suite on the steamer, complaining about having to wait at the airport for hours the day before. Salim learns that the interminable waiting was a result of the Big Man commandeering the plane for his own purposes – an experience that Salim later encounters himself. Although Indar's departure holds out hope that his waiting on others and for the future might end, Kareisha's later interruption into Salim's story fills in the blanks concerning Indar's experience in America. Kareisha is Salim's fiancée and Nazruddin's daughter, whom Salim visits in London just before the government's African nationalisation programme appropriates his shop and gives it to a Black African to manage. Kareisha relates that Indar is depressed following a 'bad experience in America'.[66] On a mission to recover funds for his business ventures, Indar instead finds himself attending social and business functions, yet '"nothing seemed to be happening. It was always just back to the hotel, and waiting."'[67] Resigned, Indar submits to the pointlessness inscribed in waiting for a future he cannot bring about himself, '"know[ing] he is equipped for better things, but he doesn't want to do them"'.[68]

Despite Salim's misgivings that he has been waiting while Indar moves ahead, Kareisha's description of a broken man being forced to wait makes 'waiting' a shared condition between the men; regardless of geographical location, the temporality of waiting inheres in the characters' relation to the future and appears to follow wherever they go. The novel's final word on Indian-Africans' position vis-à-vis the waiting rooms of history is perhaps best summarised by Nazruddin, who informs Salim in England, 'We've come here at the wrong time. But never mind. It's the wrong time everywhere else too.'[69] Indeed, Indar's violent trampling of the past does not bring him any closer to a desired future, and with both past and future truncated, he is trapped in a waiting present. As Robert Balfour observes, '[Indar] is the global citizen in the most antithetical sense; with obligations only to the present, no fixed location, no loyalties or local connection.'[70] Instead of providing an alternative to Salim at the bend in the river, however, Indar's temporality of waiting reproduces the same temporal dimensions that divorce the past and future alike from the present. Given these similarities, we are primed to read Salim's own exit from the country at the end of the novel as following in Indar's

---

[66] Ibid., 241.
[67] Ibid., 242.
[68] Ibid., 244.
[69] Ibid., 239.
[70] Balfour, 'Home as Postcolonial Trope in the Fiction of V. S. Naipaul', 26.

footsteps, burdening his departure with a sense of already guaranteed failure.

Salim's decision to leave Africa follows his epiphany that waiting is the inevitable condition of his existence at the bend in the river. His refusal to wait out the present 'troubles' is a way to manage this waiting even as he notes that he will, like Indar and Nazruddin before him, continue to wait regardless of where he is located. Salim explicitly identifies the bend in the river as a space of perpetual waiting while he is detained in jail. Salim has indicated at different points that waiting has been oppressively limiting; he thinks that for Ferdinand and Metty, the past could be shed easier, whereas for him, 'I have lost my twenties, and what I have been looking for since I left home hasn't come to me. I have only been waiting. I will wait for the rest of my life.'[71] His affair with Yvette is a temporary distraction or interruption, but her departure as well as the quickening deterioration of the country hastens Salim's surrender to waiting. After police, tipped off by Metty, discover contraband ivory tusks buried in the yard, the police take Salim into 'preventative detention' for a weekend.

Forcibly removed from the town and river, Salim must confront the fact that a future in Africa does not exist for him. Of the police headquarters, Salim remarks, 'There I learned to wait. There I decided that I had to shut out thoughts of the town and stop thinking about time, that I had as far as possible to empty my mind.'[72] As empty or dead time, the temporality of waiting and the condition of being physically outcast from society dovetail here; Salim's recognition that he is an outsider is occasioned by his most extreme moment of waiting. Salim concludes, 'I had to learn to wait, in a jail that was suddenly real, and frightening now because of its very simpleness.'[73] I contend that the jail is frightening precisely because, in its evocation of waiting, it reveals that there is no difference between the temporality of the jail and the temporality of the town at the bend in the river for Salim. Through the language of waiting, Naipaul suggests that the unnamed African country imprisons Salim. His exit from the country puts an end to his waiting at the bend in the river, but this refusal to wait leaves Salim suspended in a present, paradoxically still waiting, with neither an anchor in the past nor a grasp on the future.

Although Naipaul initially links the temporality of waiting with specific physical spaces – the bend in the river, the unnamed African

---

[71] Naipaul, *A Bend in the River*, 107.
[72] Ibid., 266.
[73] Ibid., 268.

country, the jail – by the novel's conclusion the waiting room is an existential condition for Indian-Africans rather than a concrete location in space. This extra-territorial waiting undermines Walunywa's suggestion that the novel promotes the 'relocation to globally powerful nations' as a solution for Indian-Africans marginalised in Africa[74] and Selwyn Cudjoe's conclusion that '[t]he certainties offered by London and similar places are unavailable in India or Africa because of the arbitrariness of those societies.'[75] As Indar's circumstances especially underscore, the temporalities of waiting in Naipaul's novel follow them across the globe and deconstruct the Europe/Africa binary that Indar and Salim – as well as critics like Walunywa and Cudjoe – appear to instantiate. This formulation of waiting is consistent with the waiting-room model of history, privileging progress and modernity emanating from Europe and simultaneously placing them out of reach for Salim, Indar, Nazruddin and the other inhabitants of their country. My reading here contrasts with Erica Johnson, who proposes that Naipaul 'presents a rigorously skeptical portrait of the overdetermined concept of progress', and thus 'effectively provincializes Europe' in the way Dipesh Chakrabarty calls for.[76] Johnson's unusual reading posits that the novel 'reveal[s] European signs taken as universals to be the discreet, geographically specific concepts that they are',[77] but to do so she must ignore the fact that Naipaul maps primitiveness onto Africans to render them unsuitable for the 'progress' the characters reserve for Europe. In other words, even if the novel alleges that European models of progress are geographically specific rather than universal concepts, Johnson ignores how Naipaul's characters mourn this incompatibility. Given the re-instantiation of the 'not yet' for Salim as he travels abroad, as well as the devolution into violence of the African country he leaves behind, the novel does not 'provincialize' Europe so much as reassert its centrality as a referent for measuring the myriad ways that the continent continues to wait. Naipaul does not allow other alternative configurations of modernity or civilisation to emerge. Rather, European notions of progress and modernity are still acclaimed.

In this way, Naipaul creates a foil between the temporalities of progress, history and achievement in Europe and his insistence that the temporalities of Africa are constituted by cycles of violence. Naipaul's

---

[74] Walunywa, 'The "Non-Native Native" in V. S. Naipaul's A Bend in the River', 2.
[75] Cudjoe, *V. S. Naipaul*, 187.
[76] Johnson, '"Provincializing Europe": The Postcolonial Urban Uncanny in V.S. Naipaul's A Bend in the River', 211.
[77] Ibid., 213.

declaration, cited earlier in this chapter, that 'Africa has no future'[78] is depicted within the novel as well as mirrored in its structure, which imitates 'the cycle of progress and reversion', but 'refuses to move to a point of crisis or recognition'.[79] The predictable repetition of violence 'affirms only duration' rather than the unfolding of time into an undetermined future.[80] Or, to use the operative terms in this study, the novel imposes a temporality of indefinite waiting and defers the incorporation of African and Indian-African subjects alike into modernity by returning to the waiting-room of history model of historicism characteristic of the colonial era. Naipaul adapts notions of circular time to insist that the 'not yet' will never become 'now', where the repetition of cycles of violence posit a doomed temporality emptied of the possibilities of agential action. *A Bend in the River* depicts a zero-sum temporality, where waiting and refusing to wait are both evidently self-defeating for Indian-Africans.

Perhaps the most fitting image for the temporality of *A Bend in the River* is one from Naipaul's earlier story, 'In a Free State': the broken watch. The suggestive rejections of various European histories for writing the past, present and future of the town at the bend in the river do not affirm an alternative temporality beyond a state of waiting. Time may continue to pass for Salim, as it surely does for Bobby, but the ends of both stories suggest that the characters are disoriented in time, unable either to measure it or to project beyond the present moment. The refusal to wait that concludes *A Bend in the River* guarantees Salim's isolation, and he departs the country under the cover of darkness, constructing the temporal dimensions of waiting in terms of an interminable present: as a departure where the arrival is indefinitely postponed beyond the pages of the text.

Temporal Dimensions of Waiting during the Interregnum in South Africa

According to Naipaul in a 1979 interview, 'all over the third world, the West is waiting for the helicopters that will facilitate their escape'.[81] While Salim escapes under the cover of darkness aboard a steamer instead of a

---

[78] Jussawalla, *Conversations with V. S. Naipaul*, 47.
[79] Coovadia, 'Authority and Misquotation in V. S. Naipaul's A Bend in the River', 8.
[80] Berger, 'Writing Without a Future: Colonial Nostalgia in V. S. Naipaul's "A Bend in the River"', 152.
[81] Jussawalla, *Conversations with V. S. Naipaul*, 49.

helicopter in *A Bend in the River*, the image of the helicopter is provocative and resonates with Salim's other observations about air travel. On the one hand, Salim agrees with his friend Indar that travel by air allows him 'to adjust to his homelessness', and the experience of 'being in two places at once' – between Africa and Europe – means 'you had no feeling of having made a final decision, a great last journey'.[82] In hovering over the ground and yielding a sensation of suspension between two places, Naipaul's helicopter figures as an escape from both the African continent and the pressure of making a choice. On the other hand, the helicopter is striking for the intertextual resonance it creates with Nadine Gordimer's later 1981 novel, *July's People*. Gordimer's novel concludes with an image of its protagonist, Maureen Smales, running towards a helicopter as well as an uncertain fate in the revolution that signals the possible end of apartheid.

Turning to Gordimer's *July's People* after Naipaul's *A Bend in the River* usefully illuminates some of their shared preoccupations – intertextual connections with *Heart of Darkness*, the temporal dimensions of waiting, imminent political revolution – as well as their starkly contrasting views of the postcolonial future of Africa. Gordimer's sustained interrogation of history and time, especially in contrast to Naipaul's capitulation to centring European temporal narratives of progress and modernity, is at the heart of my analysis. Although *July's People* and *A Bend in the River* both concern characters who move inward into the unfamiliar interior of their African countries, and whose flights mark the conclusion of both narratives, I contend that the difference between the two is that the kinds of waiting are qualitatively different. Unlike Salim, Maureen's waiting in July's village encourages her self-reflection and maturation, engendering a different orientation towards the new dispensation to come.

The novel opens by describing the distorted temporality that the beginning of the revolution creates for Maureen Smales, the white main character, as she escapes with her family from Johannesburg to their servant July's village. The novel's epigraph, excerpted from Antonio Gramsci's *Prison Notebooks*, positions the novel between the dying old and the new that cannot be born – the temporality of the interregnum. The rest of *July's People* wrestles with the difficulties of transitioning from the old ways to the new, especially in the context of great uncertainty over how the future might unfold; despite their progressive politics, Maureen and her husband Bam struggle to admit their own complicity in maintaining

---

[82] Naipaul, *A Bend in the River*, 228–9.

apartheid society. Maureen's relationships with her children, husband, servant July, and July's family all require reassessment as the structures and economies of the suburb become increasingly anachronistic. The village location upends their sense of time as well as their relationship to July. The novel concludes with Maureen running towards a helicopter – an ambiguous ending that has variably suggested to scholars that she is running towards revolutionaries who may kill her or rescuers who may save her, a sign of rejection or embracement, alternatively pessimistic or cautiously optimistic.

In the lecture 'Living in the Interregnum', Gordimer describes the interregnum period in terms of disruption and interruption, disorder and incoherence. The interregnum, Gordimer argues, is characterised by the winds of 'revolutionary change' and the absence of 'historical coordinates' to offer orientation.[83] Ernest Cole notes that how scholars interpret the interregnum and its temporality substantially influences their sense of the novel's rendering of South Africa's future.[84] Cole's pessimistic reading of *July's People*, for example, emphasises the ominous 'the new cannot be born' portion of the novel's epigraph, and posits a 'gap between the two transition periods [the old and new]' that ultimately 'gestures toward a process of continued interregnum'.[85] Because the interregnum is clearly a transitional time wherein the old and new intermingle and overlap, however, it would be too neat to separate these periods distinctly. The morbid symptoms result from the old and new comingling together, giving rise to a disjunctive temporality distinguished by the lingering old and the incipient new. The temporal disjunction characteristic of the interregnum manifests in the sentence structures on the novel's first page, in the enjambment of lines:

> The knock on the door
>   no door, an aperture in thick mud walls, and the sack that hung over it looped back for air, sometime during the short night.[86]

The first door is understood to be one associated with the old ways and located in the suburbs, and the absence of a door in the succeeding line reorients Maureen and the reader to the present and emerging new in July's village, where the old ways and roles are not only irrelevant, but also impossible to sustain.

---

[83] Gordimer and Clingman, *The Essential Gesture*, 263.
[84] Cole, 'Nadine Gordimer and Post-Apartheid Interregnum: An Analysis of "July's People"', 60.
[85] Gordimer, *July's People*, 60.
[86] Ibid., 1.

Significantly, and in contrast to both Conrad's and Naipaul's texts, Gordimer does not depict the movement into the interior, from the Johannesburg suburb to July's village, as a movement back to a pre-modern period. Instead, this spatial shift prompts Maureen to reflect on her personal history in relation to apartheid and the labour economy. After finding that reading fiction is impossible because she was already 'in another time, place, consciousness', Maureen reflects on the interiors of the houses in the village, which include objects that miners acquired while working in the mines.[87] The brass plaque that reads 'BOSS BOY' prompts Maureen to recall a childhood memory walking to school with Lydia, her Black nanny, who carries the young girl's school case on her head. A photographer documents the scene, promising to send the photo but never following through. Maureen remembers seeing the photo years later in a book about 'White *herrenvolk* attitudes and life-styles', and wonders, 'Why had Lydia carried her case? . . . Did the book, placing the pair in its context, give the reason she and Lydia, in their affection and ignorance, didn't know?'[88] This flashback, as well as further interactions with July and his village, pressure Maureen to confront her own position and privilege during apartheid, from daughter of a shift boss in the Western Mines area to employer of black servants – whose white boss still determines their tempos of work and leisure.

Although these memories do facilitate Maureen's critical self-reflection, they also emphasise the interconnectedness of July's village and Maureen's suburban home. Rather than separate the city and village as modern and traditional respectively, as we saw in Naipaul's presentation of London and the bend in the river, Gordimer emphasises their dependent, coeval development in time. In doing so, Gordimer not only revises the temporal relationships between the interior and exterior of Africa in *Heart of Darkness* and replicated in *A Bend in the River*, but she also addresses the specific South African context, where apartheid's creation of separate homelands instantiated 'temporal divisions of worlds of tradition and worlds of modernity', what Steffen Jensen calls 'homeland temporality'.[89] Apartheid apologists justified policies like the Promotion of Bantu Self-Government Act of 1959 with temporalising falsehoods, asserting that each group could 'develop "in its own time

---

[87] Ibid., 29.
[88] Ibid., 33. The *Oxford English Dictionary* explains that *herrenvolk* is German for 'master-race', utilised by the Nazis to describe those 'born to mastery'.
[89] Jensen, 'This House Is Not My Own . . . ! Temporalities in a South African Homeland', 991.

and in accordance with its own predispositions"'.[90] Apartheid legislation created racial groupings – white, Black, 'Coloured', and Indian – and mandated policies of separateness that dominated all aspects of life, including education, politics, healthcare and residences.[91] These racial categories, combined with theories of separate development that trafficked in the denial of coevalness, were designed to maintain white minority rule at the expense of the majority of the population. *July's People* disrupts this temporal narrative through the move from the suburb to the village, emphasising their interconnectedness in time in ways that counter apartheid's philosophy of separate development. Gordimer suggests that the interregnum – during which the old is dying and the new cannot be born – is especially suited not only to reveal the pervasiveness of these temporal narratives, but also to revise them.

Maureen and her family characterise the temporal tensions between old and new in the novel as anxious waiting. Their anxiety is heightened by the uncertainty that attends it; no one is certain how the events of the revolution will unfold. The village itself is the 'place of interregnum, between past and future', where the interregnum as Gordimer intends it is 'a space of transition, suspension, or displacement, where co-ordinates are dislodged, horizons uncertain, perception distorted in the very instruments it depends on'.[92] Historical coordinates, returning to Gordimer's description in 'Living in the Interregnum' above, are not able to orient during the interregnum, indicating that what is to come is not necessarily dictated by what has come before, despite the residual vestiges of the past. This vision is radically different from Naipaul's *A Bend in the River*, where the future is known and anticipatable because it will be a repetition of what has come before. Given the great uncertainty attending Maureen's refuge in July's village, her temporal experience of waiting is predominantly characterised by anxiety and dread.

In making 'waiting' central to Maureen's temporal experience as she negotiates the interregnum, Gordimer's novel underscores the pervasiveness of waiting in white South Africans' experiences during the turbulent 1980s. Just four years after the publication of *July's People*, anthropologist Vincent Crapanzano came to similar conclusions about white South Africans' impressions of time in the early 1980s. In *Waiting: The Whites of South Africa*, Crapanzano observes 'that South Africa today is caught

---

[90] Crapanzano, *Waiting*, xix.
[91] Posel, 'What's in a Name? Racial Categorisations under Apartheid and Their Afterlife', 56.
[92] Clingman, *The Grammar of Identity*, 212, 206.

in a deadened time of waiting'.[93] This waiting was associated with different affects, however, because fear attends to waiting by whites, hope for Blacks, and a mixture of fear and hope for 'Coloureds' and Asians. Two of Crapanzano's subjects, Ruth and Carl, are representative of the white South African experience of waiting. Ruth remains in South Africa, and in response to a question about the future, she responds,

> 'Ah, you ask me about the future. I don't like to think about it . . . .When I think about the future, I get scared. We are all acting out of fear, and so we are not doing the right thing. We didn't pay enough attention in the past, and now no one knows what to do.'[94]

Gordimer's Maureen similarly turns to the past while she waits for the future in July's village, turning to childhood memories of her relationship with Lydia to make sense of the inequalities unspoken in 'affection and ignorance'.[95] Crapanzano's Carl, however, left South Africa to teach in the United States of America, and he articulates passionately, '"I left South Africa because I couldn't stand the waiting any longer for something, anything, to happen."'[96] Carl's comment causes Crapanzano to realise that '*Waiting for something, anything, to happen* was a constant preoccupation', and 'provide[d] a thematic unity to what I heard, observed, and read'.[97]

Although Crapanzano does not cite *July's People* directly, he does close the chapter 'Waiting' with a reference to Gordimer's essay 'Living in the Interregnum' and notes that while waiting certainly captures the absence of 'historical coordinates' in South Africa, he would 'caution against overplaying the *morbidity*', which threatens to overly pathologise apartheid and make 'what is a question of morality a matter of disease'.[98] Nevertheless, the reference to Gordimer's essay, itself an elaboration of the interregnum temporalities that are explored within *July's People*, links both literary text and anthropological study in a shared consideration of South African whites waiting for the post-apartheid future. While Crapanzano's investigation is restricted to white South Africans' impressions of time in 1985, Gordimer's novel imaginatively envisions the function of 'waiting' once the anticipated event of revolution commences. Crapanzano's account of the temporality of waiting

---

[93] Crapanzano, *Waiting*, xxii.
[94] Ibid., 18–19.
[95] Gordimer, *July's People*, 33.
[96] Crapanzano, *Waiting*, 42.
[97] Ibid., 43.
[98] Ibid., 47.

situates the waiting subject in an uneasy position vis-à-vis this awaited future:

> Waiting means to be oriented in time in a special way. It is directed toward the future – not an expansive future, however, but a constricted one that closes in on the present. In waiting, the present is always secondary to the future . . . It is a sort of holding action – a lingering. (In its most extreme forms waiting can lead to paralysis.) In waiting, the present loses its focus in the now . . . Its only meaning lies in the future – in the arrival or non-arrival of the object of waiting. Waiting is always waiting for something . . . It is a passive activity.[99]

Part of the reason that waiting constricts the present is that the future weighs so heavily on the mind, but a growing awareness of the past during the time of waiting also contributes to this constriction. Crapanzano observes that we draw from the past in order to assess whether 'what we are waiting for will or will not come. Our expectations become "realistic"'.[100] This assessment of probability, drawn from experience, ensures that 'in waiting [there is] always this backward glance, this seeking security in the experience of the past'. This waiting can either be positively configured as desire and longing for something, or negatively configured as dreading something undesired.

It is my contention that Gordimer explores white South African waiting in *July's People*, and that Maureen's refusal to wait can be understood as a rejection of the temporality shared by parts of white South Africa. *July's People* situates 1980s South Africa as a time of suspension and anxious waiting, and the beginning of the revolution that causes Maureen's family to flee intensifies their waiting experiences. Given South Africa's complicated colonial history – conflicts between Britain and the Afrikaner inhabitants, the establishment of a Cape Colony, the Boer Republics, a South African Republic, and later the institution of apartheid – it is difficult to speak of colonial time and *July's People* in the same way that Naipaul evokes it in *A Bend in the River*.[101] Instead of the larger umbrella term 'colonial time', I see the novel specifically

---

[99] Ibid., 44.
[100] Ibid., 45.
[101] Derek Hook summarises, 'It is worth conceding that for some, apartheid South Africa is not necessarily a paradigmatic instance of "the postcolonial." The "neo-colonialism" of apartheid occurs within what is, strictly speaking, an already postcolonial state, an independent republic, free of imperial rule' (*A Critical Psychology of the Postcolonial*, 10). This is not to say that colonial and apartheid practices and discourses have nothing in common – in fact, Hook notes that these distinctions between 'apartheid' and 'colonial' are 'stopgaps against the making of unwarranted generalizations' – but that care should be taken

grappling with 'apartheid time', especially given the temporal dimensions inscribed in apartheid policies. The Smales family is at the end of apartheid time, both because of the imminent revolution and because the temporality that governed and justified apartheid is quickly becoming anachronistic. In traveling to July's village,

> the vehicle had made a journey so far beyond the norm of a present it divided its passengers from, that the master bedroom *en suite* had been lost, jolted out of chronology as the room where her returning consciousness properly belonged: the room that she had left four days ago.[102]

In this confused chronology, the master bedroom with all of its trappings – not only amenities but also the power of 'master' associated with it – is left behind. The hallmark of apartheid, separateness, is disrupted both by the close proximities in the village as well as the overlapping temporalities of there and then and here and now.

July's village is thus a revolutionary waiting room, in the sense that the spatiotemporal experience of waiting prompts Maureen's eventual refutation of the temporal and historical coordinates of apartheid policies and discourses. Temporality, as the 'psychical and social experience of time', Derek Hook argues, 'might express a variety of underlying (psycho)social contradictions' through its 'paradoxes and apparent distortions'.[103] Hook praises Crapanzano's study for decoding the 'paradoxical temporality of waiting', where 'the present is very much premised upon the future' but also 'diluted' by the 'generality of "the present" and the specificity of "the now"'.[104] Waiting, in Gordimer's novel, is not just characteristic of apartheid South Africa's temporality, but also a temporal modality that directly exposes the structures of power in the novel: an interrogative temporality, pushing characters to ask, who waits, and for what?

While waiting in the village for something, anything, to happen, Maureen newly comprehends and appreciates the extent to which time has always structured relationships, specifically between herself, July, and his wife Martha. As the family's servant, July's time is contingent on the Smaleses's needs and requests. Maureen's middle-class life and leisure, part-time work and vacations shape her sense of time. When the Smales family flees to July's village, this economic relationship between

---

when discussing the colonial dimensions of the apartheid context, and the 'postcolonial' aftermath.
[102] Gordimer, *July's People*, 3–4.
[103] Hook, 'Indefinite Delay: On (Post)Apartheid Temporality', 48.
[104] Ibid., 54.

white employer and black servant is disrupted; their arrival 'disturbs not only the established economic arrangements of July's family (since money will no longer be remitted from the city each month); their arrival also disturbs July's family's relationship to time and its lived patterns'.[105] For Martha, time's rhythm depends on July's returns to his village in his 'free' time. The seasons of being with and without a man

> overlaid sowing and harvesting, rainy summers and dry winters, and at different times, although at roughly the same intervals for all, changed for each for the short season when her man came home . . . The sun rises, the moon sets; the money must come, the man must go.[106]

A contrast can be drawn between Maureen and Martha's waiting; whereas Martha waited for July during apartheid, in the revolutionary moment Maureen now also waits. In upsetting the temporal structures of apartheid, however, the novel stops short of depicting what the new structures and new time might look like.

The future that Maureen no longer waits for, but instead runs towards, is ultimately open; the kind of utopian future that will succeed the dystopian apartheid present is anticipated but not prescribed in *July's People*. As Stephen Clingman argues, while the novel

> appears to be a projection from the present into the future . . . [it] is from another point of view *seeing the present through the eyes of the future*; it is after all the present that falls apart in the revolutionary context the novel proposes.[107]

Despite the anticipation of a post-apartheid future, the novel works within a limited horizon for seeing beyond the present. The novel's early reflection on emergency supply kits is particularly suggestive:

> In various and different circumstances certain objects and individuals are going to turn out to be vital. The wager of survival cannot, by its nature, reveal which, in advance of events. How was one to know? . . . The circumstances are incalculable in the manner in which they come about, even if apocalyptically or politically foreseen, and the identity of the vital individuals and objects is hidden by their humble or frivolous role in an habitual set of circumstances.[108]

---

[105] Nicholls, *Nadine Gordimer's July's People*, 23.
[106] Gordimer, *July's People*, 83.
[107] Clingman, *The Novels of Nadine Gordimer*, 201–2.
[108] Gordimer, *July's People*, 6.

The future to come is similarly indecipherable, even if the signs are becoming visible now. It is impossible to predict what objects will be useful because it is equally impossible to predict how events will unfold. In this sense, the narrative is non-teleological, what Elangbam Hermanta Singh calls a 'postmodern utopia', in its rejection of 'prescription, teleology, and naïve optimism' that anticipates rather than dictates the 'outlines of freedom'.[109] There is a sense that linear time and history are insufficient for imagining the post-apartheid future, and that such a future requires a radical reconstruction of the very categories of past, present, future, old and new, white and black, master and servant that the apartheid narrative of history depends on. The novel ends with Maureen refusing to wait any longer, closing mid-run towards a helicopter. We are told that Maureen 'could not have said what colour it was, what markings it had, whether it holds saviours or murderers; and – even if she were to have identified the markings – for whom.'[110] The novel's final words, 'She runs', maintain an image of movement in suspension, appropriate for the novel's transitional interregnum temporality. Whatever her fate, Maureen's run underscores that a return to 'back there' is impossible.

Broken Watches: Dismantling the Waiting Rooms of History

In closing, I want to return to my claim that Gordimer isolates the clock as a distorting instrument of perception in this interregnum context. Soon after their arrival in July's village, Maureen notes the obsolescence of the calendar and her watch, two markers and anchors of time. Whereas Bam 'kept glancing at his watch', Maureen instead 'knew hers was a useless thing'.[111] This significant difference in their conceptions of time coincides with the gradual devolution of their marriage; Maureen's sense of being 'in another time, place, consciousness' is heightened, compared to her husband's.[112] Likewise, the calendar's utility to link the passing of days with the body's natural rhythms is undercut in July's village when Maureen realises that she is menstruating a week earlier than usual.[113]

---

[109] Singh, 'Utopian and Dystopian Visions of the Future in Nadine Gordimer's July's People', 61.
[110] Gordimer, *July's People*, 158.
[111] Ibid., 43.
[112] Ibid., 29.
[113] Ibid., 67.

Neither the watch, which marks time as it passes, nor the calendar, which marks the passage of years as well as the return of anniversaries, allows Maureen to anchor herself in time. By the end of the novel, the watch evolves from being useless to broken:

> At about midday (from the height of the sun and the quiet of the bush – her watch was broken) Maureen Smales, who is alone at the hut although not alone in the settlement, no one was ever alone there – feels some change in the fabric of subconsciously identified sounds and movements that make the silence. There is a distant chuddering as of air being packed in waves of resistance against its own destiny.[114]

Scholars have noted the shift from the past to the present tense that sets the novel's final chapter apart from the preceding ones, but they neglect to link this shift with the image of the broken watch. Not only does the present tense indicate a more decisive break with the past, but also the broken watch suggests a radically open future not governed by the temporalities regulated by and associated with the clock and calendar. The helicopter – at the centre of scholarly debate concerning the novel's lasting hope for or pessimism about the future – arrives simultaneously with the text's acknowledgement that the time of the past is irrevocably broken; apartheid's temporalities are not only impractical now but also inaccessible entirely.

Through the temporalities exhibited in the final chapter, *July's People* illustrates the confluence of several temporal strands: the old time is broken, the new has yet to manifest (although the helicopter seems to be a harbinger of the new time), the past tense is wholly unavailable for narration, and the run towards the helicopter signals a refusal to wait and see; Maureen instead runs to see for herself. In this way, Maureen, like Salim, refuses to wait. But the temporality of waiting here is inflected with not only Maureen's specific South African historical context and its attendant temporality of waiting, but also a general commitment to an as-yet obscured future. Given the profound inconclusiveness of *July's People*'s final chapter, we might then read the novel's much-discussed 'ending' as marking a beginning, rather than a conclusion, what Clingman calls 'a flight from, but also . . . a flight towards'.[115] My reading of Maureen's refusal to wait underscores Clingman's reading of the end as a beginning, marking movement towards a post-apartheid future that gestures beyond the interregnum even if it does not depict it as fully realised. Gordimer's novel rejects the principles of apartheid time by deciphering

---

[114] Ibid., 157.
[115] Clingman, *The Novels of Nadine Gordimer*, 203.

how the characters' relationships were impacted by the time of the suburb and the relation of employer and servant, and by the waiting that shapes Maureen's experience of July's village. Waiting in the village not only permits the difficult and painful negotiation of the relationships between whites and Black people, as well as within the families, but also uncovers the sense of time tacitly governing these socioeconomic dependencies. Maureen thus achieves the moment of crisis and recognition that Naipaul's Salim never does, even as their 'escapes', on the surface, appear to be similar.

Both writers employ the imagery of the broken watch in their fictional works, though the function of the image in *July's People* is different from its role in Naipaul's 'In a Free State'. The watch, especially coupled with the calendar in *July's People*, evokes the time-keeping and synchronising mechanisms of the clock and calendar, so integral to Benedict Anderson's 'homogeneous empty time' required for imagining a national community.[116] To suggest the obsolescence of the clock and calendar in *July's People* is not simply to reject both the nationalism and historicism described by Anderson and Chakrabarty respectively. The clock and calendar, as symbols and instruments of time-keeping alike, 'have been coupled with processes of colonialism and globalization'.[117] The homogeneity posited by clocks and calendars, Kevin Birth suggests, elides the existence of multiple temporalities coexisting with the temporalities produced by these standardising mechanisms.[118] By coupling Maureen's observation that her watch is broken with her decision to run towards whatever awaits, Gordimer makes room for coexisting and alternative temporalities that underscore the heterogeneity of the interregnum and posit a future that is not predetermined by the past. As Gordimer's emphasis on the lingering old and the only-just-emerging new stresses, this future cannot be wholly divorced from the past, which must be grappled with and continuously interrogated. But Maureen's refusal to wait signals a turn away from apartheid temporalities and towards a revolutionary one – where Black-majority rule may break from the waiting rooms of history in ways that Naipaul's country in *A Bend in the River* never will.

Neither Gordimer nor Naipaul present an uncomplicated vision of the temporalities of waiting and the transition to Black-majority rule in Africa. Naipaul's retrospective view on the end of colonial rule and Gordimer's proleptic vision, imagining the future from the stormy

---

[116] Anderson, *Imagined Communities*, 24.
[117] Birth, *Objects of Time*, 5.
[118] Ibid., 32.

vantage of the interregnum, present villages as 'waiting rooms' that contend with the 'waiting rooms of history model' in strikingly different ways. In neither of these novels, where the protagonists refuse to wait any longer, is waiting imbued with overtones of resistance; waiting permits Maureen to reflect and to confront, but is not in itself a temporality she inhabits willingly. In the next chapter, the pairing of Alejo Carpentier's *The Kingdom of This World* and J. M. Coetzee's *Life & Times of Michael K* explores waiting as a temporal modality of disruption and resistance – one at odds with the colonial regimes of time depicted in the texts.

Chapter 3

Marooned Time: Disruptive Waiting and Idleness

> Specifically I want to notice how the idea of alternative or subaltern modernities operates by constructing a normative expectation of resistance or overcoming. Notably it does this, at least in part, by imagining the conditions of the modern as a largely passive or negative environment merely waiting to be surmounted or mastered or translated or displaced by preconstituted subjects: modern transformations occur, and subalterns respond in more or less creative ways.
>
> David Scott, *Conscripts of Modernity* (2004)

Toussaint L'Ouverture, famed leader of the slave rebellion that would become the Haitian Revolution, is a towering figure in the historical chronicles of the Haitian struggle for independence. C. L. R. James's 1938 *The Black Jacobins* portrays L'Ouverture not only as a central figure in the slave revolt's success, but also as the embodiment of it. In the preface to the first edition of his classic historical account, James proclaims that 'the individual leadership responsible' for the Haitian Revolution 'was almost entirely the work of a single man – Toussaint L'Ouverture'.[1] This close focus on L'Ouverture threatens to minimise the efforts of other well-known figures in the decades that comprised the rebellion, as well as those whose names and individual participation remain unrecorded for posterity. Another effect of this version of history, David Scott argues in *Conscripts of Modernity*, is that it posits an anticolonial 'narrative mode of Romance' that plots a relationship between the past and future as 'a narrative of revolutionary overcoming'.[2] According to Scott, anticolonial resistance is problematically constructed in *The Black Jacobins* in two ways; the conditions of modernity are 'merely waiting' for the revolutionary subject to overcome them,

---

[1] James, *The Black Jacobins: Toussaint L'Ouverture and the San Domingo Revolution*, ix.
[2] D. Scott, *Conscripts of Modernity*, 209.

rather than dynamically negotiated, and second, the implicit teleology of overcoming determines in advance what ought to be recognised as acts of resistance.³ This accounts, in Scott's view, not only for James's fixation on L'Ouverture as a 'romantic' hero of the Revolution, but also for the limited set of questions posed to the 'problem-space' of the revolutionary moment.⁴ Instead, Scott calls for analyses 'more attuned to the productive ways in which power has shaped the conditions of possible action, [and] more specifically, shaped the cognitive and institutional conditions in which the New World slave acted'.⁵ In turning to the power dynamics of the slave plantation, he urges, we ought to consider

> less what [the regime of the slave plantation] restricts and what resists this restriction, less what it represses and what escapes or overcomes this repression, and more the modern conditions it created that positively shaped the way in which language, religion, kinship, and so on were reconstituted.⁶

While I do not share Scott's enthusiasm in setting aside questions of escape, his argument is nevertheless important for illuminating historiography's and critical theory's reliance on romantic narratives of overcoming, and his framework suggestively reconstitutes revolutionary subjects and their contexts in active and dynamic interplay. This negotiation is not 'a Romantic one in which history rides a triumphant and seamlessly progressive rhythm', but rather 'a broken series of paradoxes and reversals in which human action is ever open to unaccountable contingencies – and luck'.⁷ In both retelling and interpreting narratives set in revolutionary times, historians and literary scholars would do well to resist the determinism of romance, and embrace the 'tragic' times of instability, ambiguity, and open-ended temporality. Writing about Atlantic slavery specifically, Saidya Hartman too cautions against 'the redemptive narratives crafted by the state in its orchestration of mourning, the promises of filiation proffered by petty traders, and the fantasies of origin enacted at these slave sites'.⁸ The 'time of slavery' Hartman continues, 'negates the common-sense intuition of time as continuity or progression, then and now coexist; we are coeval with the dead'.

---

³ Ibid., 114.
⁴ Ibid., 4. By 'problem-space', Scott intends 'to demarcate a discursive context' as well as 'an ensemble of questions and answers around which a horizon of identifiable stakes (conceptual as well as ideological-political stakes) hangs'.
⁵ Ibid., 106.
⁶ Ibid., 115.
⁷ Ibid., 13.
⁸ Hartman, 'The Time of Slavery', 759.

Together, Scott and Hartman reframe revolution and progress through their attention to temporality. This approach will also allow us to read the potential resistive strategies and negotiations of actors that are otherwise illegible through the lens of romantic anticolonial overcoming.

To that end, Alejo Carpentier's 1949 novel of the Haitian Revolution, *The Kingdom of This World* (*El reino de este mundo*), offers a useful contrast to James's focus by imagining the Revolution through the eyes of a slave, Ti Noël. Other scholars have compared James with Carpentier, but all stop short of discussing the significance of the Haitian maroon for modelling alternative relationships to the (post)colonial state and strategies of resistance in the novel. And rather than pairing Carpentier's novel with other texts and studies of the Haitian revolution, I examine *The Kingdom of This World* in conjunction with *Life & Times of Michael K*, a 1983 novel by South African author J. M. Coetzee. My aim is not simply to demonstrate that the temporal dimensions of waiting manifest differently in these two novels, as the comparison of Nadine Gordimer and V. S. Naipaul in Chapter 2 argued with respect to the waiting-room model of history. Rather, I elaborate the interpretive strategies of reading the maroon, derived from the fields of literary criticism, history, and anthropology, through my reading of the first novel, *The Kingdom of This World*. These insights allow me to extend the framework of marronage beyond the immediate Caribbean setting in order to understand the eponymous character of *Life & Times of Michael K* as another maroon figure.

This chapter makes two interventions: First, I develop a framework for reading the maroon as a trans-historical figure and literary trope, and second, through the lens of marronage, I challenge the dominant scholarly interpretations of *The Kingdom of This World* and *Life & Times of Michael K* as pessimistic and politically disengaged respectively. By arguing that the maroon is central to *The Kingdom of This World*, I suggest that the temporal dimensions of the maroon's flight offer a less pessimistic reading of the novel's ending than previously allowed by critics. The strategies of the maroon encourage important reconsiderations of Michael K's relationship to the apartheid state as well, beyond the usual frame of Giorgio Agamben-indebted criticism on the novel, and create a 'line of flight' between the Caribbean and South Africa. This device, 'lines of flight', offers a model of comparative analysis that attends to south–south links within Global South studies, and opens up possibilities for analysis and comparison beyond direct connections between texts' production or initial reception. The lines of flight between Carpentier's and Coetzee's novels show that the temporalities of waiting structure time-consciousness and resistance strategies in a transnational frame.

The maroon's separateness or withdrawal, I argue, is characterised by spatial distance that also engenders a challenge to the authority of colonial regimes of time and the colonial state, or in the case of *Life & Times of Michael K*, the apartheid state. Through the lens of marronage, the flight, labour and idleness of Carpentier's and Coetzee's protagonists become newly legible dimensions of resistive waiting.

Timelessly Recurrent: Reading the Revolutionary Maroon

The Haitian Revolution was, and through its echoes in contemporary literature continues to be, a global event. Enslaved Africans, free men, and maroons fought from 1791 to 1804 to achieve the first and only slave-led revolt to become a modern state. The Revolution ignited white concerns throughout the Americas that insurrection could spread, which in Ifeoma Kiddoe Nwankwo's view, 'forced people of African descent throughout the Americas . . . to name a relationship to the Haitian Revolution, in particular, and to a transnational idea of Black community, in general'.[9] The Revolution affected other countries and colonies in the Caribbean as well; the Haitian Revolution compelled the global sugar industry to shift its epicentre from Haiti to Carpentier's native Cuba, increasing Cuba's reliance on enslaved Black labour and creating conditions similar to colonial Haiti.[10] Despite the shortcomings of the Revolution – Jean-Jacques Dessalines's order after Independence to exterminate white Haitians, the stratification of society into labourers and soldiers, the return to forms of slavery under the guise of serfdom – the historical moment remains an influential and deeply symbolic event in Caribbean literature and scholarship. The Revolution has become, in Víctor Figueroa's words, 'a floating signifier within the Caribbean region' that writers return to 'with their own preoccupations and obsessions'.[11] The Haitian remains a rich and contested historical and symbolic moment with import not only for contemporary Haiti, but also for the larger Caribbean and Black diaspora.

The contested etymology of the word 'maroon' is itself emblematic of the Caribbean's interculturation. Most scholars locate the word's origin in the Spanish *cimarron*, a word equally applied to cattle and

---

[9] Nwankwo, *Black Cosmopolitanism: Racial Consciousness and Transnational Identity in the Nineteenth-Century Americas*, 7.
[10] Paravisini-Gebert, 'The Haitian Revolution in Interstices and Shadows: A Re-Reading of Alejo Carpentier's "The Kingdom of This World"', 5.
[11] Figueroa, *Prophetic Visions of the Past*, 1.

enslaved Africans who escaped to the hillsides in Hispaniola.[12] But others such as Richard Price and Cynthia James speculate on its Amerindian (Arawakan/Taino) roots as well.[13] Tracing the usage of 'maroon' through the *Oxford English Dictionary*, James argues for 'a distinctly Caribbean application of the word, as well as corroboration for its application to people of African descent living in primal conditions in their flight from an imperial master'.[14] Marronage occurred in both *petit* and *grand* forms, where the former included short-term flights and absenteeism, and the latter indicated permanent or long-term flights, often with the goal of establishing separate maroon communities.[15] The history of marronage in the Americas demonstrates that the topography of the landscape proved instrumental to the proliferation of marronage; enslaved Africans escaped more easily into the wilderness of hills and mountains in countries like Jamaica and Haiti. Even in *grand-marronage*, however, maroons exhibited a complicated relationship with the plantation through their periodic returns to raid for food, recruits, and women to increase their numbers.[16]

The implicit emphasis on movement in marronage – the initial flight or escape, the returns, the guerrilla tactics of retreat and ambush and lying in wait – suggest a complicated rendering of maroon autonomy. While the maroon has become, particularly in Jamaica, a popular symbol of resistance post-independence, the history of maroons in the Caribbean exemplifies the complex positions maroons negotiated between plantations and colonial governments. As Patrick Geggus notes in his important *Haitian Revolutionary Studies*, marronage in some ways functioned as a 'safety valve' for plantation societies, permitting the small-scale escape of rebellious enslaved Africans in order to prevent large-scale insurrection.[17] Once they escaped, maroons in Jamaica 'maneuvered as third parties' between enslaved Africans and the colonial government, working to quell uprisings in exchange for recognising the sovereignty of maroon communities. Acknowledging a history that encompasses moments of complicity and resistance, Erin Skye Mackie concludes that

> this failure of 'pure' oppositionality . . . does not invalidate the socio-cultural power of [maroons]; rather, if anything, it constitutes one feature central to

---

[12] James, *The Maroon Narrative*, 11.
[13] Ibid., 11.
[14] Ibid., 11.
[15] Weik, 'The Archeology of Maroon Societies in the Americas: Resistance, Cultural Continuity, and Transformation in the African Diaspora', 82.
[16] Mullin, *Africa in America*, 46.
[17] Ibid., 62.

their continuing currency in a postcolonial world where lines between law and outlaw, black and white, inside and outside, disappear almost as quickly as they are, often opportunistically, calculated and imposed.[18]

In other words, maroons remain relevant as both symbolic and historical figures for their real, complex and even contradictory negotiations between enslaved African communities, plantation owners and colonial governments in pursuit of freedom.

This acknowledgement of maroons' special history in the Caribbean can revise the limited formulations of freedom and slavery often assumed by contemporary political theory. Neil Roberts argues that maroons function as 'heretical, non-state actors' who 'cultivat[e] freedom on their own terms within a demarcated social space that allow[s] for the subversive speech acts, gestures, and social practices antithetical to the ideals of enslaving agents'.[19] Maroons thus represent not only physical but also ideological opposition to the state and its slave institutions. The very act of flight – not simply the arrival at a destination or sustained state of being – challenges theories of freedom that assume freedom and slavery to be ontologically stable.[20] Roberts concludes that a theory of freedom modelled on marronage emphasises continual flight, and suggests that 'freedom materializes in the liminal and interstitial social space between our imaginings of absolute unfreedom and the zone of its opposite'.[21] In linking marronage to models of fugitivity, I follow Tina Campt's lead in conceiving of spatial and temporal fugitivity as 'an extension of the range of creative responses black communities have marshaled in the face of racialized dispossession', part of 'practices honed in response to sustained, everyday encounters with exigency and duress that rupture a predictable trajectory of flight'.[22] While I use the language of resistance along with refusal in this chapter, Campt's own rendering of fugitivity 'is defined first and foremost as a practice of refusing the terms of negation and dispossession'.[23] For Campt, both fugitivity and refusal are linked through 'the tense relations between acts of flight and escape, and the creative practices of refusal – nimble and strategic practices that undermine the categories of the dominant'.[24] Marronage, as I conceive of it in

---

[18] Mackie, 'Welcome the Outlaws: Pirates, Maroons, and Caribbean Countercultures', 35.
[19] Roberts, *Freedom as Marronage*, 5.
[20] Ibid., 15.
[21] Ibid., 173–4.
[22] Campt, *Listening to Images*, 10.
[23] Ibid., 96.
[24] Ibid., 32.

this chapter, is a form of fugitivity whose resistive potential inheres in its refusal of the terms of both the colonisation of time and space that contributes to the dispossession of the enslaved.

In their analyses of fugitivity and marronage, Roberts and Campt highlight several characteristics of maroons and their legacies that will be central to my reading of literary maroons: the actions of historical Maroons establish 'flight' as a movement that embeds both opposition and accommodation, challenges dominant terms of freedom and resistance, and threatens either to disrupt the state or to manufacture an alternative to it. While Roberts relies heavily on the Haitian maroon to theorise marronage and freedom, he insists that it is not a concept to be 'provincializ[ed] . . . as relevant merely to Caribbean regional discourse' and acknowledges that the term marronage 'is a normative concept forged in a historical milieu, yet it has trans-historical utility'.[25] Drawing from both American and African geographies, Matthew Omelsky similarly notes that 'Black fugitivity is hardly an exclusively American historical experience', but rather 'names that desire to flee the confines not just of the nineteenth-century southern plantation or the contemporary American carceral state, but of colonial and postcolonial regimes that have suppressed Black life globally'.[26] Implicit in the practices of Black fugitivity, which in Omelsky's account encompass both physical and psychological movements, is anticipation: a future-oriented expectation that imagines the not-yet in the here-and-now. Fugitivity, moreover, 'does not only name material practices of escape from bondage, but is a theoretical and methodological orientation toward freedom . . . always in process, always in motion'.[27] These suggestive links allow me to distinguish flight across two distinct settings and times, yet also gesture towards how the concepts of flight and marronage – and the waiting embedded in them both – can travel.

For these reasons, the maroon is an enduring trope especially in Caribbean fiction, serving as a vehicle for the imaginative reconstruction of the past and inspiration of continued resistance in the postcolonial present. At the same time, however, I do not want to emphasise maroons' symbolism at the expense of their roles as historical actors and agents of resistance. It is especially important to note maroons' symbolic

---

[25] Roberts, *Freedom as Marronage* 14, 4.
[26] Omelsky, 'African Fugitivities', 56.
[27] Kelley, '"Follow the tree flowers": Fugitive Mapping in Beloved', 184. See also Moten, 'The Case of Blackness'; Moten, *Stolen Life*.

role in cultural discourse as well as their real and continued existence in postcolonial Jamaica, where the state continues

> to deny the validity of the Maroons' claims regarding their special legal status and their right to self-determination, while at the same time pays tribute to the 'Maroon heritage' through periodic visits to present-day Maroon communities and other symbolic gestures.[28]

Perhaps underscoring Roberts's claims that marronage is a perpetual state of flight, present-day descendants of Maroons continue to exist in antagonistic relation to the state. My intention in elaborating both the historical and literary discourses surrounding marronage in the Caribbean is to augment the study of literary marronage by including insights derived from marronage as it was and continues to be practised. Through a study of marronage in *The Kingdom of This World* and *Life & Times of Michael K* that is attentive to the narratives' representation of history and time, I hope to undo some of the violence that is perpetuated when the maroon is relegated only to the symbolic plane. This approach will balance the maroon as a figure who is historically situated as well as a symbol that is, in Juris Silenieks's words, 'timelessly recurrent'.[29]

Although unusual at first glance, the proposal to link diverse times, spaces and texts through the image of the maroon is not unprecedented. In identifying marronage in *The Kingdom of This World* and *Life & Times of Michael K*, I build from scholars such as Barbara Lalla and Cynthia James, who conceptualise marronage in terms that are more general in order to identify maroon practices in fiction outside of the Caribbean. Drawing primarily from Jamaican fiction, Lalla creates a list of maroon attributes and character types derived and yet distinguished from the historical maroons, including fugitives, strays, recluses, rejects, outcasts and 'rebels in physical or psychological wildernesses'.[30] Marked in equal measure by displacement and resistance, the maroon, according to Lalla, is identifiable through a 'withdrawal from the mainstream of civilization as defined by others, into the wilderness, to make a last stand for freedom'.[31] Likewise, Cynthia James ascertains both positive and negative markers of the maroon condition, including abandonment, an ambivalent relationship with the past, dispossession, survival skills and the continuation of ancestral practices, syncretism, resilience and

---

[28] Bilby, *True-Born Maroons*, 43.
[29] Silenieks, 'The Maroon Figure in Caribbean Francophone Prose', 122.
[30] Lalla, *Defining Jamaican Fiction*, 2.
[31] Ibid., 2.

improvisation.³² If, as James observes, the prototypical maroons are 'the African slaves who harried the British during the seventeenth and eighteenth centuries from forested enclaves, eventually securing autonomous existence', then the maroon's antagonistic opposition to the state, and the potential alternative social and political configurations that inhere in the founding of these autonomous communities, are central to the maroon's historic and symbolic significance.³³

The maroon's flight, then, involves a double movement: first, a move away from or rejection of slavery and its crushing power structures, and second, a move towards or affirmation of contrasting principles or practices. Roberts likens the maroon communities to James C. Scott's 'zones of refuge', which 'describe maroons' regions of existence and cultivation away from state power' and are opposed 'to the zones of governance and appropriation intrinsic to existing state regimes of slavery'.³⁴ According to Scott, zones of refuge offered shelter to maroons, but threatened the state, as these ungovernable zones 'represented a constant temptation, a constant alternative to life within the state'.³⁵ Although Scott's study is limited to Southeast Asia, he maintains that the hill peoples in his study are 'best understood as runaway, fugitive, maroon communities'.³⁶ In evading the state, the hill people adopted social and cultural practices such as mobility, egalitarianism and orality that continued to aid them in resisting incorporation or capture.³⁷ For my purposes, I want to stress Scott's observation that practices or acts that stigmatise a community from one point of view may, from another perspective, be seen as effective and deliberate strategies of resistance. The first characteristic of marronage that I stress in my study of *The Kingdom of This World* and *Life & Times of Michael K* is thus deliberate isolation in opposition to an oppressive state.

The second characteristic of marronage as I conceptualise it here is the commitment to a struggle for freedom, with the recognition that freedom is, following Roberts and Scott, a state of continual flight from oppression rather than a destination. This view is consonant with Édouard Glissant's discussion of the rhizome and marronage together. The rhizome is, Roberts summarises, 'a metaphor for Relation and lines

---

³² James, *The Maroon Narrative*, 15.
³³ Ibid., 8.
³⁴ Roberts, *Freedom as Marronage*, 5.
³⁵ J. C. Scott, *The Art of Not Being Governed: An Anarchist History of Upland Southeast Asia*, 6.
³⁶ Ibid., ix.
³⁷ Ibid., 9.

of flight [that] explain[s] further the act of marronage as a continual process of becoming in order to underscore freedom as a relational concept'.[38] Because lines of flight can change direction unpredictably, the maroon's emblematic flight is anti-teleological. Following Deleuze and Guattari, rhizomatic marronage connotes an anti-hierarchical approach that resists binaries and the re-instantiation of the power dynamics the maroon has fled. This sense is consistent with Roberts's emphasis on flight as transitional and dynamic movement, and enables us to identify Ti Noël's acts of resistance. To read Ti Noël, as Roberto Gonzalez Echevarría does, as a 'passive presence' who 'is certainly not a protagonist in the sense of a maker of events or a character who polarizes the action', assumes a narrow view of what activity or resistance can look like.[39] In the first place, to recall David Scott's critique of romantic narratives of heroism, Echevarría's assessment of Ti Noël depends on a particular metric of resistance premised on a construction of power as a negative force that must be overcome in particular, active, and assertive ways. But resistance need not be configured in such narrow terms; as W. E. B. Du Bois suggested in the context of the United States, enslaved Africans refusing to work and fleeing, neither direct acts of insurrection, can change the tide of a war.[40] More crucially, Ti Noël's acts of *petit-marronage* in the text, as well as his role in the sacking of Sans Souci, create links between the historical and fictional Ti Noël to position him as anything but a passive witness to the Revolution.

Although theorisations of marronage typically highlight the maroon's relationship to space, the final characteristic that I want to emphasise is the maroon's relationship to time – not only how the maroon challenges the totalising time of the modern state, but also how the maroon is fictionalised, manoeuvring through the postcolonial present. By absconding, maroons set themselves in opposition to slave plantations. Though the jurisdiction of slave plantations was relatively limited, the plantation itself – drawing materials, labour, and technology from eastern North America, western Africa, Europe and southern Asia – was 'a global, not a regional, enterprise'.[41] The Haitian Revolution rejected French rule, 'abolish[ed] the plantation system in Haiti and stop[ped] the recruitment of slaves', breaking with colonial rule and the slave plantation system simultaneously.[42] In 'Plantation Futures', Katherine McKittrick

---

[38] Roberts, *Freedom as Marronage*, 166.
[39] Echevarría, *Alejo Carpentier: The Pilgrim at Home*, 157, 135.
[40] Roberts, *Freedom as Marronage*, 47.
[41] Richardson, *The Caribbean in the Wider World, 1492–1992*, 38.
[42] Stinchcombe, *Sugar Island Slavery in the Age of Enlightenment*, 107.

demonstrates how, 'in both slave and postslave context, [the plantation] must be understood alongside complex negotiations of time, space, and terror'.[43] By charting a history from the plantation to the prison, McKittrick's reading of plantation time-space is informed by the 'interlocking workings of modernity and blackness' across the Atlantic, yet she provocatively notes that 'the *idea* of the plantation is migratory'.[44] Enslaved Black resistance to the time-space of the plantation took many forms, including a range of tactics such as 'emigration, mockery of planters, "laziness," and the establishment of independent village settlements', as well as 'balking, malingering, feigned stupidity, self-inflicted wounds, and even suicide'.[45] Both marronage and deliberate idleness were tactics to withhold labour and disrupt the temporal regimes of the slave plantation and, by extension, the larger regimes of colonial time, power and trade that shaped daily life in the eighteenth-century Caribbean.

I contend that the maroon signifies both spatial difference *and* temporal difference in its antagonistic relationship with colonial power and regimes of time. The term 'temporal difference' is not meant to reproduce the Orientalising tendencies of colonial historiography that relegates colonial others to the waiting room of history, discussed in detail in the previous chapter.[46] Nor is it intended to collude with similar tendencies that Johannes Fabian famously identified in anthropology, where he found that ideological and epistemological biases in scholarship entailed 'the affirmation of difference as *distance*' – a distance comprised of spatial and temporal separation alike.[47] This spatialisation of time results in a progressive view of history that divides epochs into discrete units occurring sequentially. Instead, with the term 'temporal difference' I intend to capture how maroons positioned themselves to be deliberately disruptive to the totalising temporality of the colonial state and the limited liberalism that inspired the French revolution's 'liberté, egalité, fraternité', yet continued to postpone equal rights to Black freed men and enslaved Africans alike.[48] By insisting that temporal difference is an

---

[43] McKittrick, 'Plantation Futures', 3.
[44] Ibid., 3.
[45] Richardson, *The Caribbean in the Wider World, 1492–1992*, 160–1.
[46] Chakrabarty, *Provincializing Europe*, 9.
[47] Fabian, *Time and the Other*, 16.
[48] In this spirit, Article 4 of the 1987 Haitian Constitution establishes 'liberté, egalité, fraternité' as the country's national motto. For more on the relationship between Enlightenment principles and the Haitian revolution, see Buck-Morss, *Hegel, Haiti and Universal History* and Fischer, *Modernity Disavowed*.

integral characteristic of marronage, I recuperate the maroon's vexed relationship to the state's space and time. The European narrative of modernity, as Chakrabarty describes for the Indian context, mandated that the 'primitive' colonial subject must wait to progress through stages of civilisation before integration into world history as a modern political subject; the anticolonial response (and, I would add, the maroon response) is predicated on an interruption of this historical chronology. It is with the rejection of this appeal to wait, the refusal of the 'not yet' of European liberalism, and the positing of different temporal modalities, that I turn to marronage in Carpentier's *The Kingdom of This World*.

Countertemporalities: History, Circularity and Flight

Although the Haitian Revolution and its legacies have inspired writers from across the Caribbean, Martin Munro notes that 'Haitian fiction writers have rarely revisited the founding moment of their nation in any extended way.'[49] Writers who hail from other Caribbean islands and abroad, Munro muses, have '[p]erhaps the dispassionate distance – in terms of time, place, and "race"' to approach the Revolution's 'epic heroism, extravagant violence, and outlandish bloodletting'.[50] Born in Switzerland but raised in Cuba, Alejo Carpentier's interest in the Haitian Revolution was inspired by his own revolutionary activities in Cuba in opposition to Gerardo Machado's dictatorship, his political and aesthetic interests in Afro-Cuban art and attempts to develop 'authentic modes of expression' to 'evoke the marvelous real of the Americas',[51] and a trip to Haiti in 1943 that he describes in a foreword to *The Kingdom of This World*. Though much separates Carpentier's context as a Cuban intellectual in the twentieth century from his character Ti Noël in the eighteenth century, Carpentier's own experiences with exile and return across the Caribbean – both author and character find themselves in Haiti and Cuba during decades of revolutionary upheaval – suggest the appeal of Ti Noël as a focalising force. As Lizabeth Paravisini-Gebert notes, Carpentier borrows the name Ti Noël from a real historical leader of maroon rebels, who temporarily pledged allegiance to Dessalines and ensured the success of the Revolution.[52] This choice links Carpentier's

---

[49] Munro, 'Haitian Novels and Novels of Haiti', 163.
[50] Ibid., 166, 163.
[51] Warnes, 'Magical Realism and the Legacy of German Idealism', 492–3.
[52] Paravisini-Gebert, 'The Haitian Revolution in Interstices and Shadows: A Re-Reading of Alejo Carpentier's "The Kingdom of This World"', 117.

protagonist to the larger history of marronage in the Caribbean in general, and the role of maroons in the Haitian Revolution in particular.

Beginning, then, with Carpentier's inspiration for Ti Noël's name, it becomes difficult to ignore how marronage shapes the novel, from moments of *petit-* and *grand-marronage*, to the direct depiction of the maroons Macandal and Bouckman.[53] Literary scholarship, however, tends to highlight the historical figures conspicuously absent from Carpentier's narrative, and how the novel maintains the 'cycles of oppression' that foreclose the possibility for independence to be 'truly meaningful'.[54] These approaches to the text are useful starting points to understand Carpentier's manipulation of historical research and narrative, but by focusing on who or what is absent, they cannot fully account for the maroon presence that punctuates the novel and offers the possibility to break cycles of oppression through rational political action.[55] Ti Noël is connected to marronage first through his historical namesake, and second, directly through his close relationship to Macandal. Unlike Ti Noël, Macandal's character shares much with his historical counterpart; Macandal was the most famous maroon in Saint Domingue, managing to avoid capture for anywhere between ten and eighteen years, and he was responsible for the poison campaign that ultimately led to his execution in 1758.[56] Macandal the maroon, rather than Toussaint the soldier, becomes the heroic centre of Carpentier's tale, the 'true precursor of the struggle for independence'.[57] Prior to his *grand-marronage* flight, Macandal spends time with Ti Noël, visiting the witch Maman Loi and learning the art of poison. Each rendezvous is made possible by Ti Noël's own acts of *petit-marronage*, as he 'would absent himself for hours from the Lenormand de Mézy plantation', using 'bathing the horses' as his excuse.[58] The chapter that depicts Macandal's execution is titled 'The Great Flight', recalling the language of marronage that is further reinforced in the description of his death: 'The bonds fell

---

[53] Other spelling variations of Macandal and Bouckman include Mackandal, Makandal and Boukman; throughout this chapter, I will use the variations that are consistent with Carpentier's fictional text. Where critics have used alternative spellings, I maintain their variations.

[54] Paravisini-Gebert, 'The Haitian Revolution in Interstices and Shadows', 123. See also Figueroa, 'The Kingdom of Black Jacobins', 62–3.

[55] Readers interested in the production of silences and absences in history (and Haitian history in particular) should consult Michel-Rolph Trouillot's immensely important *Silencing the Past: Power and the Production of History* (1995).

[56] Geggus, *Haitian Revolutionary Studies*, 75.

[57] Silenieks, 'The Maroon Figure in Caribbean Francophone Prose', 117.

[58] Carpentier, *The Kingdom of This World*, 18.

off and the body of the Negro rose in the air, flying overhead, until it plunged into the black waves of the sea of slaves. A single cry filled the square: "Macandal saved!"'[59] Most critics read this scene for its use of what Carpentier calls the *real maravilloso*, the comingling of real and extraordinary elements in '"harmonious contradiction"'.[60] But it is also the moment where Macandal's continued inspiration for Ti Noël is most clearly embodied in the figure of the maroon – not only through his purported escape, but also through the direct association of his escape with flight.

After Macandal's death, the Jamaican Bouckman reignites maroon-led rebellion and conducts a ceremony at Bois Caïman to create a pact between the gathered and the *loas* (spirits) of Africa. Historical accounts corroborate Carpentier's depiction; however, Carpentier frames the ceremony by stressing that acts of *petit-marronage* – absconding in secret from plantations without permission – constitute the conditions of the ceremony's possibility in the first place: 'In spite of the darkness, there was no possibility that a spy might have sneaked into the gathering. The word had been passed around at the last minute by men who could be trusted.'[61] Ti Noël returns to his plantation before the overseer rises for the day, 'sitting and singing' as if nothing had occurred the night before.[62] *Petit-marronage* strategies create the space and time to plan a surprise insurrection, which will occur eight days after the Bois Caïman pact, and strike a balance between orderly execution and the element of surprise.

The actual moment of Haitian independence, however, occurs silently in the gap between parts two and three and is not witnessed directly by Ti Noël, who is labouring as a slave in Cuba. Rather than focusing narrowly on this omission, I am interested in how Carpentier uses the Cuban chapters to emphasise the role of the maroons in keeping the revolution alive. At the beginning of the chapter 'The Ship of Dogs', Ti Noël learns that the French are transporting hundreds of mastiff dogs to Saint Domingue to chase down slaves and quell the rebellion.[63] Successive pages recount events in Saint Domingue as learned from the Dufrené family's slaves, focusing on the arrival of Pauline Bonaparte on the island with her husband General Leclerc. Bonaparte's departure

---

[59] Ibid., 46.
[60] Webb, *Myth and History in Caribbean Fiction*, 18.
[61] Carpentier, *The Kingdom of This World*, 59.
[62] Ibid., 63.
[63] Ibid., 84.

signals a shift back to Ti Noël's narrative, and the omniscient narrator relates,

> The day the ship Ti Noël had seen rode into the Cap, it tied up alongside another schooner coming from Martinique with a cargo of poisonous snakes which the general planned to turn loose on the Plaine so they would bite the peasants who lived in outlying cabins and who gave aid to the runaway slaves in the hills.[64]

The minor details underscore the persistent threat of runaway slaves, and remind us that acts of marronage persist in Ti Noël's absence as the Haitian Revolution continues.

Importantly, *The Kingdom of This World* holds out the promises and possibilities of marronage even as Jean-Jacques Dessalines (first leader of an independent Haiti) and Henri Christophe (self-styled monarch of Haiti after Dessalines was assassinated) begin new cycles of oppressive rule. When the new mulatto elite arrive to survey and appropriate the land, 'hundreds of peasants were leaving their cabins . . . to seek refuge in the hills. Ti Noël learned from a fugitive that farm work had been made obligatory'.[65] Several details here are significant. Images of marronage reappear with the flight to the hills for refuge, signalling a rejection of mandatory labour and the new rule. Importantly, the text observes that Ti Noël's informant is a fugitive; this designation places him in antagonistic relation to the state and its laws, and continues the practice of word-of-mouth networking among runaways, fugitives and potential maroons. The threat of 'this rebirth of shackles, this proliferation of suffering' causes Ti Noël to lose hope in resistance, and he attempts to follow Macandal's lead by turning himself into a bird, among other animals.[66] His metamorphosis leads him to seek refuge with geese, described in the language of marronage, who 'escaped the sack because the Negroes did not like their meat, and . . . had lived as they pleased, all this time, among the canebrakes of the hills.'[67] Ti Noël had 'taken notice of their model habits when M. Lenormand de Mézy had attempted years before, without much success, to acclimate them'. The geese, however, reject him, which Barbara Webb interprets as his 'punishment for having betrayed the legacy of Mackandal; the rebel

---

[64] Ibid., 97.
[65] Ibid., 170.
[66] Ibid., 172.
[67] Ibid., 175.

slave had undergone a series of metamorphoses to *serve* his people, not to forsake the world of men.'⁶⁸

I want to suggest that we can read this betrayal of Macandal in terms of marronage, specifically that Ti Noël and others have forgotten the revolutionary promise embodied in the act of flight, which was a movement with the potential to found alternative communities antagonistic to the colonial state and slavery by way of *grand-marronage*, or to spark a revolutionary overthrowing occasioned by *petit-marronage*. Flight as metaphor or image in the novel additionally registers the temporal disruption represented by suspension – a caesura that interrupts and produces possibilities for an abrupt change of direction. When Ti Noël lies in wait as a mode of *petit-marronage*, his short-term flight allows him to be open to opportunities for a larger insurrection, as well as to contingencies and luck – very much counter to the Romantic narrative of overcoming that Scott describes in *Omens of Adversity*. In *The Kingdom of This World*, the leaders of the Haitian Revolution faltered when they reject such openness, and began to assume the same practices and pageantry of the ousted French planters, whereas the geese 'denied all superiority of individual over individual of the same species' and the oldest gander maintained order 'after the manner of the king or head of the old African assemblies'.⁶⁹ By harkening back to precolonial African forms of government, the geese present a model of egalitarian community at odds with the former colonial state as well as Dessalines's new republic, and to which Ti Noël might aspire. Ti Noël consequently realises the value of struggling in the kingdom of this world and shouts a 'new declaration of war against the new masters'.⁷⁰ While presumably Ti Noël meets his end in old age and senility as the plantation crumbles and a storm rolls in, the novel concludes with one final image of renewal amid death, and flight: a vulture dries his wings in the sun before taking flight to Bois Caïman, the site of Bouckman's solemn pact that initiated the Haitian Revolution.

Idle Time: Laboring Against the State

Carpentier and Coetzee share European heritages, but whereas Carpentier vehemently identified as Cuban and actively supported the Cuban Revolution, Coetzee unsuccessfully sought to emigrate from

---

⁶⁸ Webb, *Myth and History in Caribbean Fiction*, 40.
⁶⁹ Carpentier, *The Kingdom of This World*, 176.
⁷⁰ Ibid., 179.

South Africa during apartheid. This distancing has been read into Coetzee's works as well; unlike Carpentier's novel, whose engagement with historical time most critics acknowledge, reviewers of Coetzee's work, and *Life & Times of Michael K* in particular, have accused him of ahistorical allegorising and passive disengagement.[71] David Attwell attempts to rehabilitate Coetzee's political engagements, and asserts that '[e]very attempt in the novels to hold South Africa at arm's length, by means of strategically nonspecific settings or socially improbable protagonists, simply confirms the intensity and necessity of this struggle.'[72] I am less motivated by an urge to defend Coetzee from his critics than by an interest in the unexpected (and certainly unintended) correspondences between Carpentier's Ti Noël and Coetzee's Michael K in their oppositions to oppressive regimes.

In order to offer a fuller reading of Michael K as a maroon figure, I want to contextualise Coetzee's preoccupations in the novel – with waiting, history, time and idleness – in light of his other writing projects in the 1980s. Especially relevant is Coetzee's novel *Waiting for the Barbarians*, published four years before *Life & Times of Michael K*. In a study of waiting and Coetzee's fiction, *Waiting for the Barbarians* would be an obvious choice; waiting seems less apparent in *Life & Times of Michael K*, but as we will see, the preoccupation with waiting that begins in the earlier novel is extended and complicated in the later text. Composed entirely in the present tense, *Waiting for the Barbarians* tracks the Magistrate's complicated relationship with the Empire he serves, meditating on the nature of truth, justice and barbarity. The first half of the novel describes the Magistrate's preoccupation with another unnamed character, a barbarian girl, and the inaccessible story of her torture and history prior to arriving at his outpost. The text pivots on the Magistrate's decision to return the girl to the barbarians. Subsequently, he is identified as a traitor, imprisoned and tortured. He is released as the Empire's conscripts retreat after a failed offensive in the desert.

When the barbarians are first physically present in the narrative, they are victims of torture whose confessions are extracted by the Empire's agents to provide support for a foregone conclusion that the barbarian

---

[71] Criticism on Coetzee frequently points to Nadine Gordimer's oft-cited review in the *New York Review of Books*, where she charged that Coetzee's protagonists 'ignore history, not make it'. Gordimer, 'Idea' 3. Interestingly, Gordimer also characterized *Life & Times*'s temporality as 'ultimate malaise', a time of suspension where history's course is utterly undetermined – what we might consider a kind of waiting that links Coetzee's earlier *Waiting for the Barbarians* with *Life & Times*.
[72] Attwell, *Rewriting Modernity*, 3.

attack is imminent. The 'waiting' that preoccupies the Empire, which disrupts the relative ease in which the Magistrate worked and waited for his retirement, is the Empire's own creation. As an example, early in the novel, a young barbarian boy's father is tortured to death, and when it is the boy's turn, he confesses to Joll's men that the barbarians are planning an imminent attack. Stunned, the Magistrate confronts the boy: '"They tell me you have made a confession . . . Are you telling the truth? Do you understand what this confession of yours will mean?"'[73] The Magistrate has already introduced doubt regarding the reliability of the confession; he questions how Colonel Joll can discern 'the tone of truth' in a man's voice, and notes that throughout his years on the frontier, he has never seen the unrest that the Empire insists must be prevented through 'precautionary measures'.[74] The Empire's anxious waiting for an imminent attack must be understood in the context of this coerced confession. Given that 'once in every generation, without fail, there is an episode of hysteria about the barbarians', this heightened sense of waiting is characteristic of the Empire's machinery and modus operandi; by insisting that the barbarians will attack – that they lie in wait – the Empire can justify its own pre-emptive measures and attacks.

While I locate waiting as essential to the Empire's justification of its own use of pre-emptive force, other critics have instead turned to the characters and considered how waiting marks an ethical engagement with the other. Drawing from the scene where the Magistrate washes the barbarian girl's feet, Patrick Hayes argues that the Magistrate enters an 'anxious and productive state of "waiting"' that allows him, through the disorientation that attends the experience, to 'becom[e] open to other ways of perceiving – ways that had hitherto been felt to be "nothing", or "beside the point"'.[75] Although the temporality of waiting justifies the Empire's suspension of the rule of law and pre-emptive acts to defeat the rumoured barbarian threat, waiting here is experienced by the Magistrate as a temporality where the extreme openness to another[76] means losing awareness of the girl as well as himself. While the temporal descriptor that both the Magistrate and agents of Empire evoke – 'waiting' – is the same, its political implications are not. The subtlety to this difference, in one case consolidating the Empire's power, and in the other inviting a tentative openness to the Other, underscores the need to

---

[73] Ibid.; Coetzee, *Waiting for the Barbarians*, 10–11.
[74] Ibid., 5, 8.
[75] Hayes, *J. M. Coetzee and the Novel*, 62, 70.
[76] There are echoes here of the kind of waiting Nadine Gordimer's Maureen experiences in *July's People*, described in Chapter 2.

attend to waiting's multivalent function in Coetzee's work specifically and its signification as a cultural practice or strategy of resistance more generally.

At the same time that he was drafting *Waiting for the Barbarians* and *Life & Times of Michael K*, Coetzee was also at work on non-fiction essays eventually published in the 1988 collection *White Writing: On the Culture of Letters in South Africa*. The first chapter, 'Idleness in South Africa', describes the evolution of the discourse of idleness in the Cape, first ascribed to the natives, and then denounced in European settlers. Influenced by the European Reformation's emphasis on work over idleness, the discourse of idleness on the Cape excluded natives from the civilisational paradigm that leads 'from Adam via a life of toil to civilized man'.[77] Idleness marks a lack of self-improvement and a sinful nature; for the 'native', idle time is spent 'sleeping, while among other savages who have passed through the toolmaking revolution free time becomes leisure.' Powerfully, Coetzee suggests that the charge of idleness displays an anxiety about the ability of idleness to challenge and scandalise because of its illegibility.[78] Rejecting the labour economy of European settlers and ethnographers, idleness becomes 'an authentically native response to a foreign way of life, a response that has rarely been defended in writing, and then only evasively.'[79] This 'unreadable' idleness in the Cape system of signification marks a limit of comprehension and as such, is a site of anxiety.[80] Both idleness and waiting are coded as unreadable in Coetzee's work, and in their instability, they present possibilities for reading difference or resisting the imposition of meaning. Like idleness, waiting's potential to scandalise lies in its refusal to be read as active or passive, and its potential to disrupt systems of meaning. This 'discourse of waiting', Laura Wright observes, is shared by both *Waiting for the Barbarians* and *Life & Times of Michael K*.[81]

By the time Coetzee was writing *Life & Times of Michael K*, then, waiting had accumulated various valences in Coetzee's work: waiting is related to idleness, called forth in the time of Empire through the

---

[77] Coetzee, *White Writing*, 25.
[78] Ibid., 34.
[79] Ibid., 35.
[80] See also Clifton C. Crais's *White Supremacy and Black Resistance in Pre-Industrial South Africa*, which also affirms that '[f]rom the end of the 1820s Africans were increasingly represented [by the British-settler elite] as libidinous, uncontrolled, lazy and disrespectful . . . . The growth of negative appraisals initially centered on two issues . . . violations of private property ('thievishness') and the unwillingness of Africans to labour for whites ('indolence').' Crais, 129.
[81] L. Wright, *Writing 'Out of All the Camps'*, 94.

suspension of law, but also a temporality that permits ethical engagement with the Other. *Life & Times of Michael K* recounts the eponymous character's birth – born with a harelip and classified as 'not quick' – his attempt to return his dying mother to the mythic farmland of her youth, and his evasions and escapes, from hospitals, labour and refugee camps. Unlike *Waiting for the Barbarians*, *Life & Times of Michael K* is largely written in the past tense, but the narrative paradoxically produces an openness to time rather than a sense of time foreclosed. In Cape Town with his mother, frustrated by 'waiting for permits' that 'would never come', Michael K's narrative announces, 'Now was the time.'[82] The tension produced by the 'now', an indicator of the present moment, and the past tense of 'was' creates 'an indeterminant [sic], endless newness, a resistance to other defining restrictions beyond the narrative attachment "was"'.[83] The past tense is unable to capture the slipperiness of 'now', yet the present is 'more elusive, for it exists perpetually, yet cannot be recorded, for it is gone as soon as it arrives.'[84] As *Life & Times of Michael K* progresses, Michael K begins to inhabit this temporality more and more, opening himself up to time and embracing the possibilities of idleness.

Interpretations of the novel that speculate on Michael K's import for political critique, however, tend to emphasise his relationship to space over his relationship to time. Often, scholars turn to Giorgio Agamben's theorisation of bare life to understand Michael's continual incorporation and rejection by the state. Agamben argues that the *homo sacer*, the sacred man 'who may be killed but yet not sacrificed', is integral to modern politics.[85] Coetzee's novel does concern a man, marked and consistently set apart, confronting the mechanism of the apartheid state through run-ins at check points and camps. These thematic links between Agamben's political theory and Coetzee's literary text help to 'explain why, four decades after its first publication, a never-ending stream of commentaries still, and in vain, attempt to stitch up Michael K into the latest nomenclatures of "bare life" and "*homo sacer*"'.[86] Scholarship on the novel tends to impose concepts from European political theory on

---

[82] Coetzee, *Life & Times of Michael K*, 18.
[83] Heider, 'The Timeless Ecstasy of Michael K', 83.
[84] Ibid., 83.
[85] Agamben, *Homo Sacer: Sovereign Power and Bare Life*, 8.
[86] Van Niekerk, 'The Literary Text in Turbulent Times: An Instrument of Social Cohesion or an Eruption of "Critical" Bliss. Notes on JM Coetzee's Life and Times of Michael K.', 22.

the text, with the effect that the novel becomes a site for Western political theory to illuminate its own assumptions about state power.

Coetzee's own interest in state power circles around its ubiquity and the difficulty one encounters in trying to think of alternatives to it. As Rita Barnard notes, Coetzee is preoccupied with the temporality that inheres in our understanding of ourselves as state subjects; the state is an utterly naturalised idea that appears prior to us and to which we are, in Coetzee's words, '"born subject"'.[87] If, as Barnard summarises, '[w]e cannot reverse the narrative of our acquiescence and think entirely outside the structures of the state', we can nevertheless employ alternative generic modalities, such as the fable or the allegory, to 'imagine the unimaginable'. Timothy Wright agrees that Coetzee's interest lies in the 'narrative form taken by the state', and that that state's 'production of its own temporal anteriority' is central to its function.[88] The interest in exposing the mechanisms of temporal anteriority may explain Coetzee's use of the past tense; Michael K is consistently hailed by state actors as a thief, a deserter or a terrorist, and each of these words names a specific, but deviant, relationship to state power. Michael K's mode of refusal is more than simply an evasion of the space of the camp or the logic of the checkpoint, but also a rejection of the state's apparatus of time and history.

Michael K's sense of time puts him at odds with the state and the logic of capitalistic labour, which privileges productivity and condemns idleness. After returning to the Visagie farm and taking up residence in a cave, Michael K remarks that the sound of fighter jets seem to come from 'the other time in which the war had its existence', but as for himself, 'he was living beyond the reach of calendar and clock in a blessedly neglected corner, half awake, half asleep.'[89] Living outside of state power, here, is determined not only by physical distance from centres and agents of power, but also by temporal distance, where the clock and calendar have not penetrated. In citing the clock and calendar specifically, Coetzee's novel presciently identifies the same mechanisms that Benedict Anderson argues underlie the temporality of the modern state. In *Imagined Communities*, published the same year as *Life & Times of Michael K*, Anderson argues that the nation-state's temporality is shaped by the conception of '"homogeneous, empty time," in which simultaneity is, as it were, transverse, cross-time, marked not by prefiguring

---

[87] Barnard, 'Tsotsis: On Law, the Outlaw, and the Postcolonial State', 543.
[88] T. Wright, 'The Art of Evasion: Writing and the State in J. M. Coetzee's Life & Times of Michael K', 57.
[89] Coetzee, *Life & Times of Michael K*, 116.

and fulfilment, but by temporal coincidence, and measured by clock and calendar.'[90] In placing himself outside of those strictures, Michael K resists the mechanisms necessary for imagining the modern nation-state. Instead, he explicitly refuses to 'master time' or 'impose a personal frame of reference onto the things exterior to him'.[91]

As a result, Michael K's sense of the past and the future is at odds with the temporality of the state. His apparent idleness and extreme focus on the immediate present yields a radical open-endedness towards the future. Once his mother dies, the vague notions of what Michael K will do next and where he will go dissolve into aimless wandering and indefinite pauses. The idleness he embraces on the farm and in the veld is prefigured in the text's earlier description of his first experience with unemployment. Michael K leaves his first gardening post for reasons unspecified, and spends a 'spell of unemployment . . . lying on his bed and looking at his hands'.[92] Later, Michael K will describe freedom in terms of idleness and the absence of work, in the same paragraph where he delineates the time on the farm from the time of war:

> But most of all, as summer slanted to an end, he was learning to love idleness, idleness no longer as stretches of freedom reclaimed by stealth here and there from involuntary labour . . . but as a yielding up of himself to time, to a time flowing slowly like oil from horizon to horizon over the face of the world.[93]

Michael K's idleness, however, is not 'a betrayal of humanity', as the discourse of idleness on the Cape asserted, but rather 'divorced from his economic status', separating value and labour.[94] As Coetzee makes clear in recounting Michael K's time on the farm, this 'idleness' includes acts of gardening and tending to his pumpkins. What sets this idle time apart is how Michael K refuses to master or own the land. Michael K's desertion of 'involuntary labour' and refusal to possess the land as private property echo early accounts of African labourers who fled the British settlement of Theopolis in South Africa. Clifton Crais recounts that in the 1820s, these 'refugees frequently squatted on unused or unclaimed land and established, like mission stations, "artificial communities" where they violated private property rights and lived "in a state of

---

[90] Anderson, *Imagined Communities*, 24.
[91] Monson, 'An Infinite Question: The Paradox of Representation in Life & Times of Michael K', 95.
[92] Coetzee, *Life & Times of Michael K*, 4.
[93] Ibid., 115.
[94] Heider, 'The Timeless Ecstasy of Michael K', 96.

idleness without possessing property sufficient for their subsistence"'.[95] Those who escaped conditions of unfree labour were called *drosters*, and included 'runaway slaves, deserted sailors, absconding soldiers' and others in the Cape, forming 'groups, bound together in a particular form of resistance to oppression – flight'.[96] In the Cape, just as in Haiti, the mountainous geography 'beckoned to fugitives, offering . . . a wild and alluring place of refuge seemingly removed from colonial control'.[97] Through his refusal to 'work' and to possess the land, as well as his flight from unfree labour, Michael K draws on tactics of resistance with a long history in South Africa.

The refusal to work, as Kathi Weeks notes, 'can make time and open spaces – both physical and conceptual – within which to construct alternatives' to capitalism's organisation and imposition of work.[98] 'The utopian aspect of the refusal to work', Weeks elaborates, is 'its insistence that we struggle toward and imagine the possibilities of substantial social change', where 'paths to alternative futures' can be opened.[99] Michael K's idleness is characterised by an openness to time that neither dwells on making sense of the past nor anticipates the future in concrete terms. Whereas the 'ordering of knowledge and history associated with society require fixing references to break the ceaseless flows of time', Michael K welcomes the flow of time.[100] When there is work to do, Michael K is indifferent because 'it was all the same'; leisure and labour are indistinguishable outside of the labour economy.[101] This sense of time frustrates all of the state agents he encounters. To the roadblock guards who ask him to wait, he replies, '"I don't want to stop, I don't have time."'[102] Although he is forced to work on the railway tracks for a few days, Michael K escapes '[w]ithout waiting . . . duck[ing] through

---

[95] Crais, *White Supremacy and Black Resistance in Pre-Industrial South Africa*, 131.
[96] Penn, 'Drosters of the Bokkeveld and the Roggeveld, 1770–1800', 41.
[97] Ibid., 41.
[98] Weeks, *The Problem with Work*, 100.
[99] Ibid., 101.
[100] Heider, 'The Timeless Ecstasy of Michael K', 91.
[101] Coetzee, *Life & Times of Michael K*, 115. See Richard Waller's 'Rebellious Youth in Colonial Africa' for an historical account of youth, defiance, leisure and labour. Waller notes that colonial rule promoted 'the ideals of productive masculinity, tamed by work and made responsible through the obligations of marriage and citizenship, and of modern wifehood and motherhood that taught girls the disciplines of a new but still subordinate domesticity'. Waller, 78. Michael K's 'idle time', spent tending to his plants, not only opposes the colonial regime's 'productive masculinity', but also the dichotomy of male labour and female nurturing.
[102] Coetzee, *Life & Times of Michael K*, 40.

a hole in the fence'.[103] His sense of urgency derives less from a sense of things he must do, and more from a sense of how he must be: outside the reach of the state and its temporality. In the rehabilitation camp, Michael K is continually pressed to tell the truth and answer a battery of questions ranging from the political to the philosophical and temporal: 'What is your stake in the future?'[104] Once again, Michael K refuses to comment or elaborate. His sense of time is stubbornly irreducible to the time of state, but also irreducible to seasonal or natural cycles. Although Michael K's first visit to the farm finds him living 'by the rising and setting of the sun, in a pocket outside time', by the second time he arrives he 'kept no tally of the days nor recorded the changes of the moon'.[105] Michael K seems to pass his time in a state of non-intentional waiting, a waiting characterised by an unassuming openness to the future.[106] While Heider notes that Michael K 'is removed from recorded time, from language, and from work', the implication of her passive-voice construction is that Michael K is neither deliberate nor intentional in his actions.[107] But on the contrary, Michael K moves constantly and evinces a deliberate intention to seek out both spaces and times more amenable to his sense of freedom.

Michael K's nomadism and acts of escape constitute his resistance. Though he does not articulate, to potential interlocutors, an affirmative theory of freedom, we can nevertheless look to how freedom is negatively defined in the narrative through acts of escape; what Michael K does not prefer can give insight into his predilections. When he leaves the Visagie farm, it is because the Visagie grandson 'tried to turn him into a body-servant'.[108] When Michael K refuses to carry on in the same manner as the Visagies by establishing 'a new house, a rival line',[109] Coetzee 'engages with and writes, through the lens of the pastoral . . . the larger ideological underpinnings of the modern state as such'.[110] Michael K also

---

[103] Ibid., 44.
[104] Ibid., 140.
[105] Ibid., 60, 115.
[106] To be clear, Michael K is not always waiting in the novel; he refuses to wait in the various camps, for example. These enclosures, however, make particular demands on Michael K's space and time, and to be free from the camps makes possible a more utopian way to wait and to dwell in the present. Rather than ignore these moments of activity, my reading of the novel instead accounts for the oppositional nature of Michael K's ostensible passivity.
[107] Heider, 'The Timeless Ecstasy of Michael K', 84.
[108] Coetzee, *Life & Times*, 65.
[109] Ibid., 104.
[110] T. Wright, 'The Art of Evasion', 58.

escapes from the Jakkalsdrif resettlement camp and infirmary, which are significant spaces where staff and medical officers attempt to interpret him, fill in his history and make sense of his intentions. Because the soldiers and police persistently assume that Michael K is an insurgent giving aid to rebels in the mountains, they can only imagine his 'protest' as a direct response in opposition to the state, choosing one side instead of the other. But in fact, Michael K's refusal to signify puts him 'at odds with the discourse of war' and 'outside of such categorizations'.[111] In the same way, camps attempt to fix freedom and imprisonment as opposing nodes, as if the matter were settled merely by the presence of a fence. In the hospital ward, Noël is perplexed that Michael K is malnourished despite '"living by himself on that farm of his free as a bird, eating the bread of freedom"'.[112] Likewise, at Jakkalsdrif camp, the guards are emphatic that '"This isn't a prison"', despite the fact that being found vagrant again will guarantee penal servitude in Brandvlei camp, and that Michael K will be shot if found climbing the fence.[113] In order to make sense of the form of resistance he embodies, we need a framework or paradigm that will account for his ambivalent relationship to the various 'sides' in the war, his constant movement, the way he frustrates the easy delineation of freedom and unfreedom, and his developing sense of time.

If we read Michael K in the tradition of marronage, we can better understand how Coetzee reworks the concepts of freedom and resistance in *Life & Times of Michael K*, and the role of waiting in configuring Michael K's counter-temporality. If we revisit the characteristics of marronage developed in the first part of this chapter, we see that Michael K fulfils the criteria of deliberate isolation, of seeking freedom in flight, and of reconfiguring the totalising time of the state. His escape from Jakkalsdrif is instructive in all three regards; he scales the camp's fence and trembles 'with the thrill of being free'.[114] At the same time, each subsequent fence he encounters reminds him that his sense of freedom is contingent, and that he is 'a trespasser as well as a runaway'. When Michael K contemplates the meaning of freedom in the novel's third part, he concludes, 'Perhaps the truth is that it is enough to be out of the camps, out of all the camps at the same time.'[115] The changing landscape of South Africa in the novel ensures that the space outside of the camps will be a constantly shifting environment, requiring Michael K to be on the move or in flight always.

---

[111] L. Wright, *Writing 'Out of All the Camps'*, 89.
[112] Coetzee, *Life & Times*, 146.
[113] Ibid., 78.
[114] Ibid., 97.
[115] Ibid., 182.

Like historical maroons, Michael K too escapes to the mountains. Here, his sense of time again is influenced by idleness:

> He spent a day in idleness, sitting in the mouth of his cave gazing up at the farther peaks on which there were still patches of snow . . . When he awoke in the morning he faced only the single huge block of the day, one day at a time.[116]

Michael K acknowledges that previously, he relied on other people in positions of authority to give him orders, but 'now there was no one, and the best thing seemed to be to wait'.[117]

The possibility of waiting expresses, for Michael K, a freedom outside the confines of the workday in the Cape or the camp. Concerning *Waiting for the Barbarians*, Patrick Hayes notes that the novel is 'truly amenable to an anti-foundational imagining of moral community – one that, like the Magistrate himself, is placed in a sustained condition of "waiting"', and that freedom is experienced 'as a continued slipping of the chains'.[118] The relationship between waiting and freedom is similarly configured in *Life & Times of Michael K* through idleness, which renders Michael K illegible to the state that would like to incorporate him in its system of meaning. In this, Michael K is a mystery to himself, admitting that his story is 'full of the same old gaps that he would never learn how to bridge'.[119] He is utterly resistant to interpretation and unable 'to interpretively colonise himself', which in Timothy Wright's view 'makes him a problematic subject not only within the context of the South African state, but, potentially, for any future state'.[120] Rita Barnard comes closest to reading Michael K as a maroon figure when she writes that the 'brilliance of the survival strategy Michael K devises is that he finds a way to reclaim displacement and tracklessness as a form of freedom'.[121] Even within the camps, Michael K exhibits a sense of time hostile to the state by slowing down or refusing to work.

To recall Coetzee's writing on idleness in the Cape, the discourse of idleness separated natives from colonists based on the perception that the natives wasted their time doing nothing. Or as Charles Mills

---

[116] Ibid., 66.
[117] Ibid., 67.
[118] Hayes, *J. M. Coetzee and the Novel*, 71.
[119] Coetzee, *Life & Times of Michael K*, 176.
[120] T. Wright, 'The Art of Evasion: Writing and the State in J. M. Coetzee's Life & Times of Michael K', 72.
[121] Barnard, *Apartheid and Beyond: South African Writers and the Politics of Place*, 31.

observes more widely, European ideologies of time, what he calls 'white time', became a moralising assessment 'of the appropriate use *of* time, conceptions of daily rhythms of work and leisure, as opposed to the general misuse of time Europeans found elsewhere'.[122] The parallels between the native constructed through the discourse of idleness and the novel's characterisation of Michael K are difficult to miss; Michael K spends much of his time on the farm, in the camp, and at Sea Point sleeping, and in the Jakkalsdrif camp, Robert presses him, '"You've been asleep all your life. It's time to wake up."'[123] Robert advises Michael K to slow down, since he will be paid one rand for his day's work no matter the output: '"Just go slow . . . They can't make you do what you can't do."'[124] Other times, Michael K refuses to work entirely, telling the guard, '"I don't want to work. Why do I have to work? This isn't a jail"' and '"When I need to eat, I'll work."'[125] His refusal posits a temporality that is in sync with the rhythm of the body rather than the ticking of the clock; by inhabiting this temporal mode, Michael K's decision to work or not is utterly unpredictable to others. In effect, his idleness forces others to wait, which as Pierre Bourdieu discerns in another context, 'is an integral part of the exercise of power'.[126]

Although Michael K does not take up arms for the insurgency or react in expected ways to protest the state and its emergency powers, his continual flight from the state's camps, hospitals and roadblocks shares affinities with Ti Noël's practice of marronage and its attendant formulation of freedom. The Medical Officer learns that from an early age, Michael K dreamed of the freedom of flight. Of life in Huis Norenius, Michael K remembers,

> 'I used to think about flying. I always wanted to fly. I used to stretch out my arms and think I was flying over the fences and between the houses. I flew low over people's heads, but they couldn't see me.'[127]

In his imagination, flying would enable him to bypass the barriers of fences, which create separations and boundaries, and to inhabit in-between spaces. This decision to seek freedom in flight rather than fighting with the guerrillas struck a dissonant chord with the novel's first readers as the struggle against apartheid intensified. I want to suggest

---

[122] Mills, 'White Time: The Chronic Injustice of Ideal Theory', 31.
[123] Coetzee, *Life & Times of Michael K*, 88.
[124] Ibid., 87.
[125] Ibid., 85.
[126] Bourdieu, *Pascalian Meditations*, 228.
[127] Coetzee, *Life & Times of Michael K*, 133.

that Michael K's mode of resistance is not necessarily a normative one; as the contrast with Ti Noël underscores, there are moments when what is more easily recognised as direct, active resistance is necessary. But what I take Michael K to model in his refusals and flight is a line of critique that South African society after apartheid continues to grapple with, and those are the terms and foundations of oppression, power, and freedom. Michael K's flight draws attention to the ostensibly apolitical or 'passive' actions of ordinary characters – actions that may prove surprisingly disruptive to state power and its agents.

Lines of Flight: States of Freedom in Marronage

Ti Noël and Michael K, despite the vast distances in space and time between Carpentier's 1949 fictionalisation of the Haitian Revolution and Coetzee's 1983 novel set during the Emergency in South Africa, share a commitment to freedom and the future through their affirmation of flight, fugitivity and marronage. For *The Kingdom of This World*, marronage offers a way of reading the novel's historical and revolutionary investments through the evocation of real life maroons and the continual references to runaways that give the plot its shape. For *Life & Times of Michael K*, the strategies of marronage that Michael K adopts enable his mode of resistance, allowing us to read his temporal mode as refusal in the context of the Cape's discourse of idleness. Both characters are marked by their ostensible passivity, but reading the texts in terms of marronage reveals accents of active opposition. Their respective deliberate, intentional acts are disruptive to state or colonial power, exposing the underpinnings of the state mechanism even if not directly or successfully abolishing it. But where Ti Noël and the other Haitian revolutionaries seem to have forgotten the revolutionary promise embodied in the act of flight, Michael K's relentless movements and escapes permit him a kind of freedom in flight.

Reading Michael K as a maroon figure allows us to return to *The Kingdom of This World* with the notion of marronage's association with waiting. Michael K embraces waiting as idleness in his refusal to work or to follow the expected patterns of time dictated by the labour camp workday or even the natural cycles of the moon. To wait can also mean to lie in wait with hostile intent or ambush, or to look forward or continue in expectation.[128] Both meanings are applicable to the

---

[128] *Oxford English Dictionary*, 'Wait, v. 1'.

practice of marronage derived from the Haitian Revolution, where survival strategies included ambushing plantations and waiting for opportune moments to launch offensives, as well as a commitment to an alternative, free future. The juxtaposition of the two novels shows how the maroon's flight, especially the *petit-marronage* form that challenges the ontological categories of free and unfree, makes newly legible the myriad ways that Ti Noël and Michael K mobilise waiting to resist the plantation and the state's claims on their spaces and times. Michael K refuses to master time; Ti Noël wrests time from the time-space of the plantation and posits other ways of being at odds with the cycles of oppression he observes. For each protagonist, time itself is a battlefield. Idleness and lying in wait are the temporal modalities that prove disruptive to the plantation and state regimes of time. Yet Ti Noël and Michael K configure 'lying in wait' in meaningfully different ways; while Ti Noël and other maroons evince quintessential maroon tactics in their relationship to the plantation, and then later the state, Michael K lies in wait – in the sense of reclining, and dwelling in the temporality of waiting. Earlier passages depict Michael K as waiting *for* specific objects or events, such as for the passes to be issued to enable him to travel, but as the novel progresses, he increasingly lies in wait for its own sake.

If we broaden out our considerations of lying in wait in *The Kingdom of This World*, we might also interpret Carpentier's choice to reach back to the Haitian revolution, in his twentieth-century present, to be motivated by a revolutionary promise that still lies in wait for postcolonial Haiti and Cuba to manifest. The theory and practice of marronage illuminates not only the totalising temporality of the state, but also the varied ways resistance to it might be embodied through flight; marronage can disrupt the naturalised progression of time associated with the temporal regimes of nation-states. The temporality assumed by state structures, according to James Scott, 'consists of a historical series arranged as an account of economic, social, and cultural progress', and the structures of maroon societies, like the hill peoples he studies, are illegible as agents of deliberate choice when confronted with the state's 'powerful civilizational narrative'.[129] If the philosophy of marronage is, following Glissant and Roberts, one of continual becoming and movement and 'counter to the idea of fixed, determinate endings', then marronage opposes not only the slave plantation, but also the temporality of the modern nation-state.[130] The modern state naturalises its existence

---

[129] J. C. Scott, *The Art of Not Being Governed: An Anarachist History of Upland Southeast Asia*, 187.
[130] Roberts, *Freedom as Marronage*, 174.

by professing 'to give political expression' to nations that 'always loom out of an immemorial past, and still more important, glide into a limitless future'.[131] Marronage's strategic mobilisation of waiting – as lying in wait, and lying in ostensible idleness – posits an alternative sense of time in both texts. Ti Noël and Michael K share an affinity for nonintentional waiting, in the sense that they are open to the future without explicitly anticipating how the future will become manifest.

This chapter, together with Chapter 2, considered novels set during revolutions and anticolonial movements, or anti-apartheid struggles for freedom and black-majority rule. Thus far, we have observed how refusing to wait was a response to the waiting-room model of history, which characterised colonial regimes of time and in turn affected what kind of future – if any at all – the text is able to anticipate or imagine. Waiting can be an oppressive and limiting temporal experience, as Salim in *A Bend in the River* illustrates, but waiting can also be a tactic or practice of resistance, as this chapter's discussion of marronage suggested. The following chapter builds from these insights but pivots to a new context: postcolonial disillusionment in the second half of the twentieth century. Although Michael K and Ti Noël, as maroon figures, couple flight with a spatial and temporal politics of resistance, Chapter 4 explores the extent to which the temporal experience of waiting can empower protagonists in novels of disillusionment. This discussion raises the following questions: If refusing to wait was central to anticolonial nationalist movements' urgent insistence for independence, could waiting possibly signify differently after independence had been achieved? How might gendered ideas about waiting, women and passivity generate new critiques of postcolonial states, illuminate their failings, and also trouble the association of waiting with passivity and femininity?

---

[131] Anderson, *Imagined Communities*, 11–12.

Chapter 4

Gendered Timescapes of Waiting: Patience and Urgency in Novels of Disillusionment

> The anteriority of the nation, signified in the will to forget, entirely changes our understanding of the pastness of the past, and the synchronous present of the will to nationhood.
>
> Homi K. Bhabha, *The Location of Culture* (2004)

> As Homi Bhabha points out in his work on nationhood, these performances of synchrony may seem to consolidate collective life, but the coherence they provide is fragile.
>
> Elizabeth Freeman, *Time Binds* (2010)

To date, the label 'novels of disillusionment' has been applied almost exclusively to fiction from the African continent that reflects the disappointment with several unrealised hopes: for a full representative government after independence, a unified nation and state, an even promotion of political, social and economic welfare across all segments of society, and a cultural, institutional and political break with the colonial past. Despite the initial euphoric optimism of independence, the fiction of the immediate postcolonial period depicts the struggles of the people, still waiting for these promises to be fulfilled. Given that 'high-sounding rhetoric' at the time of independence predominated where 'framing political principles or social visions' ought to have guided, Derek Wright remarks, it was 'not surprising' that independence was an uneven process, benefiting a handful of professional elites.[1] The fiction written during this '"disillusionment" period' levelled criticism at the 'indigenous ruling elite' who exploited the masses and often exacerbated intra-national conflict.[2] Arthur Ravenscroft's early 1969 account of the proliferation of disillusionment themes, 'Novels of Disillusion', was published less than a decade after large swaths of the African

---

[1] D. Wright, 'African Literature and Post-Independence Disillusionment', 797.
[2] Obi, 'A Critical Reading of the Disillusionment Novel', 400.

continent achieved independence, and focused on Chinua Achebe's 1966 *A Man of the People* and Wole Soyinka's 1965 *The Interpreters*. Writing in 1976, the Ghanaian writer Kofi Awoonor remarked that Ayi Kwei Armah, among other African writers, seemed 'to epitomize this era of intense despair'.[3] Thus, Armah's novels, beginning with his first, *The Beautyful Ones Are Not Yet Born,* have long been associated with postcolonial disillusionment. Neil Lazarus's *Resistance in Postcolonial African Fiction*, a study of Armah's oeuvre, contends that Armah's work is 'exemplary of the passage from messianism to disillusion', marking the disappointment that succeeded the optimism of independence.[4] The affects of disappointment and disillusionment that Ravenscroft and others have identified in African postcolonial literature after independence depends on a narrative of anticolonial nationalism that, according to Hugh O'Connell, 'posits a frenzy of Utopian nation-building texts in the 1960s that eventually turn dyspeptic and critical due to the failure of postcolonial states in the 1970s.'[5]

While O'Connell and others overwhelmingly reference African fiction in their discussions of novels of disillusion, postcolonial literatures from around the globe also reflect the various shortcomings of postcolonial governments. In contrast to African novels of disillusionment, many works of Indian fiction register disillusionment immediately after or simultaneously with independence. R. K. Gupta elaborates the parallels and contrasts between these two traditions, noting that 'In India, as in many African countries with a colonial past, the new native rulers turned out to be no less rapacious than the colonial masters they had supplanted' and that in Indian fiction 'the sense of hopes belied and aspirations not fulfilled began to appear as a literary theme soon after 1947'.[6] Significantly, Gupta links the African and Indian traditions of disillusionment fiction, but also acknowledges an important departure: that the trauma of Partition effectively inaugurated disenchantment concurrently with independence.

The dominant affects of disillusionment fiction – dashed hopes and unfulfilled aspirations – tend to produce a sense of time as stasis, or indefinite waiting. As we will see in this chapter's discussion of gendered nationalisms and (re)productive time, characters who desire integration and participation in newly independent nations – nations that elevate

---

[3] Awoonor, *The Breast of the Earth*, 303–4.
[4] N. Lazarus, *Resistance in Postcolonial African Fiction*, x.
[5] O'Connell, 'A Weak Utopianism of Postcolonial Nationalist Bildung: Re-Reading Ayi Kwei Armah's The Beautyful Ones Are Not Yet Born', 372.
[6] Gupta, 'Trends in Modern Indian Fiction', 303.

only elites or men as wielders of power – find themselves frustrated and further alienated by the terms of belonging. Sara Ahmed usefully evokes 'waiting' to describe the desire for national belonging and a reciprocal love between self and nation:

> One loves the nation, then, out of hope and with nostalgia for how it could have been. One keeps loving rather than recognising that the love that one has given has not and will not be returned. One could even think of national love as a form of waiting. To wait is to extend one's investment and the longer one waits the more one is invested, that is, the more time, labour and energy has been expended. The failure of return extends one's investment. If love functions as the promise of return, then the extension of investment through the failure of return works to maintain the ideal through its deferral into the future.[7]

While this discussion of national love is more expansive than my more narrow focus on newly independent, postcolonial nations, these latter 'disillusioned' contexts underscore the dynamics of desire, attachment, and waiting for fulfilment Ahmed describes above.

In this way, disillusionment fiction indexes what Lauren Berlant calls, in another context, the 'cruel optimism' of the immediate post-independence period. Cruel optimism arises 'when something you desire is actually an obstacle to your flourishing'.[8] Though Berlant anchors their analysis in post-1980 United States and Europe, postcolonial disillusionment fiction from the 1960s and 1970s has much to offer as scenes of desire and attachment to political projects that stagnate in an 'impasse'.[9] Berlant's concepts and framework are useful for theorising the relationship between fiction and the world outside the text. Of their analysis of literature and affect, they write,

> The key here is not to see what happens to aesthetically mediated characters as equivalent to what happens to people but to see that in the affective scenarios of these works and discourses we can discern claims about the situation of contemporary life.[10]

---

[7] Ahmed, *The Cultural Politics of Emotion*, 131.
[8] Berlant, *Cruel Optimism*, 1.
[9] Impasse is one way Berlant characterises the present, in language deeply resonant with the mood and affect of disillusionment fiction: 'impasses in zones of intimacy that hold out the often cruel promise of reciprocity and belonging to the people who seek them – who need them – in scenes of labor, of love, and of the political.' Berlant, *Cruel Optimism*, 21. Both *Fragments* and *Cry, the Peacock* include all three 'scenes' in their depiction of disappointment and waiting to belong.
[10] Berlant, *Cruel Optimism*, 9.

In my analysis of disillusionment fiction that follows, the affective scenarios depicted in Ayi Kwei Armah's *Fragments* and Anita Desai's *Cry, the Peacock* enable us to detect disappointment and the attendant temporality of continued waiting as not simply a critique of the postcolonial nation, but also an affective response. This waiting can engender new rhythms of being that deliberately syncopate with the frenetic tempos of accelerated, productive time in Armah's Accra and with the suspension of women's belonging in Desai's India.

While the category 'novels of disillusion' has been generative for theorising postcolonial fiction, including a range of novels not limited to Africa that register disenchantment with postcolonial states after independence, its employment has resulted in two major scholarly omissions. First, there has been insufficient attention paid to the complex role of waiting in disillusionment novels, especially insofar as waiting appears in relation to post-independence experiences of patience and urgency. Novels of disillusionment depict the postcolonial subject in a continued state of waiting in vain; in what is often characterised as literature of disillusionment, scholars note a marked pessimism about the future in a seemingly stalled present that is doomed to replicate the power dynamics of the colonial past. The urgency that characterised the independence-era's state and nation-building dissipated in the Cold War era, and with many of the structures of the former colonial state still intact, postcolonial state rulers replicated the marginalisation of 'weaker or subnational groups'.[11] By collapsing waiting and disillusionment, scholars overlook how individuals may employ waiting to criticise the state and, in some cases, to empower themselves still. Second, scholars have neglected to consider the gendered dimensions of waiting – that waiting might signify differently in relation to discourses of gendered nationalism. Many of the classic 'disillusionment' novels feature male protagonists, and scholarship has then reproduced this focus. In contrast, this chapter argues that in post-independence novels by Armah and Desai, women evoke the temporal dimensions of waiting in ways that challenge the simplistic opposition of revolutionary urgency, replaced by disappointed waiting, that dominates the scholarly narrative of 'postcolonial disillusionment'.

In order to arrive at a more expansive rendering of waiting and gender in these two disillusionment novels, I turn to the concept of 'timescapes' as a way to capture the interplay between different temporalities

---

[11] Amin-Khan, *The Post-Colonial State in the Era of Capitalist Globalization*, 48–9.

and temporal modes in the texts, which produce the seemingly opposed modes of urgency and patience. Barbara Adam coined the term timescape to refer to 'the embodiment of practiced approaches to time', and, unlike other 'scapes' (such as land, city, and sea) that privilege the spatial, the concept of timescapes 'emphasize their rhythmicities, their timings and tempos, their change and contingencies'.[12] A focus on timescapes in the texts aims to avoid a reductive comparison of Western linear temporalities to indigenous cyclical temporalities. Scholarly studies of African temporality and fiction in particular have often fallen into such a reduction, which as Adam Barrows observes, tends to impose 'a stark dichotomy between African time as cyclical and Western time as linear'.[13] As I traced in the Introduction to this book, Orientalist studies similarly pitted the East and West in dichotomous opposition, fixing the East in time and place such that the West is further ahead and the East is always further behind.[14] V. Y. Mudimbe notes that this practice also occurred with respect to Africa, which was 'represented in Western scholarship' through constructions that 'simplif[y] cultural complexities'.[15] Orientalist and Africanist discourse alike exoticise the 'other' temporalities, emphasising their irreducible difference and complete incompatibility with Western notions of time.

Drawing on the concept of timescapes, I read Armah's 1970 novel *Fragments* and Desai's 1963 novel *Cry, the Peacock* for their representations of waiting in relation to patience and urgency. While timescape scholarship thus far omits any explicit discussion of gender, the novels themselves emphasise their mutual imbrication, especially with regard to representing patience and urgency, which have been traditionally coded as feminine and masculine respectively. In these novels, women register the interaction of multiple temporalities, including the temporal regimes of capitalism, history, prophecy, Hinduism, Akan and ancestral time, and the reproductive accents of national time. The reinscription of masculine national identity in these postcolonial settings after independence creates additional tensions for the women in the novels, and their embodied dramatisations of patience and urgency challenge the dominant narrative of disillusionment and its attendant, underlying association of waiting with passivity and femininity.

---

[12] Adam, *Timescapes of Modernity: The Environment and Invisible Hazards*, 10.
[13] Barrows, *The Cosmic Time of Empire*, 633.
[14] Said, *Orientalism*, 108.
[15] Mudimbe, *The Idea of Africa*, iv.

Engendering Timescapes: Patience and Urgency

Clocks and calendars effectively produce sensations of simultaneity and homogeneity across space – an impression that globalisation has deepened. In *Time Passing*, Sylviane Agacinski remarks that 'contemporary chronotechnology' – that is, the 'extension of production methods and the establishment of [the West's] temporal architecture' – results from 'the unification of the world's rhythms, all adjusted to the Western clock'.[16] Yet because of the ubiquity of the clock and calendar in the industrialised West, and the increasing hegemony of 'industrial time' in the globalised world, Barbara Adam counters, people around the world are not sufficiently attuned to the 'multi-dimensional' temporalities embedded in 'socio-environmental life'.[17] Just as industrial time suppresses alternative temporalities, homogenising and synchronising temporal experience to the mathematical time of clocks and calendars, national time, accordingly to Benedict Anderson, relies on these same external time-keeping mechanisms to produce the 'homogeneous empty time' required for the nation to be 'conceived as a solid community moving steadily down (or up) history'.[18] Anderson notes that national revolutions tend to ground themselves 'firmly in a territorial and social space', but his attention to the simultaneity undergirding national time redirects us to the ways that temporal landscapes, or timescapes, are integral to consolidating national identity.[19] Of course, the clock and calendar also suppress alternative and coexisting temporalities in an effort to 'achieve temporal standardization and uniformity'.[20] In order to avoid the tendency of making calendrical and clock time stand in for universal and homogeneous time, Byron Ellsworth Hamann advises, we ought to examine 'times and places where that calendar functions alongside other, alternative forms of time reckoning'.[21] To contest the

---

[16] Agacinski, *Time Passing*, 5–6.
[17] Adam, *Timescapes of Modernity: The Environment and Invisible Hazards*, 8.
[18] Anderson, *Imagined Communities*, 26.
[19] Pertinent to the elaboration of timescapes as the heterogeneous comingling of temporalities, Partha Chatterjee notes in 'Anderson's Utopia' that the homogeneous, empty time of the nation-state is 'utopian', and that the 'real space of modern life is a heterotopia . . . Time is heterogeneous, unevenly dense' ('Anderson's Utopia', 131). Chatterjee asserts that the strongest case can be built with reference to the postcolonial world, where 'there more than anywhere else in the modern world' we can see the 'the presence of a dense and heterogeneous time' (132).
[20] Birth, *Objects of Time*, 123.
[21] Hamann, 'How to Chronologize with a Hammer, Or, The Myth of Homogeneous, Empty Time', 279.

myth that Western temporality is 'inescapably "homogeneous, empty time"', Hamann argues, we must both 'desecularliz[e]' and 'provincialize' the notion of Western time.[22] The concept of timescapes can address both concerns, because attending to timescapes entails acknowledging the multiple temporalities that coexist within and alongside dominant temporal regimes that otherwise posit homogeneity through standardisation, and illuminating the suppressed or overlooked temporalities interacting in a given setting or experience.

Timescapes enable us to see temporal heterogeneity, which is especially important in national contexts that emphasise synchronicity, as the epigraphs from Homi Bhabha and Elizabeth Freeman suggest. The women in Armah's and Desai's novels dramatise asynchrony with their newly independent nations, and they describe their modes of being in time as different forms of waiting. To be sure, Baako's experience of time will also be a focus of my reading of *Fragments*, as his inability to navigate the post-independence timescape helps us to understand the alternative ways of being in time represented most clearly by Naana, his grandmother. This study of gendered waiting in disillusionment fiction will show that these characters' waiting is the locus for the novels' political and social critique and, at least in the case of *Fragments*, also a temporality of possibility. Naana, drawing from several temporal modes activated in the timescape of Accra, is able to reconcile the past, present, and future in ways that Baako is unable.[23]

While the growing body of scholarship on timescapes thus far has been attuned to various temporalities in conjunction with industrialisation, modernisation, the environment and nature, none has interrogated how gender is mapped on to temporalities, or the ways in which time and temporal experiences are gendered – especially with regard to waiting. A growing body of scholarship in mobility studies, however, addresses how patience and urgency, immobility and mobility, are gendered and associated with waiting. Combining these two areas of research highlights the intersections between waiting, gender, movement and passivity, and will enable a robust reading of timescapes in *Fragments* and *Cry, the Peacock*. Waiting, David Bissell observes in his widely cited

---

[22] Ibid., 286.
[23] Comingling temporalities can be distinguished according to the kind of discord or harmony they produce; another word for the coexistence of temporalities is polyrhythmia, which can be eurhythmic (consonant) or arrhythmic (conflicted). Birth, *Objects of Time*, 101. The euphoric timescape of independence privileges the consonant; in my reading of disillusionment fiction I am interested in how arrhythmias signify.

article 'Animating Suspension: Waiting for Mobilities', complicates commonplace notions of activity and passivity; he argues that waiting need not be reduced to 'slowed rhythms or somehow opposed to speed', but rather entails 'rich durations' replete with 'multiple temporalities'.[24] Configured as a mix of urgency and delay, patience and impatience are central to this reformulation. Patience is, in a way, the 'apotheosis of waiting' as a subject positively endures the present.[25] Patience is the ability to reconcile the tempo of the self in duration with the tempo of the world; impatience, however, '"stems from [an] inability to reconcile the two temporalities . . . that grate and jar"'.[26] Urgency is closely linked to impatience, as that which cannot wait any longer.

Impatience and patience, as well as activity and inactivity, tend to be coded male and female respectively. In a study of waiting and migrancy, Deirdre Conlon finds that regardless of gender identity,

> those who wait in refugee camps in the global South are feminized, considered passive, immobile and more likely [to be] deemed 'authentic' refugees. In contrast, individuals who move are produced in accordance with masculinist assumptions; they are coded as politicized self-serving subjects who represent a threat to security and resources in the global North.[27]

Conlon observes that 'the feminization of "staying put" has a positive valence that allows women to come to terms with the place of waiting in their lives in strategic ways', such that 'waiting can be appropriated as part of a feminist political project'.[28] This view prompts us not only to reconsider the opposition between waiting and movement, immobility and mobility, but also to attend to the 'multi-faceted' temporalities of waiting, which include waiting as 'an active and intentional process'. The coding of mobile migrants as masculine, threatening and potential national security threats assumes that there is a correct, ethical way to wait; patience will be rewarded, as in the platitude 'Good things come

---

[24] Bissell, 'Animating Suspension: Waiting for Mobilities', 279.
[25] Ibid., 290.
[26] Schweizer, quoted ibid.
[27] Conlon, 'Waiting: Feminist Perspectives on the Spacings/Timings of Migrant (Im)Mobility', 355. The North/South divide that Conlon notes structures the relationship between the waiting refugees in the Global South, and the Global North's role in delaying movement or migration reproduces a dynamic similar to Dipesh Chakrabarty's 'waiting room of history', described in the Introduction and Chapter 2, and reintroduced in this chapter's section on *Cry, the Peacock*.
[28] Ibid., 258.

to those who wait.' In the field of human geography, Elizabeth Olson has found that

> [h]ow a person waits can also produce judgments about both her culture and her character. As it organizes the routines of our daily lives, waiting can serve – rightly or wrongly – as a measure of lawfulness and civility, and potentially as a justification for the removal or denial of rights. A worthy citizen waits appropriately or faces consequences.[29]

The assumption that patient waiting reveals moral character plays out not only on an international scale, such as for Conlon's asylum seekers, but also within national borders, as we will see in Armah's *Fragments*, and within the home, in Desai's *Cry, the Peacock*. In this way, national governments leverage the distinction between patience and impatience to dismiss urgent criticisms and calls for change. This 'ethical dimension of waiting' was underscored by Martin Luther King Jr, who argued 'that a demand to wait can be immoral and therefore requires an apposite counterforce, what he called "the fierce urgency of now"'.[30]

In *Fragments* and *Cry, the Peacock*, the gender-coding of patient waiting as feminine and commendable intersects with the gendered nationalisms of postcolonial states. The gendering of the nation-state is well documented; Elleke Boehmer's *Stories of Women: Gender and Narrative in the Postcolonial Nation* summarises that 'gender forms *the* formative dimension for the construction of nationhood, if in relation to varying contextual determinants across different regions and countries'.[31] Benedict Anderson's own formulation in *Imagined Communities* is also suggestive of the link, despite not being otherwise concerned with the gendered dimensions of nationalism: '[I]n the modern world, everyone can, should, will have a nationality, as he or she "has" a gender.'[32] In Boehmer's comparative study, she finds that 'women's externalized, static and a-historic relationship to power', as well as their association

---

[29] Olson, 'Geography and Ethics 1: Waiting and Urgency', 517.
[30] Ibid., 518. See also Mario Feit's 'Democratic Impatience', which argues that King 'rejects the binary logic that casts patience and impatience as mutually exclusive opposites', and advocates for 'democratic impatience.' Feit, 3. In language that echoes the findings of Chapter 3 regarding resistive waiting, Feit suggests that 'democratic impatience *contains* subordinate elements of *operational patience* in the form of strategic delays and long-term programs of transformation'. Ibid.
[31] Boehmer, *Stories of Women*, 22. See also Sangeeta Ray, *En-Gendering India: Woman and Nation in Colonial and Postcolonial Narrative* which attends to the Indian context specifically, as well as Andrew Parker et al.'s edited collection *Nationalisms and Sexualities*.
[32] Anderson, *Imagined Communities*, 14.

with 'past, tradition, nature', are distinguished from men's occupation of 'the dimension of time-linear, future-directed' temporalities 'associated with change and progress'.[33] Here again, the gendered temporalities of national time dovetail with the coding of immobility and stasis as feminine, timeless and ahistorical. The following analyses of timescapes in *Fragments* and *Cry, the Peacock*, however, dramatise disruptions of these associations. *Fragments* not only challenges the male-dominated dimensions of future-oriented national time, but also troubles the association of women with tradition and the past. In *Cry, the Peacock*, the constraints of the woman/tradition bind become more pronounced, and deadly; the protagonist, Maya, responds to the imposition of waiting by insisting on the fierce urgency of now.

Waiting Impatiently: Timescapes of Accra

While Michael K, in my reading of *Life & Times of Michael K* in Chapter 3, embraces waiting as idleness, Baako Onipa in Ayi Kwei Armah's 1970 novel *Fragments* suffers acute anxiety as he experiences waiting and delays in post-independence Accra. When we first encounter Baako, he is waiting. In the Paris airport and *en route* from studying abroad in the United States, Baako 'avoided the initial stampede of passengers in a hurry'.[34] Titled 'Awkwaaba', the Akan word for welcome, the chapter pits the excitement and eagerness of other 'been-tos' returning from abroad against Baako's increasing anxiety that his arrival will be disappointing for his family, who expect ostentatious distributions of wealth. His immediate family – mother Efua, sister Araba, and grandmother Naana – expects that his return to Ghana will entail prosperity for the entire family, but Baako balks at the idea of success '"at the expense of the community."'[35] He meets Juana, a psychiatrist and his eventual lover, with whom he confides his growing despair not only for himself, but also for his country. While the first and final chapters are focalised from his grandmother's point of view, the rest of the novel concerns Baako's anxieties, fears, and disappointments.

Like the native intellectual in Frantz Fanon's *The Wretched of the Earth*, Baako dreams of returning to Accra and awakening the masses

---

[33] Boehmer, *Stories of Women*, 32.
[34] Armah, *Fragments*, 38.
[35] Ibid., 103.

to their exploitation by the educated elite.[36] Instead, he is discouraged by the general malaise and stagnancy he observes across the country. As Baako's grandmother Naana adeptly observes in the novel's final chapter, Baako has crumbled under the pressure of others' 'heavy dreams and hopes filled with the mass of things here and of this *time*'.[37] Fanon cautioned of a 'time lag, or a difference of rhythm, between the leaders of a nationalist party and the mass of the people', and Baako's return evinces these arrhythmias as he feels out of step with both the masses and the new nationalist elite.[38] Indeed, the dissonance between the temporalities engendered by national development and 'progress', disillusionment, deferral, Akan time, and tradition contribute to Baako's eventual mental breakdown and his institutionalisation in a mental asylum. This confluence, I will demonstrate in this section, creates a timescape wherein waiting is reduced to stasis, and neither Baako's patience nor impatience assists him in achieving his goals and disrupting the cycles of greed and corruption implicit in 'productive time'.

Baako's family assumes that he spends his time abroad 'productively', and that his return home will constitute a return on their investment. The intrinsic value of traveling abroad overlaps with the ways that mobility is generally valued over immobility, a residual effect of the 'generally competitive neo-liberal rationales of productivity and a concern that time needs to be utilized more productively in order to be more profitable'.[39] This in turn produces 'chronological time as a container waiting to be filled', and 'must be used wisely' and not wasted.[40] This sense of productive time is additionally informed by the legacies of colonialism and the creation of African labour forces by colonial authorities on the continent. Using Kenya and Malawi as case studies, Alamin Mazrui and Lupenga Mphande trace the creation of African labour pools through the imposition of capitalist conceptions of time. In language resonant with J. M. Coetzee's writings on idleness on the Cape in *White Writing*, Mazrui and Mphande note that activities that 'may be seen as idleness and time-wasting' had value in the Kenyan and Malawian communities,

---

[36] In language particularly relevant for reading Armah's *Fragments*, Fanon notes that 'the violent collision of two worlds has considerably shaken old traditions and thrown the universe of the perceptions out of focus', and that the native intellectual's 'family very often proves itself incapable of showing stability and homogeneity' in the face of the 'various assaults . . . of Western culture'. Fanon, *The Wretched of the Earth*, 195.
[37] Armah, *Fragments*, 198, emphasis mine.
[38] Fanon, *The Wretched of the Earth*, 107.
[39] Bissell, 'Animating Suspension: Waiting for Mobilities', 280.
[40] Ibid., 280.

and that the 'idea of time as a linear object that could be gained, saved, or lost was alien' to the African cosmologies colonists encountered.[41] In order to bind Africans to a standard workday, colonial governments passed vagrancy laws and imposed penalties for unemployment and failure to pay taxes.[42] Upon Baako's return, he is pressured to capitalise on his mobility – his time abroad and the cultural capital associated with Western ties – and turn time spent elsewhere into financial returns. Commodified time is, as John Mbiti points out, discordant with traditional African life, where in some settings 'time has to be created or produced' rather than 'utilized, sold and bought'.[43] During his journey back, Baako is consistently perplexed by this valuation of time and he confesses that he does not have a job waiting for him, or connections with 'big men' who can facilitate rapid socioeconomic mobility. Baako's foreign education and inability to integrate into Accra's workforce prefigure the proliferation of gymmers in twenty-first-century Accra, discussed in the Introduction to this book. The gymmers Quayson describes are unemployed or under-employed young men whose 'attempt[s] to move between life phases' are restrained by 'a state of expectant waiting'.[44] Unlike Quayson's gymmers, however, Baako in this earlier era does not turn to activities to manage, navigate and control the dissonance between his impatience and the economy of waiting.

The detrimental effects of these tensions are evidenced in Baako's meditations on the cargo cult and its resonance in contemporary Ghanaian society, which occur during his most acute exhibition of mental distress. The chapter 'Dam', the Akan word for madness, opens with Baako immobilised by fever.[45] Agitated by thoughts and reflections that flit quickly through his mind, Baako attempts to 'trap' them with his typewriter. In the fragmented text that follows, Baako meditates on the similarities between the Melanesian cargo cults – the 'ritualistic religious expression of the fetishization of material goods introduced to Melanesia by Europeans'[46] – and the expectation that the been-to will similarly act as an intermediary and human export. Baako writes, 'A return is expected from his presence there: he will intercede on behalf of those not yet dead,

---

[41] Mazrui and Mphande, 'Time and Labor in Colonial Africa: The Case of Kenya and Malawi', 100.
[42] Ibid., 105.
[43] Mbiti, *African Religions & Philosophy*, 19.
[44] Quayson, *Oxford Street, Accra*, 210.
[45] Zabus, *The African Palimpsest*, 165.
[46] Murphy, 'The Curse of Constant Remembrance', 63.

asking for them what they need most urgently.'⁴⁷ The been-to, as Baako describes, '[m]eets established, well-known expectations handsomely' and 'is and has to be a transmission belt for cargo'. He then elaborates the cargo mentality in terms of waiting:

> CARGO MENTALITY. The expectancy, the waiting for bounty dropping from the sky through benign intercession of dead ancestors, the beneficent ghosts . . . The waiting not a simple expectation, but something more active. An integral part of the waiting is an active expression of strong belief that the cargo will come, i.e., the phenomenon of hope is incomplete without an incorporated act of faith.⁴⁸

The waiting Baako describes here is without end; in this active expression of strong belief, the absence of bounty, which might disrupt such steadfast certainty, can still be reconciled through continued hope and faith. In the same way, Baako's return, despite falling short of expectations, is not enough to dispel his family's faith in the been-to narrative and the wealth that is expected. The expectations centred on returns, of the spatial and material kind alike, reveal that waiting and return here are mutually constitutive and contribute equally to Baako's growing mental instability.

One way to understand the relationship between this meditation on cargo mentality and the text's larger timescape is through the recurring images of the slave trade – a past that Baako attempts to link with Ghana's present, but that others continually suppress. Disappointment, or to use the language of the period, disillusionment, can, in Saidya Hartman's view, 'create an opening for a counterhistory, a story written against the narrative of progress'.⁴⁹ Hartman, in suggestive language that resonates with *Fragments*, observes that the 'time of slavery persists in this interminable awaiting – that is, awaiting freedom and longing for a way of undoing the past'.⁵⁰ Turning to how slavery is figured in the novel, Laura Murphy argues that the trauma of the slave trade causes 'Baako's stress and existential nausea', and that the text makes 'explicit links between the materialism of postcolonial Ghana and the earlier vicious and deadly consumption of human lives'.⁵¹ Linking the slave trade with the cargo cult mentality of awaiting the been-to, *Fragments*

---

⁴⁷ Armah, *Fragments*, 157.
⁴⁸ Ibid., 160.
⁴⁹ Hartman, 'The Time of Slavery', 769–70.
⁵⁰ Ibid., 769–70.
⁵¹ Murphy, 'The Curse of Constant Remembrance', 56.

creates a 'layered temporality' in which present-day consumerism 'is no modern, post-independence malady'.⁵²

Building from this observation, I want to suggest that the waiting and return that the characters evoke supplement the slave trade imagery to provide temporal continuity between colonial and postcolonial Ghana. In the rush to embrace a break with colonial government, the characters in *Fragments* avoid coming to terms with the history of the slave trade, and inadvertently perpetuate its atrocities through what Murphy calls 'the slave trade's commodification of human life and his [Baako's] family's vision of him as the deliverer of consumable "cargo."'⁵³ The expectation of returns on investments works on both the scale of the individual – the family's hopes for Baako's return – and the larger national population, who hope for a return on their investment in the nation's future. This 'failure of return for investment', Ahmed explains,

> extends one's attachment to the nation: the endless deferral of happiness takes the form of waiting. So 'justice' becomes the promised return for investment in the nation, but one that must not be realised for the investment to be sustained. The nation, in other words, becomes the 'agent' of justice, the one that can deliver justice through happiness, but this *capacity is sustained only through its failure to be actualised in the present*.⁵⁴

Much of the waiting that we see in *Fragments* involve this interplay between investment and deferral. In addition to this future-oriented deferral of happiness and belonging – a promise that must be indefinitely withheld in order to sustain one's very investment in the nation – *Fragments* also exposes the problematic speed at which the nation eschews the past. Rather than confront slavery, and I would argue the existing geopolitical and economic realities that are the legacies of colonialism, producers at Ghanavision tell Baako, '"Look, we're a free, independent people. We're engaged in a gigantic task of nation building. We have inherited a glorious culture, and that's what we're here to deal with . . . Look, don't waste time."'⁵⁵ This forward-looking mentality, however, excises the past prematurely by mobilising the language of 'wasted time', and allows similar dynamics of dispossession and privilege – acceleration for some and waiting for others – to continue.

Armah frames *Fragments* with Naana's perspective, which operates as a corrective to the commodification, greed and corruption informing the

---

⁵² Ibid., 63–4.
⁵³ Ibid., 63.
⁵⁴ Ahmed, *The Cultural Politics of Emotion*, 196–7, emphasis original.
⁵⁵ Armah, *Fragments*, 147.

sense of capitalist, productive time. A grandmother figure, Naana evokes the circular relationship between the living, the unborn, and the ancestors, what Chukwunyere Kamalu calls 'a cyclical process of becoming'.[56] Naana's point of view evokes both circularity and return at odds with the forward-only thrust of modern Accra's environment, and also offers a promise of forging continuous connections despite interruptions in the construction of time and history. Derek Wright's work on the Akan background to *Fragments* helpfully addresses Naana's role in the text. In his view, Naana's final call to the ancestors, whom she will shortly join,

> holds in simultaneous [o]pposition contrary ideas of cyclicality and terminality, process and endings, leaving uncertain the final value which is to be attached to Naana's religious vision. Naana's death, in her own view, is subsumed into a cycle of renewal and restoration, and the historical decline of which it is part is only another development in the unceasing process of the spirit. But from the quite different and more material viewpoint of her age, the deteriorative historical process has already subverted this circular progress.[57]

As she awaits her own return to the ancestors, she represents and enacts a dynamic relationship with the past in defiance of her contemporaries' viewpoints. Naana's vision of the present and future engenders a different temporality than that assumed by narratives of linear history or disillusionment, allowing her to wait rather than despair, not only for herself but for Baako: 'The returned traveler also – in all that noise I thought he would surely die, but there must be strong spirits looking after him ... I know no way of reaching him and letting him know as I go that my spirit has been filled with thoughts of his happiness, that I have wished for him a life of good things done and a great peace at the end.'[58]

In this way, Armah uses Naana to shift the definition of 'success' for Baako from the acquisition of material goods and status to 'a powerful unifying understanding', one that resists the temporality of waiting as stasis and instead makes the past present as the characters turn towards the future to come.[59] In this way, the temporal mode she espouses starkly contrasts with the oppressive pressures of 'productive' time. The temporal modality that Naana inhabits, according to Wright's reading, is neither inflexibly cyclical nor absolutely linear; in her negotiation of time and culture in contemporary Ghana, Naana evokes waiting to wrestle with these competing temporalities. In her, we see that 'the traditional

---

[56] Kamalu, *Person, Divinity & Nature*, 31.
[57] D. Wright, 'Fragments: The Akan Background', 188.
[58] Armah, *Fragments*, 199.
[59] Lawson, *The Western Scar*, 71.

order is given a dynamic continuity with the present'.[60] Additionally, the Akan temporalities conjured by Naana do not exist in isolation from capitalist time. She admits:

> I too have had my dreams of his return, and they too have been filled with things to give rest to tired flesh heavy things, things of heavy earth. I have also dreamed of riches and greatness for Baako, and they were not for him alone.[61]

The complex timescape forged from Naana and Baako's perspectives reveals that the Akan rituals that formerly provided cohesiveness to temporal and communal experience have, in interactions with competing temporalities, produced temporal arrhythmias, resulting in the sensation that actions inevitably occur too soon, too late or both at once. Taking a closer look at moments of temporal arrhythmias and their effects on Baako will enable us to see how waiting, passivity, and patience come together to drive Baako towards a nervous breakdown.

The temporal arrhythmias are most apparent in the conflicts arising during two traditional ceremonies, which mark Baako's departure and the birth of his nephew. Both Akan ceremonies 'not only locate individuals in the past, present, and the future but also become vehicles for historical recall, interpretations, and reappraisals', creating a palimpsest of temporalities.[62] Naana remembers the ceremony celebrating Baako's departure, which was similarly rushed by the 'hot desire impatient at his departure for his return'.[63] The ceremony itself, led by Uncle Foli, was marred by selfish greed; Foli withholds a generous pour of alcohol from the ancestors, as well as Naana and Baako, in favour of saving more for himself. Even before Baako's departure, then, Armah indicates that growing greed, selfishness and impatience threaten not only the respect and traditions that underpin Baako's family structure, but also the sense of time that inheres in the rituals themselves. From the perspective of Akan ritual, the premature ceremony bodes ominously for the baby's future, and it appears that Baako and his family would have done well to wait, or at least slow down.

Like the departure ceremony, the outdooring ceremony for Araba's baby establishes links between the newborn in the world of the living in relation to the world of the ancestors. Also called a naming ceremony, this tradition 'locate[s] individuals into the world of their contemporaries

---

[60] D. Wright, 'Fragments: The Akan Background', 176.
[61] Armah, *Fragments*, 3.
[62] Adjaye, 'Time, Identity, and Historical Consciousness in Akan', 71.
[63] Armah, *Fragments*, 4.

with whom they share a community of time'.⁶⁴ Both the unborn and the ancestors occupy the spirit world, and so the outdooring ceremony acknowledges a cyclical process of continuity between the physical and spirit worlds.⁶⁵ In this way, Akan temporalities contain both linear and cyclical elements. As Joseph Adjaye writes, 'Akan time perceptions are at once and the same time linear and cyclical. In the long continuum from protohistoric times through the present to the future, there is a linear view of an unbroken chain linking all phases.'⁶⁶ But then Adjaye clarifies,

> Yet, it is clear that the Akan do not see this linear perception of history as conflicting with the view of time as being cyclical from the present to the future and back to the present, which becomes the past of tomorrow. There is not only an awareness of the contribution of the ancestors in times past towards the growth and well-being of the present group but also a realization of the duty to preserve the present for future times.⁶⁷

The outdooring ceremony is emblematic of this temporal orientation, as the family welcomes the child to the physical world and looks forward to its future. It is important to note *Fragments* recounts the outdooring ceremony in a flashback, after Baako has a mental breakdown and is institutionalised in an asylum. The actual planning of the outdooring ceremony, however, is narrated much earlier in the text. We learn that traditionally the outdooring ceremony occurs one week after the birth, but that Efua and Araba move it earlier to coincide with the first weekend after payday.⁶⁸ Naana foreshadows the baby's premature death, warning that the child '"is not yet with us . . . His birth can be a good beginning . . . But for this he must be protected. Or he will run screaming back, fleeing the horrors prepared for him up here."'⁶⁹ The child's premature outdooring ceremony parallels its premature birth and death alike. Baako botches his responsibility of calling for gifts for the baby, and as the guests leave, Naana remarks, '"It was too sudden, whatever you did . . . Everything is wrong now."'⁷⁰ After a paragraph break, the text continues, matter-of-factly reporting, 'Three weeks after the child was buried Efua asked for help and [Baako] asked her what for.' Baako is disturbed to learn that '"[t]he time has come to put an announcement

---

⁶⁴ Adjaye, 'Time, Identity, and Historical Consciousness in Akan', 63.
⁶⁵ Kamalu, *Person, Divinity & Nature*, 31, 49.
⁶⁶ Adjaye, 'Time, Identity, and Historical Consciousness in Akan', 73.
⁶⁷ Ibid. 73.
⁶⁸ Armah, *Fragments*, 88.
⁶⁹ Ibid., 97.
⁷⁰ Ibid., 187.

in the papers"' to report the baby's death. This new ritual, which Baako believes to be motivated by a desire to keep up appearances, is governed by a sense of time and customs of propriety with which Baako is, again, unfamiliar.

Because of Baako's time away, the discrepancies in temporal schemes and rhythms are especially jarring. In the instance of the outdooring ceremony, the time of the workweek that controls when the men are paid conflicts with the ritualistic time that traditionally dictates when the ceremony occurs. Likewise, new traditions such as farewell announcements in the newspapers require temporal adjustments; the announcement is expected three weeks after the death, a conventional mourning period, but its timing will additionally depend on the newspaper's publication schedule. Unable to negotiate these different temporal modes, Baako's actions are arrhythmic, or 'too sudden'. Subsequently, Baako's temporal experience devolves into an impression of stalled time, manifested in flashbacks to earlier moments during bouts of mental breakdown. The narrative itself reflects this temporal fragmentation, jumping between Ghanavision's rejection of Baako's television scripts about slavery, the outdooring ceremony, and fevered meditations on the cargo cults of Melanesia. In this timescape, where the rhythms of various temporalities variably overlap and conflict, the new postcolonial elite tell Baako to wait patiently.

Over time, Baako develops a sense of stalled time, of waiting as stasis, through the continued circling back to the past. Neil Lazarus similarly argues that Baako is unable to bridge the past and future in the present moment. Baako's problem, according to Lazarus, is that he is unable

> to sustain his activism in the concrete here-and-now while appreciating that it is not in the present but only in the 'not yet', in the as-yet unforeseeable and uncertain future, that this activism will be seen to have been constructive.[71]

Juana, on the other hand, 'understand[s] that the present is in so many wearying respects barely more than an extension of the past', and so she 'live[s] not merely with future in mind, but as though it were already here'.[72] In other words, Baako faces a disjunction between acting in the present and knowing that the results will only be realised in the future: a discouraged sense of waiting.

On the other hand, the women in the novel – Baako's mother Efua, his grandmother Naana, and his lover Juana – pry apart the ways in

---

[71] N. Lazarus, *Resistance in Postcolonial African Fiction*, 101.
[72] Ibid., 105, 116.

which waiting and patience tend to be associated with immobility and passivity. In doing so, they disrupt the gender-coding of passive waiting with femininity, and suggest methods of inhabiting the temporal dimensions of waiting in order to reach out towards the uncertain future. The Akan are distinct among 'Ghanaian ethnic groups [for their] matrilineal descent systems', which in my view, further supports increased attention to their voices and roles in the text, despite the fact that the novel largely lingers on Baako's experiences.[73] Efua, Baako's mother, has waited a long time for her son to return and her expectations of socioeconomic mobility are unsatisfied. Despite her disappointment, Efua has one moment where she exhibits a spirit of reconciliation towards Baako that configures waiting as a temporality open to the future, but does not dictate its outcomes. This tentative reconciliation occurs in a short chapter that bears her name, and immediately after the chapter 'Dam'. As Baako remembers this encounter, he is in the hospital, lying in the acute ward after running across Accra, tortured by the image of a successful been-to's business card that reminds him of his failures. In contrast to the immediately preceding chapters, Baako's memory is clear here and he more or less linearly remembers the events of an earlier Sunday with Efua. She warns Baako 'not to let the waiting make him angry' as they take the bus to a deteriorating building that she hoped he would renovate to be a house for her.[74] As part of her 'soul-cleaning', she tells him that she had previously cursed him for his failures, but now relinquishes the dream of the extravagant house. She continues with her 'happy laugh' throughout their return home, 'waiting in the sun for whatever would come'.[75] In her admonition to Baako to resist anger, and the following characterisation of her laugh as 'happy', the text marks an affective change in Efua's orientation towards waiting. In contrast to the attachment to the future she imagined, her openness to whatever would come signals detachment. To be clear, Efua's hopeful expectation becomes disappointed disillusionment, a transition consistent with the larger mood of the 'disillusionment' era in which *Fragments* was published. But when Efua releases Baako, reiterating that 'it's all over now', we might also read through her disappointment to a new orientation towards the future, heralded and more fully realised in Naana's concluding voice that announces, 'The time has come.'[76] Put another way, the 'not yet' has become 'now'.

---

[73] Adjaye, 'Time, Identity, and Historical Consciousness in Akan', 57.
[74] Armah, *Fragments*, 176.
[75] Ibid., 179.
[76] Ibid., 195.

Given the ways that the novel's women negotiate Accra's timescape, what the novel may model is a way to harness a different kind of patience – one that is not the same as that demanded by those in positions of power, nor one that requires inactivity or acquiescence. Naana, again, is an exemplary figure in this regard. Unlike many of the other characters preoccupied with materiality, wealth, and waste, Naana is certain that 'All that goes returns and nothing in the end is lost.'[77] This perspective starkly contrasts with the producers at Ghanavision, who are quick to call 'unproductive' time 'wasted time'. Naana's voice, both structurally and thematically in the novel, bookends the text. Rather than signifying a supplementary position, however, I contend that Naana's voice becomes central to the text's renegotiation of time and patience. While patience is often understood as 'calm, uncomplaining endurance', patience can also connote 'calm, self-possessed waiting'.[78] The latter allows for critique, and we see this most clearly in Efua's waiting, where she airs her dissatisfaction but is able, nevertheless, to wait 'for whatever would come'. As David Bissell contends, while waiting might be experienced as a slow rhythm, it may also 'take *effort* and therefore some form of intentional action to wait', and this 'active *doing* . . . could be seen as an achievement of a specific set of ongoing embodied tasks'.[79] Waiting, he concludes, can instead be understood 'as an anticipatory consciousness that is inherently intertwined with the present but with the excessive pressing immanence of the "not yet"'.[80] The language here resonates with Lazarus's appraisal of Juana's sense of time in contrast to Baako's, and this orientation towards the future is similarly applicable to Efua and Naana. If one lives as if the future is already here, as Juana seems to do, then each moment in the present is potentially imbued with a renewed sense of urgency – which Anita Desai's protagonist, Maya, underscores.

'Now' is Here: Fierce Urgency

Despite their many differences, *Fragments* and Anita Desai's first novel *Cry, the Peacock* share striking similarities in their explorations of the themes of madness, restraint, waiting, and despair. Both novels register dissatisfaction with their respective postcolonial societies, but this

---

[77] Ibid., 1.
[78] *Oxford English Dictionary*, 'patience, n.1 (and int.)'.
[79] Bissell, 'Animating Suspension: Waiting for Mobilities', 285.
[80] Ibid., 292.

disillusionment is more complex than simply a period of stasis for characters marginalised in the new nation. As an organising category, the term 'novels of disillusionment' risks flattening these differences and histories by positing a homogeneous period of waiting. Together, *Fragments* and *Cry, the Peacock* lend nuance to the temporalities shaping disillusionment, exhibiting multifaceted timescapes in which waiting becomes variably a source of strength and a cause of destruction.

Because scholars tend to focus so narrowly on *Cry, the Peacock* as an exploration of female consciousness, especially Maya's 'emotional' responses in contrast to her much-older husband Gautama's 'rational' takes, they have missed how the novel comments on the national mood of disillusionment in postcolonial India, especially as articulated by women. An early collection, *Perspectives on Anita Desai* (1984), is representative of the general trend. The editor declares that 'there are no significant historical incidents, let alone contemporary ones, in her novels', and scholars' narrow concentration on her early works as explorations of female consciousness, largely separate from the external world that shaped it, has certainly contributed to this impression.[81] In contrast to this prevalent trend, Josna Rege argues that *Cry, the Peacock* and other early Desai novels reflect the paralysis and malaise of post-independence India, which resulted from 'contradictions within the Indian nationalist discourse'.[82] In my view, Maya shares Baako's growing sense of the sociocultural, as well as socioeconomic restrictions that condition the monotony of her daily life. Like Baako, Maya experiences extreme mental and emotional strain, and most critics agree that Maya suffers from a mental breakdown as well.

Anita Desai's prolific career spans nearly five decades, and *Cry, the Peacock* was her first published novel. Organised into three parts of unequal lengths, the novel's part one is just over two pages long, but efficiently establishes the tensions between the protagonist Maya and Gautama after the death of Maya's dog. Maya is deeply troubled, but Gautama is coldly brisk in arranging the dog's disposal. Part two

---

[81] Srivastava, 'Introduction', xix. The studies that focus explicitly on *Cry, the Peacock* tend to reproduce the dichotomous oppositions of male and female, outside and inside, modern and traditional, West and East in pitting Maya against her husband Gautama. See, for example, Sudhakar R. Jamkhandi's 'The Artistic Effects of the Shifts in Point of View in Anita Desai's Cry, the Peacock', and Som. P. Sharma and Kamal N. Awathi's 'Anita Desai's Cry the Peacock: A Vindication of the Feminine.'

[82] Rege, 'Codes in Conflict: Post-Independence Alienation in Anita Desai's Early Novels', 317.

comprises the majority of the novel, and shifts from the omniscient third-person perspective of part one to Maya's first-person perspective, interrupted by several flashbacks or memories. The first memory introduces the horoscope, prophesised by an albino astrologer when Maya was a child, that death would come early either to Maya or to her husband after four years of marriage.[83] Scenes where the couple argue about life, logic, religion and emotions dramatise the differences in their worldviews and values, and Maya's increasing desperation is reflected in the text's frantic pacing, moving quickly between their charged disagreements and Maya's own internal commentary. This section concludes with Maya killing Gautama by pushing him off the roof. In the final section, which mirrors the first in its brevity, Maya's mother-in-law and sister-in-law discuss Gautama's death and their plans to place Maya in a mental asylum. Maya's voice and independent perspective are completely silenced, and the novel ends with the suggestion that Maya and her mother-in-law perish together after falling off the balcony.

In my examination of Maya's timescape, I aim not only to contextualise Maya's waiting in post-independence India, but also to argue that Maya's relationship with other women – not strictly her relationship with Gautama and her father – exacerbate her isolation and alienation. I argue that Desai's novel directly engages with its historical and temporal context, specifically the legacies of gendered nationalism and the association of women with motherhood, the home, and continued waiting for the equality promised at independence to be codified in laws that extend to the private sphere. While *Fragments* is more concerned with political stasis and the psychodynamics of waiting and patience, I find that *Cry, the Peacock* emphasises urgency as a temporal dimension of waiting, and that Maya's actions, while certainly self-defeating in the most literal sense, affirm a fierce urgency of the now.

The landscape that anchors Maya's timescape is, overwhelmingly, the home. With few exceptions, Maya's movements are restricted to her present-day home with Gautama, her childhood home with her father, and brief visits to the homes of acquaintances. Maya's associations with 'home' evolve from the idyllic childhood of carefree indulgence to that of restriction and anxiety. As scholars from Partha Chatterjee to Elleke Boehmer have shown, the home occupies an ambivalent position in the context of Indian nationalist discourses. While the home was viewed as the domain of tradition during independence movements, for women who expected full civic participation after independence, the home was

---

[83] Desai, *Cry, the Peacock*, 31.

not necessarily a liberating space. Scholarship on Indian nationalisms, especially after Chatterjee's influential 'Whose Imagined Community?' has revealed how 'the female domestic sphere' during the independence struggle functioned 'as storehouse of traditional attitudes ... one which enables male nationalists to appropriate the forms of European modernity while simultaneously conserving an apparent cultural authenticity'.[84] In Chatterjee's rejoinder to Anderson's *Imagined Communities*, he admits that anticolonial nationalist discourse in India created a 'domain of sovereignty within colonial society' from which nationalism gained its force as well as its difference, but in the process instated a different patriarchal order wherein the new Indian woman would display the signs of national tradition – what he calls 'false essentialisms'.[85] Women occupied a vexed position in the new nation; elevated as symbolic signifiers, they tended to be denied full participation in political and social life.

Despite the insistence on 'now' and anticolonial nationalism's rejection of the waiting room of history, as Dipesh Chakrabarty put it in *Provincializing Europe*,[86] marginalised segments of India's citizenry continued to experience the deferral of full equality and participation in the new nation, which re-established the rhetoric of 'not yet' in a new context. Christine Keating traces the development of democracy in India, and, in language that echoes Chakrabarty, notes that the 1946 Indian constitution signified 'a radical rejection of the racialized logic of colonial rule, which held that Indians were not "ready" for democratic self-rule'.[87] Simultaneously, however, a new 'not yet' was introduced, as the constitution 'reject[ed] measures that would have ensured adequate political representation for minority groups, in particular Muslims, and 'consolidated women's legal subordination in property ownership, inheritance, marriage, and divorce'. Given her attention to gender and equity, Keating's view complicates Uday Mehta's argument about the Indian Constitution, discussed in Chapter 2, ushering in a revolutionary disruption of time and history. While women were granted universal suffrage in India and included in the public sphere after independence, the dominance of men in the family and home was maintained 'by preserving the system of personal laws developed under the British'.[88]

---

[84] Boehmer, *Stories of Women*, 8.
[85] Chatterjee, *The Nation and Its Fragments*, 6, 9, 134.
[86] Chakrabarty, *Provincializing Europe*, 8–9.
[87] Keating, *Decolonizing Democracy*, 5.
[88] Ibid., 73. Rajeswari Sunder Rajan similarly remarks that while 'suffrage and other forms of political representation and participation were relatively easily won for women in India ... the acceptance of women's equality in actual political and

The history of the Hindu Code Bill, which would have codified Hindu personal laws, is a concrete example of deferring the promises of independence for women. Radha Kumar observes that women raised the issue of codifying the Hindu personal laws as early as the 1930s, and a committee drafted a code in 1944.[89] However, under pressure from influential Congressmen, including then-President of India Rajendra Prasad, Prime Minister Jawaharlal Nehru stalled the bill until it was passed in piecemeal fashion between 1955 and 1956, a decade after independence, and over twenty years after the issue was first broached.

In placing Maya almost exclusively within the confines of the home, and emphasising her restless unhappiness, Desai makes literal the gendered discourse of nationalism and reproductive feminism in the setting of the novel. Maya's father's influence is overbearing, her husband Gautama is dismissive of her views, and as I will demonstrate further below, her childlessness indexes her anxieties as well as her subtle criticism of traditional Indian womanhood that had become so central to anchoring women's role in the nation. To achieve political visibility, as Elleke Boehmer, Rajeswari Sunder Rajan and Asha Nadkarni, among others, observe, Indian women increasingly turned to the rhetoric of gendered nationalism to stake a claim in the emerging Indian nation in the twentieth century.

The influential gendered nationalism of Sarojini Naidu, a prominent Indian politician, is a case in point. Throughout her speeches and writings, she relied on 'highly traditional images of Indian womanhood' in her insistence that women 'were central to the nation-building project in India'.[90] Despite pre-independence documents like the Women's Role in the Planned Economy report from 1939 to 1940, which proposed 'a radical mode of citizenship for women as workers', the first five-year plan was limited to 'provid[ing] women with adequate services necessary to fulfil what was called a "woman's legitimate role in the family"'.[91] Nadkarni traces this development in gendered Indian nationalisms through the lenses of eugenic feminism and reproductive nationalism, and she shows that Indian women became legible in the language of development in India through their maternal roles.[92] 'The decades

---

socioeconomic structures comes up against resistance and opposition in powerfully entrenched patriarchal structures.' Sunder Rajan, *The Scandal of the State*, 17.

[89] Kumar, *The History of Doing*, 97.
[90] Boehmer, *Stories of Women*, 77.
[91] Sunder Rajan, *The Scandal of the State*, 27.
[92] Nadkarni, *Eugenic Feminism*, 17.

following independence', she notes, 'have been labeled the "silent period" of the women's movement'.[93] This very period, which also saw 'accelerating modernization'[94] in India, overlapped with what Josna Rege calls 'post-independence malaise' or disillusionment.[95] Given the persistence of gender-based discrimination after independence, it is not surprising then that Desai's novels register 'a progressive sense of disillusionment'.[96] Although Elleke Boehmer does not discuss *Cry, the Peacock*, I draw on her general observations about postcolonial women writers in my reading of Maya's timescape: these writers 'strategically play off [the] different narratives [of the homogenising nation] – of patriliny and matriliny, of modernity and tradition – against one another'.[97] The concomitant, diverse temporalities assumed by these narratives are also put into dialogue and discord in the novel, pushing Maya inexorably towards the only action available to her in moments of fierce urgency.

The narrative's organisation, with interruptive flashbacks that provide context and a sense of causality, create a mood of inevitable tragedy and disillusionment. The narrative present in part one opens with the grisly image of Maya's dog rotting in the afternoon sun and Maya 'sobbing, and waiting for her husband to come home'.[98] Whereas Maya is depicted as overly emotional and inarticulate, Gautama does 'all that was to be done, quickly and quietly like a surgeon's knife at work'.[99] Part two shifts from the omniscient third-person perspective of part one to the first-person perspective, interrupted by several flashbacks or memories that assist in contextualising the present. The first memory introduces the horoscope that death would come early either to Maya or to her husband after four years of marriage, to which Maya responds, "No! . . . I will never marry."'[100] This outburst is tragic and ominous, given that the narrative opens four years into her marriage. A subsequent flashback reveals that Maya's childhood was 'idyllic' and protected, in no small part because of her doting father. The childhood flashbacks, which recur several times throughout the novel, reveal Maya's present concern with women and domestic dispossession.

---

[93] Ibid., 133.
[94] Ibid., 166.
[95] Refe, 'Codes in Conflict: Post-Independence Alienation in Anita Desai's Early Novels', 317.
[96] Ibid., 323.
[97] Boehmer, *Stories of Women*, 16.
[98] Desai, *Cry, the Peacock*, 7.
[99] Ibid., 8.
[100] Ibid., 31.

In one memory, Maya recalls a desperate woman, the wife of her father's friend, asking futilely for assistance in escaping her husband. At the conclusion of another memory, Maya reflects:

> (Yes, now that I go over it in my mind, my childhood was one in which much was excluded, which grew steadily more restricted, unnatural even, and in which I lived as a toy princess in a toy world. But it was a pretty one.).[101]

Further flashbacks revisit her brother Arjuna's troubled relationship with their father and Maya's desperate but ineffective attempts to connect with her childhood friends Leila and Pom. Combined with her sister-in-law's visit, which was occasioned by her desire to divorce her husband (and a process she must accomplish on her own, as her brother Gautama refuses to help), the novel's seemingly strict focus on Maya's psychological decline expands to include all women in developing the theme of entrapment.

These analeptic moments heighten Maya's sense of impending doom and despair, and complement the dominant temporal scheme in the narrative, which is shaped by Hinduism's concepts of fate and free will. Rege notes that the concept of karma 'was recast under colonialism, partially secularized to denote selfless action in the service of the nation, and eventually, embedded in Indian nationalist discourse and public discourse more generally'.[102] For the protagonists of Desai's novels specifically, karma entails the 'selfless performance of domestic duty'.[103] In Rege's view, Maya's husband Gautama espouses 'an inexorably logical theory of cause and effect, which denies the possibility of all independent agency' to the extent that 'for Maya, karma comes to mean, not action, but its impossibility'.[104] Here, karma and inaction dovetail in a gendered configuration of indefinite waiting. Nationalist discourse, which collapses karma and gendered nationalist symbols in order to postpone the self-determination of the modern Indian woman, goes unchallenged in the novel because 'Desai both resists and reproduces the dominant structures and symbols of nationalism.'[105] I depart from Rege's analysis by suggesting that the novel's representation of waiting and Maya's developing sense of urgency registers the very challenge that Rege believes 'remains unvoiced'.

---

[101] Ibid., 78.
[102] Rege, *Colonial Karma*, xi.
[103] Ibid., 81.
[104] Ibid., 93.
[105] Ibid., 90.

Significantly, in *Cry, the Peacock* the advocates of this particular post-independence rendering of Hindu theology are also the most imposing male figures in Maya's life: her father and Gautama. Karma, in the Hindu tradition, ought not to be conflated with irreversible fate; karma's 'round of rebirths, of world creations and destructions in an endless series, offers the possibility of ever new changes in decisions being made', and as such, 'does not cancel free will and genuinely free decisions'.[106] The concept of karma as described in the Upanishads reveals an interplay between fate and free will, as karma 'keeps in motion the vicious circle of action, desire, reward, and new action'.[107] Real disagreement on the relationship between fate and karma exists among scholars and practitioners of Hinduism, and the everyday practices of religious belief vary across the Indian subcontinent. Nevertheless, popular discourse exhibits a tendency to conflate fate and karma, and we see Desai's male characters do the same when they frame acceptance and detachment in fatalistic terms.[108] Previous literary scholars have remarked on fate's function in the novel, but instead of considering how fate pervades Maya's timescape, scholars tend to corporealise fate and transform it into Maya's adversary in a battle over her mind.[109] While I am interested in fate's role in shaping her temporal experience, my reading is also attuned to how the temporality of fate is espoused and imposed by the men in Maya's life.

The astrologer's initial prophecy of Maya's fate includes a caution that her life will not necessarily take this path, and he advises her to pray and sacrifice to avoid the undesired outcome. This rendering of fate is consistent with the concept of karma as theorised in the Upanishads, where fate and free will exist in dynamic interaction. However, the possibilities of alternatives are continually dashed or suppressed with each new urge to accept and submit uttered by Gautama and her father. When Maya first receives the unfortunate horoscope, her father burns the paper in response. At first glance, this act might suggest that he rejects the notions that fate and prophecy are immutable. However, as Maya's memories of her father's advice are elaborated throughout the novel, we can understand the act as one of denial, suppression and intentional forgetting,

---

[106] Klostermaier, *A Survey of Hinduism*, 176.
[107] Ibid., 175.
[108] As Judith Pugh notes, fate is often not only treated synonymously with karma, but that 'popular ideas of fate . . . are oriented to a comprehension of everyday life'.'Astrology and Fate: The Hindu and Muslim Experiences', 132.
[109] See, for example, Jamkhandi, 'The Artistic Effects of the Shifts in Point of View in Anita Desai's Cry, the Peacock', 35.

rather than a radical rejection of fate and its attendant, deterministic temporality. In adolescence, Maya found her father's point of view soothing:

> 'It is best to accept, Maya. What good does it do to cry?' 'Why must you get so upset? Surely it is for the best.' 'It cannot be undone now, and it must be accepted as it is – you will find that to be the wisest course' . . . I felt them soothe me like a stream of cold water that tumbled through the ferns of Darjeeling, like the cold, pearl mists that crept over the blue hills and poured into the valley.[110]

The admonition to accept circumstances and outcomes is palatable for young Maya, but as she develops a stronger sense of her own desires, she chafes under similar directives, this time uttered by Gautama, who emphasises detachment and logic in contrast to her emotional attachments.[111] He too urges her, 'Let it go – it must be so', and this appeal produces a jarring dissonance between her outer calm and inner turmoil, a 'dance within [that] grew more urgent, more significant'.[112]

While fate is the dominant temporal scheme in the novel, Maya's sense that she has been left behind to wait in the home while others actively contribute to Indian society additionally accentuates her perception of urgency. Gautama's family constitutes one particularly illuminating point of comparison. Like Maya's father, Gautama is a lawyer and his family shares his interest 'in parliament, in cases of bribery and corruption revealed in governments . . . of trade pacts made with countries across the seas, of political treaties with those across the mountains, of distant revolutions'.[113] Rather than engage her in welfare activities, Gautama's mother looks to Maya only as a financial resource; she inquires about receiving money from Maya's father in order to pay nurses who need the money urgently. Maya summarises, 'I knew I was . . . one of those outsiders who could be used for this purpose and were therefore necessary, though not necessarily loved.'[114] Maya's dissatisfaction is consistently registered in her recollections of family dinners, where she was excluded from political conversations 'with a naturalness I had to accept for they knew I would not understand a matter so involved, and I knew it myself'.[115] When Gautama's family does speak to her, they limit their

---

[110] Desai, *Cry, the Peacock*, 48.
[111] Ibid., 101, 104.
[112] Ibid., 50–1.
[113] Ibid., 43.
[114] Ibid., 44.
[115] Ibid., 45.

conversations to 'babies, meals, shopping, marriages, for I was their toy, their indulgence'.

The men in Maya's extended family are even more closely tied to the success of anticolonial nationalist movements; her father-in-law was 'a political prisoner while India's independence hung uncertain as an unfurled flag at half-mast',[116] and her brother was active in the Quit India movement and later in the civil rights movement in America. She imagines her brother to be 'a wild bird, a young hawk that could not be tamed, that fought for its liberty', but she perceives herself to be 'a partridge, plump, content'.[117] While most critics are quick to recognise that Maya, in contrast to the other characters, experiences intense attachment to the world and sensory experience, almost all ignore the political dimensions of Maya's desires. Repeatedly, Maya's discontent is registered in the novel by the comparisons that Maya draws between herself and others who have active roles in shaping India's, as well as their own, future.

Not only does Maya detect her exclusion in debates and activities surrounding national identity, but also she consistently rejects inclusion predicated only on images of traditional Indian womanhood. Maya's friends Leila and Pom give in to 'fate' in different ways, and both end up modelling versions of traditional Indian femininity. Leila married a man who was already suffering from tuberculosis, and Maya observes that 'she had married the fatality of his disease as much as the charm of his childish personality' and Leila's movements reflect both 'great beauty and great bitterness'.[118] Leila teaches at a girl's college, 'where she taught Persian literature to a handful of girls' who were 'waiting, coyly, for suitable marriages to be arranged'. Distance develops between the two friends because Leila no longer resists her condition; in contrast to Maya, who frantically seeks to circumvent her own destiny, Leila laments, '"It was written in my fate long ago"'.[119] Pom, on the other hand, 'did not speak of fate' directly and instead relished food, colour, and beautiful textiles, but her exuberance is dimmed, in Maya's eyes, by pregnancy and the new religiosity it inspires in her. Maya ends her reminisces, 'There was not one of my friends who could act as an anchor any more, and to whomsoever I turned for reassurance, betrayed me now.'[120] Their betrayal, Maya suggests, involves their embrace of fate,

---

[116] Ibid., 46.
[117] Ibid., 113.
[118] Ibid., 52.
[119] Ibid., 54.
[120] Ibid., 57.

and the temporality of waiting complemented by it. Leila, in particular, aids other young women in managing waiting by passing the interim time, between childhood and marriage, in school.

Taken together, these scenes detailing Maya's relationship to family – in the abstract, as well as her own – and to nation suggest that she rejects, at least for herself, the temporality of gendered nationalism, where women's significance and empowerment is tied to their reproduction of the future of the nation through child-bearing. The discourses of gendered nationalism in India are underpinned by the reproductive nationalism that Nadkarni describes. Not only is Maya childless herself – a condition she never laments – and troubled by Pom's pregnancy, but her reaction to mothers becomes increasingly agitated as the novel progresses. Maya's intense responses to women and children reach an apex when she and Gautama are out to dinner in a friend's home. Before depicting the Lal's dinner party, the chapter opens with a conversation between Maya and Gautama that occurs chronologically after the event itself. Maya declares that the whole evening was 'horrible', while Gautama asserts that it was merely boring. Incredulous, Maya demands, 'You didn't want to weep when you saw that pregnant woman? You were just – bored?'[121] Gautama tries to comfort her, asking, 'What if they do live in a grubby house? What if she is pregnant again? . . . Besides, your life is your own, so different from theirs – your world completely separate.'[122] Maya's strong reaction belies this soothing assertion, suggesting that she nevertheless sees links, or potential links, between Mrs Lal and herself.

Here again, fate intertwines with images of motherhood to create a temporality of doom and futility. Mrs Lal's young son interrupts the gathering, and Maya recalls that at his entrance,

> [a]n indescribable air of futility had entered the room with the child. It seemed to me that we alone existed upon an island in a city of the dead, and that we, too, were gripped by a fatal disease and would soon, slowly, perish since even the youngest, freshest generation was touched by it and had no hope of survival.[123]

The child's entrance represents hopelessness and death, paradoxically associating an image of birth and reproduction with disease and fatality. When Mrs Lal admits that she has four other daughters, Maya immediately imagines 'dowries, of debts, humiliations to be suffered,

---

[121] Ibid., 58.
[122] Ibid., 60.
[123] Ibid., 62.

and burdens so gross, so painful that the whole family suffered from them'.[124] These images of confinement and burden produce Maya's most intense affective responses, and combine to reveal her increasing identification with and simultaneous fear of a confined future, despite her equally strong desire to live. Throughout the novel, Desai depicts children as what Sara Ahmed calls 'sticky' objects, 'saturated with affect, as sites of personal and social tension'.[125] It is crucial to read Maya's response as indexing both personal and social tensions; her emotional rejection of pregnancy and children is not simply a matter of personal preference, but also a matter of rejecting the terms of national belonging. If we too narrowly read Maya in terms of a domestic tragedy, we miss the novel's political statements about women's indefinite waiting. As Ahmed reminds us, 'emotions "matter" for politics; emotions show us how power shapes the very surface of bodies as well as worlds.'[126] The child, she elaborates, is a particularly rich symbol for intertwining waiting as investment and national belonging: 'It is not surprising that the return of the investment in the nation is imagined in the form of the future generation . . . National love places its hope in the next generation; the postponement of the ideal sustains the fantasy that return [on the investment in the nation] is possible.'[127]

Within this progressively desperate context, Gautama reacts to Maya's anxieties by instructing her to be patient. Occupying the very centre of the novel, the third chapter of part two depicts not only the Lal's disastrous dinner party, but also introduces the motif of crying peacocks, whose poignant dance and cry signify awareness of their impending death. Maya identifies with the peacock's agonising prescience, lamenting, 'Now that I understood their call, I wept for them, and wept for myself, knowing their words to be mine. Not only their words, but their fate.'[128] Maya recognises that she will not have peace or rest as long as the prophecy haunts her present, and she is increasingly aware that Gautama's death may be required to fulfil the prophecy in a way that would still allow her to live. Tormented with the memories of the horoscope, chapter three concludes, 'There is no rest any more – only death and waiting.' Positioned as consonant with death, waiting describes Maya's temporal experience that must be terminated if she is to live.

---

[124] Ibid., 63.
[125] Ahmed, *The Cultural Politics of Emotion*, 11.
[126] Ibid., 12.
[127] Ibid., 131.
[128] Desai, *Cry, the Peacock*, 84.

Whereas the relationship between uncertainty and anxiety in a novel like *Fragments* is directly proportional (in other words, when one is more uncertain about the future, one is more anxious and fearful), here, uncertainty and anxiety are inversely proportional. That is, the more certain Maya is, and the closer the future comes to the present through the temporality of prophecy, fate, and prediction, the more anxious and mentally strained she becomes. To return to the temporal variables and constraints of waiting illustrated in Table I.1, the second category most accurately describes Maya's waiting: a long duration of waiting in dread, with a belief that the undesired outcome is certain to come about. While Maya unequivocally rejects the death predicted by the horoscope, she is still discontent with life if it implies indefinite waiting. This discontent is central, in my view, to understanding why the narrative continues beyond the moment that Maya pushes Gautama off the roof. While this act may have circumvented her own predicted death, it has not necessarily afforded her a life without waiting.

Maya's final rejection of passive waiting, and her decision to push Gautama off the roof, can be understood as both a personal and a political choice in the context of Maya's timescape. Recognising that Maya's timescape combines fate influenced by Hindu belief as well as national time shaped by reproductive time, we can see how these temporalities complement one another to promote a resigned temporality of waiting. Maya's need to act with a fierce urgency of 'now' is a direct response to the several ways that 'fate' and a sense of predetermination merge in the scenes where Maya encounters images of traditional Indian femininity. Maya's stake in her own future is not contingent on her participation in reproducing the Indian nation. Her defiant rejection of waiting occurs in tandem with her affirmation of the present moment. As the narrative builds towards its tragic conclusion, Maya's thoughts coalesce around waiting and urgency, as she ponders, 'But how long could one stand with one's eyes shut, waiting?'[129] She realises,

> And it was the end that I waited for. The beginning had begun long ago, was even forgotten. It was the end, the ultimate, the final version of the final fate that had to appear now – *had* to appear now. I had waited too long – another day would be one too many.[130]

If fate dictates this unfortunate future, then Maya is paradoxically 'free' to act as she believes she must.

---

[129] Ibid., 152.
[130] Ibid., 154.

The temporality of fate works in two ways here. On the one hand, fate is the very outcome that Maya is agitating against; she registers this resistance not only in her first, immediate response to the horoscope ('I will never marry!') but also each time her mind wanders to the option that killing Gautama could be a way to negotiate the prophecy. On the other hand, fate, in tandem with her attachment to sensuous life and Gautama's seeming indifference to it, is a source of empowerment. If the horoscope has limited her options so severely, to the point where her husband dies so that she can live, then the prophecy's inevitability softens the lines of justice and fairness, in effect mitigating her culpability in committing a 'crime'. As Maya herself imagines, 'I saw a future insanity projected before me, beyond the window in a world where guilt, sin, crime, punishment all stood stock still, struck into threatening immobility by a ruthless force of fate.'[131]

I have been arguing that Maya's sense of urgency is oriented in opposition both to the horoscope's prediction, where the future is in many ways immutable as well as undesired, and to an alternative future modelled on acceptable roles of wife and mother. Both temporalities, of prediction and reproductive time, entail an already defined future; in the first, either Maya or her husband must die, and in the second, Maya's claim to the future is dependent on reproduction. By killing her husband, Maya deftly avoids both futures, and her urgent act disrupts the temporalities that undergird both. Urgency itself is 'temporal, pushing for resolution in the immediate present or very near future, and it is also authoritative, demanding attention, compelling action or preventing us from acting'.[132] If 'the important ethical work of urgency has been to identify that which must not wait',[133] then Maya's urgency here deserves further attention. Undoubtedly, Maya's desperation is linked to her sense of impending doom and struggle against what she fears is a future lying in wait. But the ways in which Maya feels additional panic and rage when she contemplates the idealised image of traditional womanhood suggests that her 'refusal' to wait any longer should also be placed in relation to the novel's larger, mid-1960s Indian context, when, as Sunder Rajan, Keating, Boehmer, Kumar and others have demonstrated, many Indian women continued to wait.

In articulating this urgency of now, Maya subtly reconfigures the very categories of acceptance and detachment, originally promoted by her husband and father, to fit her own desires. Maya and Gautama's final

---

[131] Ibid., 154.
[132] Olson, 'Geography and Ethics 1: Waiting and Urgency', 518.
[133] Ibid., 521.

interactions are alienating and aloof, reinforcing Maya's conclusion, 'This was as it had to be.'[134] In my view, Maya's certainty here is also dependent on limiting her focus to the immediate present, because a future at odds with the horoscope is still in the making. As a conversation about the weather begins to drift to the night, which should be cooler, Maya 'bit [her] words off abruptly, having strayed too far. The present, I reminded myself fiercely, the present and not the future'.[135] The parenthetical commentary, ostensibly from the future Maya reflecting back on this moment, clarifies the power of temporal tenses to ease Maya's commitment to her own future. She explains, '(And yes, now that I remember, all the while I thought of him and of our marriage as things of the past. I thought of the past with deep, twilit, hopeless regret.)'[136] At this point, Maya has already committed herself to choosing her life over Gautama's.

Moreover, from the vantage point of the narrative present, Maya realises that because her husband and marriage are 'things of the past', she can reproduce a similar temporality of inevitability and fate for her independent actions. In Maya's conscience, the ethical and moral dimensions of killing her husband appear to be similarly diminished; when she thinks of the past with regret, it is with hopeless regret – that is, the present is rendered 'past' as if the act had already been done. Maya's impatience to endure the conditions in which she finds herself is not simply an involuntary reaction to the circumstances, but rather a calculated response to the self-effacing rhetoric of karma and fate espoused by Gautama and her father. As Mario Feit argues with reference to Martin Luther King Jr's philosophy of democratic impatience, 'impatience affirms the dignity of the oppressed' by refusing to support 'the undemocratic status quo [made possible] by compromise'.[137] Maya's impatience is her mechanism for self-determination. Though *Cry, the Peacock* presents a bleak account of Maya's possibilities for self-assertion, the urgency and impatience of her actions challenge the ways that gendered nationalism, fate, and inaction collude to present her with very little room to manoeuvre.

Underscoring Maya's heightened awareness of time, Desai fittingly depicts Maya passing a statue of Shiva – the Hindu deity associated with time – on her way to the roof. In the form of Kali, the 'goddess of destruction and all-pervasive power of time', Shiva is associated with

---

[134] Desai, *Cry, the Peacock*, 161.
[135] Ibid., 162.
[136] Ibid., 168.
[137] Feit, 'Democratic Impatience: Martin Luther King, Jr. on Democratic Temporality', 10.

'"great time" and "all-devouring time"'.¹³⁸ Maya is mesmerised by the statue, which, despite its fixed form, is not 'frozen or immobile in this pose of eternal creative movement'.¹³⁹ The Shiva statue captures the paradox of the Hindu god, who 'awakens inert matter, animates the inanimate world and brings forth the cycles of time: birth and death, creation and destruction.'¹⁴⁰ As Maya prepares to step onto the veranda, she takes solace in remembered Sanskrit passages and the image of Shiva's 'arched foot, raised into a symbol of liberation'.¹⁴¹ Linking Maya's apprehension of time to the twinned processes of creation and destruction, as well as to liberation, the novel's climax lends both weight and rationality to Maya's decision to kill Gautama in an effort to save herself.

Before concluding this reading of *Cry, the Peacock*, I want to address the scholarly readings that focus on Maya's 'madness', which appears to progress throughout the novel and culminate in Gautama's murder. Many take for granted that Maya is evidently insane.¹⁴² But Inder Kher, who explicitly addresses madness in the novel, argues,

> By focusing on Maya's clarity about Gautama's death and its purpose, by highlighting Maya's apparent serenity and happiness toward the end of the novel, Anita Desai strongly suggests that Maya is not mad and should not be confined to an asylum.¹⁴³

As *Fragments* demonstrates, a character's experience of madness or mental breakdown can still function as a social or political critique to draw attention to the external conditions and circumstances that affect the character's senses of being and time. Thus, even if Maya were clinically insane, a diagnosis that the novel does not unequivocally assert, her decision to murder her husband would not necessarily be voided of its social and political critique. In my view, however, the charge of madness is more appropriately levelled at the society in which Maya lives, rather than at Maya herself. As a first-person narrator, Maya is cognisant that her strong reactions and feelings might encourage others to consider her mad, and she succumbs at points to doubting her own sanity. But her doubts arise in the first half of the novel because of her lingering memories of the horoscope, which she was not certain

---

¹³⁸ Adam, *Time*, 7.
¹³⁹ Desai, *Cry, the Peacock*, 169.
¹⁴⁰ Adam, *Time*, 7.
¹⁴¹ Desai, *Cry, the Peacock*, 169.
¹⁴² Jamkhandi, 'The Artistic Effects of the Shifts in Point of View in Anita Desai's Cry, the Peacock', 46.
¹⁴³ Kher, 'Madness as Discourse in Anita Desai's Cry, the Peacock', 23.

truly occurred. Her brother Arjuna's letter, however, turns these otherwise unsubstantiated memories into facts, and her fears are verified. That which has made Maya doubt her sanity is then proven to be real; if she experiences a mental breakdown as a result, then it is the 'real' that drives her madness. This, in turn, suggests that we read Maya not simply as a study in an isolated individual's psychology, as many others have done, but rather in her social, familial and even national context. Given this context and the temporalities jostling to restrict her sense of the future, Maya's act takes on an aura of cold reasonableness rather than hot hysteria.

Unfortunately, the immediate result of Maya's action is that her self-affirming moment is reinscribed into the discourse of madness; her sister-in-law Nila and her mother-in-law discuss their plans to place Maya in an insane asylum, and discredit Maya's own version of the events. Unlike waiting, which 'can be productive or unproductive for radical praxis', as we saw in *Fragments*, 'urgency compels and requires response . . . Insisting that a suffering body, now, is that which cannot wait, has the ethical effect of drawing it into consideration alongside the political, public and exceptional scope of large-scale futures.'[144] While Maya's death, which presumably occurs at the novel's close, is ultimately a self-destroying act, the urgency that attends her actions throughout the novel compels us to consider the political, public and temporal contexts shaping the possibilities she identifies for action.

Gendered Temporalities of Waiting

The protagonists of *Fragments* and *Cry, the Peacock* repeatedly emphasise their impatience while waiting, and their temporalities of waiting gesture towards sociocultural and economic conditions that restrain their sense of possibility and resistance, to the point that each experiences mental breakdown or madness. Baako's impatience arises from his desire to achieve synchronicity with productive, capitalist time, whereas the women of *Fragments* start to occupy 'patient' waiting as a refusal to synchronise: a refusal to consolidate with the seemingly synchronous time of the nation that both Bhabha and Freeman note in the epigraphs to this chapter. Contrary to other analyses of the novels that focus narrowly on Baako and Maya, my reading expands to consider the communities of women who further add nuance to the novels' timescapes.

---

[144] Olson, 'Geography and Ethics 1: Waiting and Urgency', 523.

If temporal landscapes are integral to national identity, and the women dramatise arrhythmias within the disillusionment settings, then their waiting is part of the texts' political and social critique. Waiting is not a static signifier in *Fragments*; rather, it is named by Efua and Naana to describe temporal orientations that are at odds with Baako's sense of waiting as stasis. Likewise, Maya's comparison with Leila and Pom suggest that women wait differently, not only in ways that may be different from men, but also in ways that are different from one another. In both novels, the waiting dramatised by women exposes the fragile unity of performances of national synchrony. For postcolonial literary studies more generally, this chapter expands the category of 'disillusionment' fiction beyond the African continent to consider how Indian fiction might modify the relationship between disillusionment and national independence. Moreover, while the experiences of women are largely not the focus of disillusionment fiction of the 1960s and 1970s, here we see a pattern in literary representations of women, waiting and national belonging that show the cruel optimism of the attachment to nation as well as the ways that this belonging might be configured otherwise.

Thus, in terms of their representation of postcolonial disillusionment, women and the nation, both novels register discontent and critique, and new ways forward. Maya's self-assertion 'stands for change, even if it is nihilist', Fawzia Afzal-Khan suggests, 'whereas Gautama and her father symbolize the continuance of patriarchal, neocolonialist traditions'.[145] Given the various factors affecting and constricting Maya's self-determination, waiting is not a possibility, and the narrative suggests that change is needed desperately, and now. For *Fragments*, Lazarus has already described the way that Juana's sense of time is at odds with Baako's, but Efua and Naana additionally posit ways of being in time that are critical of postcolonial Ghana without giving in to disillusionment. Efua waits for whatever will come, but her acceptance is still forward-looking even as she relinquishes the expectation of financial returns on Baako's own return to Ghana. Naana's sense of return and waiting in the novel's final section creates synchronicity with the ritual time of Akan ceremonies, and might yield continuity with tradition and communal solidarity for a postcolonial context at risk of fragmentation.

The interplay of multiple temporalities comprising the novels' timescapes, structuring waiting as a combination of patience and urgency, uncovers the gendered assumptions that waiting entails immobility and passivity. Maya, Naana, Efua and Juana challenge these assumptions.

---

[145] Afzal-Khan, *Cultural Imperialism and the Indo-English Novel*, 66.

Maya's sense of waiting emphasises its urgent dimensions. For her, in this period of disillusionment, the fierce urgency of 'now' has not lost its potency to register complaint, even as Maya's refusal to wait leads to self-destruction. Baako's sense of time forces us to confront how the neocolonial, postcolonial state, as well as the new elite, use the language of patience to maintain indefinite deferral, and to exercise power over others. Yet the women in Baako's life, in diverse ways, practise patience as a way of synchronising with temporalities that contrast with 'productive' time. Together, these novels expressly draw our attention to the multiple temporalities imbricated in the characters' experience of waiting. The complex timescapes suggest that waiting does not divide people evenly into those with power and those without, but rather that gradations of power and resistance shift in relation to various temporal schemes. The relationship between women and waiting will be taken up further in the following chapter, beginning with Njabulo Ndebele's *The Cry of Winnie Mandela* – a novel that alludes to one of the most famous waiting women of all time: Homer's Penelope.

Chapter 5

'Strategic Waiting' and Reconciliation in the Aftermath of Conflict

do not eat an unripe apple
its bitterness is a tingling knife.
suffer yourself to wait
and the ripeness will come
and the apple will fall down at your feet.
now is the time
pluck the apple
and feed the future with its ripeness.
    Njabulo Ndebele, 'The Revolution of the Aged' (1981)

The speaker in Njabulo Ndebele's 1981 poem 'The Revolution of the Aged' captures the strained atmosphere of the final decade of apartheid in South Africa, bringing to the fore anxieties about timing, agency and activism. Addressing the youth of today, the aged speaker recounts lessons learned over the course of a long life, including, 'if you cannot master the wind,/ flow with it/ letting know all the time that you are resisting.'[1] To the young who are 'hot for quick results', the speaker explains that he has 'watched and listened', and while experiencing 'humiliation/ i felt the growth of strength in me/ for i had a goal/ as firm as life is endless.'[2] While the thief and oppressor, the source of his humiliations, has grown old, the speaker still has 'the weapon of youth'. The final stanza advises the youth on the utility of waiting, which allows the fruit to ripen; at the same time, the speaker urges that the time is 'now' to harvest the fruits of waiting.

The poem contains both caution and encouragement; the speaker advises the youth not to be so quick to act, nor so quick to judge the

---

[1] Ndebele, 'The Revolution of the Aged', 241.
[2] Ibid., 242.

apparent patience of the generations before them.³ When the speaker counsels, 'suffer yourself to wait', the language connotes both pain and endurance in relation to waiting. Though the verb 'suffer' is commonly understood in the transitive and passive sense of 'to have (something painful, distressing, or injurious) inflicted or imposed upon one', the history of the word's association with endurance suggests undertones of choice and agency.⁴ The word, moreover, contains religious overtones as well, which will be important for this chapter's later discussion of the Truth and Reconciliation Commission's investment in redemptive logics of waiting, confession and closure. To suffer can also entail 'to go or pass through', or 'to hold out', or 'to allow oneself, submit *to be* treated in a certain way; to endure, consent *to be* or *to do* something.' Suffering, in this sense, entails endurance and patience. The speaker suggests that to wait, rather than act before the time is ripe, can be a choice, and in this case it is a transformative process. Not only does the fruit ripen in time, but also the speaker's strength grows as he 'watched and listened', never losing sight of his 'goal/ as firm as life is endless'.⁵ To the youths who would scorn his choices, he reminds them, 'it is a blind progeny/ that acts without indebtedness to the past.' The poem enacts a complicated temporality, 'looking backward and forward at once, embracing as needed direct and indirect forms of discourse and action and the perspectives of both old and young'.⁶ Timing, here, is everything. Jennifer Wenzel enumerates several questions that preoccupy Ndebele's poem:

> [W]ould the shift from armed struggle to negotiation bring the bitterness of unripe fruit? . . . What was the difference between waiting for the apple to decide it was ripe or choosing the moment to seize it, so that its imminent ripeness might 'feed the future'?⁷

Decades later in 2003, Ndebele returned to the temporality of waiting in *The Cry of Winnie Mandela* with renewed interest in the relationship between waiting and the settlement and negotiation that had occurred in the meantime. Divided into two parts, Ndebele's novel concerns

---

³ For the larger Black Consciousness movement context and generational struggle that the poem addresses, see Tom Penfold's 'Volume, Power, Originality: Reassessing the Complexities of Soweto Poetry', which notes that Ndebele's warnings to the youth 'extends the message of Black Consciousness to a wider group, including the old' at the same time that it 'attacks the modern and the urban African youth'. Penfold, 16.
⁴ *Oxford English Dictionary*, 'suffer, v.'
⁵ Ndebele, 'The Revolution of the Aged', 241–2.
⁶ O'Brien, *Against Normalization*, 49.
⁷ Wenzel, *Bulletproof*, 159.

'Penelope's Descendants', women who waited for their men during the apartheid years, and who now struggle in the post-apartheid present to reconcile with this past. Each 'ordinary' woman in *The Cry of Winnie Mandela* has two largely uninterrupted monologues. In part one, the women introduce themselves and their particular histories and experiences of waiting for their men; in part two, they address Winnie and ask her questions. Winnie then has her own section, where she imagines her double and addresses herself. For clarity, throughout this chapter I will refer to the fictional character as 'Winnie', and the historical person as 'Mandela'. The novel concludes with the group together in a car, encountering Homer's Penelope as a hitchhiker on the road to Durban. The allusion to Penelope – the figure from *The Odyssey* who becomes a character in the novel's final section, 'The Stranger' – draws attention to how women historically have been expected to wait indefinitely, and chastely, for their male counterparts.

In the Penelope tradition of waiting, waiting is moralised and gendered as passive and feminine, and the novel's dialogue with this history suggests that these expectations have become 'timeless': inherited, transnational and trans-temporal. The four waiting women, as well as the character Winnie, describe and revise the assumptions of this gendered history of waiting. Sometimes waiting is not rewarded, sometimes the women cultivate opportunities for themselves while waiting, and other times the women refuse to wait at all, but in each case, the waiting is grounded and contextualised in the specific, ordinary circumstances in which the women live. In their probing reflections, conversations and apostrophes to Mandela herself, the waiting women raise the following questions: What role can the temporal experience of waiting play in the process of reconciliation – with self, other and nation – after trauma? Given the agony of waiting the women experienced during apartheid, how could waiting possibly signify differently in the post-apartheid present? And how might the temporal dimensions of waiting interact with the temporalities of reconciliation, especially those evoked in the narrative process of recounting memories for Truth and Reconciliation Commissions?

This chapter pairs *The Cry of Winnie Mandela*, by the South African writer Njabulo Ndebele, with *Radiance of Tomorrow*, a 2014 novel by the Sierra Leonean writer Ishmael Beah, in order to assess what I call 'strategic waiting' as a productive stage in the process of negotiating a traumatic past in order to create a shared future. Like the speaker in Ndebele's poem, *The Cry of Winnie Mandela* and *Radiance of Tomorrow* illustrate that the time of waiting may be inhabited actively and intentionally, especially in an effort to 'feed the future'. The novels are set soon after Truth and Reconciliation Commissions (TRCs) in both countries reported their findings and suggestions. TRCs are mechanisms of transitional justice that gained popularity in the later twentieth century, and aim to uncover the truth about human rights abuses perpetrated, typically, by states or military governments. The South African TRC was established by an act of Parliament in 1995, but its provisions can be traced to the negotiations for a peaceful settlement conducted between President F. W. de Klerk and the African National Congress (ANC) between 1990 and 1993. As Johnny De Lange characterises, in language that resonates with my focus on waiting, the ANC 'as the government-in-waiting' was committed to the idea of a truth commission as a way of 'dealing in the future with past violations'.[8] The South African TRC aimed to bring about reconciliation through restorative justice by investigating human rights abuses that occurred between 1960 and 1994, restoring dignity to victims and encouraging rehabilitation and reparations, and granting amnesty to violators in exchange for complete disclosure in public hearings.

The Sierra Leonean TRC began its operations in 2002, though the 1999 Lomé Peace Agreement had included provisions that called for such a Commission to bring about reconciliation after the civil war.[9] According to Abubakar Kargbo, the TRC was meant to 'break the cycle of violence' in the country, and its mandate extended back to 1991, when the Revolutionary United Front (RUF) rebelled against President Joseph Momah's government.[10] The Sierra Leonean civil war began with an attempted coup by the Revolutionary United Front, led by Foday Sankoh and supported by Liberia's Charles Taylor. Like the South African TRC, the Sierra Leonean TRC sought both written statements and testimonies in public hearings. One complication for the Sierra Leonean TRC, detailed further below, was how to reintegrate child soldiers, who uneasily straddled the line that TRCs tend to draw between 'victim' and 'perpetrator'. Rather than extensive truth-telling, Rosalind Shaw and Lars Waldorf find that '[d]uring closing reconciliation ceremonies, many ex-combatants made "apologies" that – while full of silences about specific acts of violence – nevertheless enacted moral norms critical to local processes of reintegration'.[11] In contrast to South Africa's highly standardised practice of eliciting, submitting and promulgating

---

[8] De Lange, 'The Historical Context, Legal Origins and Philosophical Foundation of the South African Truth and Reconciliation Commission', 20.
[9] Sierra Leone and Truth and Reconciliation Commission, *Witness to Truth*, 2.
[10] Kargbo, 'The Long Road to Peace: 1991–1997', 46.
[11] Shaw and Waldorf, 'Introduction: Localizing Transitional Justice', 14.

stories of victims and perpetrators, the ex-combatants and the TRC participants in Sierra Leone 'drew upon local techniques of selective integration. They thereby retooled [the truth-telling and reintegration process] "from below" into an alternative mechanism that would facilitate coexistence'.[12] Despite some variation in structure and practices, ending waiting was an important function of both TRCs: waiting for news of disappeared loved ones, for facts, for resolutions, for knowledge, for closure.

The South African TRC released the first five volumes of its report in 1998, and the last volume in 2003 (coinciding with the year that Ndebele published *The Cry of Winnie Mandela*). Sierra Leone's TRC released its report the following year, in 2004. Throughout his novel, Ndebele incorporates excerpts from the TRC proceedings in South Africa verbatim, and we will see that the text's women acknowledge and address the TRC's purview, process and conclusions as they situate their own life experiences alongside this national narrative. While not only a response to the South African TRC, *The Cry of Winnie Mandela* does explicitly discuss the TRC hearings and Mandela's controversial refusal to submit fully to its method of reconciliation. Beah's characters, on the other hand, do not refer to the Sierra Leonean TRC or the Sierra Leonean Special Court, which functioned in tandem. Nevertheless, I argue that in *Radiance of Tomorrow* themes of reconciliation and rebuilding after conflict intersect with the TRC, and the narrative explores the limitations of confession and confrontation, as well as the potentially healing function of silence. In their explorations of waiting, the novels highlight not only the limitations of TRCs, especially as some characters continue to await justice, closure or reparations, but also the work of fiction to supplement and to augment the work of TRCs.

In selecting novels as the fictional form to place in conversation with TRCs, I follow Edward Said, who asserted in another context that novels 'are forms of beginning and being in the world'.[13] I find that the same could be said of TRC processes – that they are forms of beginning (again), and enabling being in the world by giving shape to painful experiences. Mark Sanders makes a compelling case for an interdisciplinary law and literature study of the South African TRC, given that '[i]n post-apartheid South Africa local cultural formations interact with more widely shared juridical codes such as human rights to produce new kinds of legal, political, and ethical concepts and practices', and '[l]iterature

---

[12] Ibid., 14.
[13] Said, *Beginnings : Intention and Method*, xii.

is at the heart of these developments' through 'testimonial narrative'.[14] Significantly, Sanders notes that while the South African TRC was unable to take up the 'interpretative labor' of addressing the 'abuse of female comrades in the liberation struggle', such work has 'been initiated in two remarkable recent works of fiction'; Ndebele's *The Cry of Winnie Mandela* is one of these novels that 'take up predicaments of advocative storytelling'.[15] To be clear, the novels discussed in this chapter and the official TRCs in South Africa and Sierra Leone do very different work, but I contend that these fictive responses to TRCs and national projects of reconciliation expand and continue the dialogue of reconciliation in a productive, different form.

Thus, this chapter argues that these fictional narratives examine the philosophical assumptions and temporal underpinnings of TRCs, and variably serve as correctives and complements to TRC processes. Whereas Ndebele's focus on waiting women addresses lacunae in the South African TRC's method and report, Beah's limited focus on the rebuilding of a single village, Imperi, scales down the scope of the Sierra Leonean TRC to focus on sub-state reconciliations of injury and loss. Despite these differences in geographical location, scale and narrative, as well as the unique formations of the TRCs in South Africa and Sierra Leone, the texts evince instances of 'strategic waiting' as a temporal modality that can be productively inhabited in the service of reconciliation. In order to elucidate how strategic waiting intervenes in the temporalities of reconciliation as promoted by TRCs, I provide an historical account of the establishment of TRCs in South Africa and Sierra Leone in the following section, with an eye towards illuminating their narrative and temporal underpinnings. I then examine the strengths, controversies and shortcomings of the TRCs, and emphasise the temporal tensions at the heart of the reconciliation processes. Given these strengths and limitations, I turn to *The Cry of Winnie Mandela* and *Radiance of Tomorrow*, and I argue that these fictional renderings work to extend, qualify and even redirect the official national reconciliation narrative process. If, as Adam Czarnota asserts, '[r]econciliation does not merely happen in time but requires time for its happening',[16] then these novels suggest that strategic waiting can be mobilised precisely to accomplish this work.

---

[14] Sanders, *Ambiguities of Witnessing*, 4.
[15] Ibid., 82–3.
[16] Czarnota, 'Sacrum, Profanum and Social Time: Quasi-Theological Reflections on Time and Reconciliation', 160.

'Breaking the cycle': History, Memory and New Beginnings

From Bolivia to Argentina, Uganda, El Salvador and the Philippines, official national commissions that aimed to uncover the truth about state violations of human rights proliferated around the world across the twentieth century. In 1990, Chile became the first country to use the term 'Truth and Reconciliation Commission' to describe its project of investigating human rights abuses, and five years later South Africa followed suit. Sierra Leone's own TRC was established in 2000 after the country's eleven-year-long civil war. While the particular focus of each Commission, its mandate, and its purview were specific to each country, TRCs broadly share several assumptions about truth, justice and temporality.

First, TRCs require the double perspective of looking back in order to look forwards. While Commissions are often candid about the challenges that remain for the nation, and the difficulties (or impossibilities) of achieving 'harmony', the teleology of forward movement underpins the popular justifications for the work of the TRCs. Despite the difficulties of looking backwards, or remembering, doing so is necessary to moving past and beyond. As Desmond Tutu wrote in his foreword to the Truth and Reconciliation Commission of South Africa Report, the South African TRC aspired to 'hel[p] our nation to come to terms with its past and, in so doing, reach out to a new future'.[17] These efforts towards 'accounting for the past', Tutu explains, will enable the nation to 'become accountable for the future'.[18] Those who participated in the South African TRC's public hearings, which lasted from 1996 to 2001, had diverse reasons for doing so; some sought amnesty, others information about missing loved ones, and still others desired the opportunity to be heard or to tell their stories.

But in terms of the South African TRC report's own account, formally remembering and reconstructing the past is important to prevent gross violations of human rights in the future. The Chairman of Sierra Leone's TRC, Bishop Joseph Christian Humper, echoed similar sentiments in his foreword to Sierra Leone's TRC report: 'Forgetting or ignoring the past means we cannot learn its lessons and are at a greater risk of

---

[17] South Africa and Tutu, *Truth and Reconciliation Commission of South Africa Report*, 1:2.
[18] Ibid., 1:7.

repeating it.'[19] The report, he hopes, will 'serve as a roadmap towards the building of a new society in which all Sierra Leoneans can walk unafraid with pride and dignity'.[20] Likewise, according to the South African TRC report's summary of its mandate, the 'Commission was conceived as part of the bridge-building process designed to help lead the nation away from a deeply divided past to a future founded on the recognition of human rights and democracy.'[21] The metaphor of the bridge, however, elides the complicated temporalities of memory and history, which can impede easy transition from one side of the 'bridge' to the other.[22]

Second, TRCs share a commitment to victim-centred restorative, rather than retributive, justice. The TRCs in both South Africa and Sierra Leone were charged with understanding and reconstructing the past in an effort to forge national unity. In this way, the Commissions were 'both preventative and restorative', aiming 'to reconcile the old and new, and to move forward in effective harmony'.[23] South Africa's amnesty for truth arrangement – that in certain cases perpetrators of gross violations of human rights could be granted amnesty if they fully disclosed their politically motivated actions – is emblematic of this emphasis. Sierra Leone, on the other hand, added retributive elements to its reconciliation process through the establishment of a Special Court. The Sierra Leonean Special Court, the TRC report notes, 'was created after the abandonment of the amnesty provisions ... following breaches of the Lomé Peace Agreement by elements within the RUF'.[24] The Lomé Peace agreement incited protests within Sierra Leone as well as in the greater international community because it granted amnesty to all combatants, including Foday Sankoh, the leader of the RUF. The Truth and Reconciliation Act was officially passed in 2000, the same year that President Kabbah requested that the United Nations create a tribunal to pursue criminal charges against RUF combatants.[25] The disarmament of the RUF and other rebel groups was one of the goals of establishing a TRC in Sierra Leone, but the government was concerned that the TRC

---

[19] Sierra Leone and Truth and Reconciliation Commission, *Witness to Truth*, 2.
[20] Ibid., 2.
[21] South Africa and Tutu, *Truth and Reconciliation Commission of South Africa Report*, 1:48.
[22] In his essay 'Of Lions and Rabbits: Thoughts on Democracy and Reconciliation', Ndebele also draws on the imagery of the bridge, noting that the TRC 'allowed the country to cross a particular river of *time* and circumstance'. 'Of Lions and Rabbits' 155–6, emphasis mine.
[23] Rotberg and Thompson, *Truth v. Justice*, 3.
[24] Sierra Leone and Truth and Reconciliation Commission, *Witness to Truth*, 15.
[25] Ibid., 30.

would be 'perceive[d] as a court of law' and stall the process.[26] Thus, in language I find particularly suggestive for considering the temporality of reconciliation underlying the Sierra Leonean TRC process, the 'government's position, supported by most people, [was] "to make haste slowly"', utilising both a TRC and a Special Court.[27]

Third, TRCs, as temporary institutions of investigation, are necessarily limited in their temporal scopes. Not only are TRCs charged with investigating abuses within a circumscribed amount of time, but also the Commission is not intended to continue its work indefinitely. Complicating these temporal limits, the TRC and the Special Court in Sierra Leone were held to different timelines. While the Sierra Leonean TRC was authorised to address violence and abuses beginning in 1991, the date recognised as the start of the civil war, the Special Court was limited to 1996, when the Abidjan Peace Accord failed. South Africa's TRC was limited to the years 1960–94. As we will see below in the subsequent discussion of *The Cry of Winnie Mandela* and *Radiance of Tomorrow*, the demarcation of set dates for TRC mandates imposes a narrower scope that, while making the volume of claims more manageable and establishing a starting point for the narrative of reconciliation, necessarily excludes contributing events that pre-date the starting point.

In practice, then, the rigid scope of the TRCs' mandate disqualifies some abuses from being addressed, deferring closure for some individuals even as the nation ostensibly works towards unification. The South African TRC has come under scrutiny because some experiences, including the ordinary, banal experiences of abuse under apartheid, appeared to be excluded or downplayed in the process of reconciliation. While Sierra Leone followed South Africa's example in establishing a limited scope for its TRC, the country did attempt to learn from the earlier Commission's shortcomings; important differences between the two include the Sierra Leonean TRC's focus on human rights violations and its separate Special Court. Within its report, the Sierra Leonean TRC acknowledges that South Africa's experience proved an instructive example. Under 'Mandate of the Commission', the report notes that the South African TRC's scope of 'gross violations' of human rights was 'much narrower' than the 'violations and abuses' that Sierra Leone's TRC was authorised to probe.[28] The Sierra Leonean TRC report suggests that the narrow scope of South Africa's gross violations of human

---

[26] Alie, 'A Price for Peace? Justice and Reconciliation in Post-War Sierra Leone', 176.
[27] Ibid., 176.
[28] Sierra Leone and Truth and Reconciliation Commission, *Witness to Truth*, 34.

rights 'excluded a large number of victims' and potentially 'compromised truth'. In Sierra Leone, supplementary ceremonies of reconciliation occurred outside the parameters of the official TRC hearings, highlighting the role of local community-level negotiations of reconciliation that allowed, in some instances, a 'forgive and forget' approach at odds with the TRC premises of truth-telling and the rigorous reconstruction of the past.

In summary, the South African case was a useful touchstone for Sierra Leone, as it was the first commission created 'through a public and participatory process, by way of an Act of parliament'.[29] Yet transitional justice can be a messy legal endeavour, especially when neither side can claim military victory, and when amnesty is at issue. During the transition in South Africa, 'the apartheid legal order remain[ed] the law of the land, even if unconstitutional, until amended by the democratic parliament, or declared unconstitutional by the Constitutional Court'.[30] Recalling Nadine Gordimer's concept of interregnum temporalities discussed in Chapter 2, we might view the origins of South Africa's TRC as befitting the twilight of the 'interregnum' context from which it emerged, embedding the negotiation of the dying old and emerging new. As mentioned above, the amnesty for truth arrangement that was so central to piecing together South Africa's past originated in the settlement negotiated by President de Klerk and the African National Congress (ANC) between 1990 and 1993. During the regime change, Paul van Zyl notes, 'the former government retained control over a formidable military and police force', and 'maintained considerable power'.[31] The interim constitution of 1993, in fact, 'was completed without agreement on whether an amnesty provision should be included', and that provision was eventually included as part of a postamble.[32]

Rather than enabling decisive breaks with the nondemocratic past, then, the conditions for TRCs' possibility often emerge explicitly from the negotiation and settlement process. While metaphors of bridges (in the South African case) and roadmaps (in the Sierra Leonean case) implicitly acknowledge that the past and future are linked, there is also, I believe, a desire for the traffic to proceed in one direction, from the 'divided past' to the reconciled future. From the intermingling of

---

[29] De Lange, 'The Historical Context, Legal Origins and Philosophical Foundation of the South African Truth and Reconciliation Commission', 14.
[30] Ibid., 19.
[31] Van Zyl, 'Dilemmas of Transitional Justice: The Case of South Africa's Truth and Reconciliation Commission', 649.
[32] Ibid., 650–1.

legal regimes during the transition process to the provision of amnesty marked by the belatedness of a postamble, the temporal conditions for the creation of the South African TRC by no means progressed linearly or discretely.

For individuals identified in TRC processes as perpetrators and victims, the complicated reworking of the past through remembering, witnessing and testifying – acts central to TRC proceedings – can similarly produce psychological tensions between the temporal categories of past harm and future reconciliation. Many commentators on TRCs, and in particular South Africa's TRC, evoke what Claire Moon calls 'popular therapeutic platitudes about denial and mental health: that recalling buried memories or truths about past trauma can help alleviate anxiety and emotional suffering, and prevent the unsettling and disruptive "return" of the past'.[33] In her view, individual and national experiences of suffering, healing, unity and reconciliation 'were conflated . . . such that individual healing became commensurate with national reconciliation'.[34] The forward movement emphasised by the South African TRC's own narrative of bridging the past and future is here underscored by the imperative to recall in order to prevent an unbidden return of memories – language that is consistent with the above insistence that TRCs can help to break cycles of violence. Creating parallels between TRC confessional and testimonial practices and therapy, Moon observes, 'implies a teleological adjudication of trauma that necessarily engages inner psychological and emotional processes, professing to be destined, at some unknown point in the future, for wholeness or healing'.[35] Ultimately, all 'three distinct constituents of reconciliation – past atrocity, present truth-telling and future reconciliation', Moon finds, 'were constructed, indeed narrated, by the TRC as existing in a causal, linear, and inevitable relationship with one another'.[36]

Moon's analysis points to a central tension in TRC narratives: that while positing a unified, reconciled future, the Commissions nevertheless acknowledge a plurality of stories and perspectives on the past.[37] The temporality of reconciliation, then, is more heterogeneous than TRC narratives of unified reconciliation admit. And reconciliation, as Emilios Christodoulidis and Scott Veitch argue, 'is all about time'.[38]

---

[33] Moon, 'Reconciliation as Therapy and Compensation: A Critical Analysis', 165.
[34] Ibid., 165.
[35] Ibid., 181.
[36] Moon, *Narrating Political Reconciliation*, 6.
[37] Ibid., 7.
[38] Christodoulidis and Veitch, 'Introduction', 2.

Their observations about the temporality of reconciliation are worth quoting at length because they illuminate how the narrative of national reconciliation charts a teleology of closure not necessarily shared by the individual participants in the process:

> Reconciliation calls forth both a future that is uncontroversially common, but significantly also a certain past. This 'past' is one of conflict but, crucially, one where the conflict is seen as resolvable . . . In all these formulations reconciliation 'overdetermines' the past. It projects onto it the origin of a common future. But this is a future that will only be had if, and this is the *if* that reconciliation misses, the past lends itself to the overcoming of the conflict that divided it.[39]

Reconciliation, then, posits a particular future as well as a particular past; this past is not simply 'uncovered' but created. The resultant temporality posited by TRC processes also emphasises closure, temporal unity, and teleological significance, with the desired ending conditioning how the story unfolds.[40] Put another way, TRC narratives tend to 'embod[y] a liberal version of history as progress', exhibiting redemptive models where the past can always be recuperated in service of a better future.[41] One of the most widely cited critics of the South African TRC, Wole Soyinka, objected to what he viewed as the overwhelming emphasis on closure or catharsis.[42] The emphasis that TRCs placed on testifying in order to produce healing, in any case, encouraged participants to view the TRC as a mechanism towards achieving closure.

Many of the limitations of TRCs that commentators identify result from the imbrication of narrative with memory at each stage of the process, from witness statements and testimonies to the Commission's writing of the final report to be disseminated at the conclusion of the process. In order to try to understand, inasmuch as it is possible, 'what really happened', TRCs create an historical account. While TRCs place great emphasis on remembering and recounting, Hayden White among others reminds us that the production of history is 'as much about forgetting as it is about remembering'.[43] The South African TRC process attempted to address the limitations of trial court hearings – which do not present incentives for perpetrators to tell the truth, and tend to be

---

[39] Ibid., 2.
[40] Moon, *Narrating Political Reconciliation*, 59, 61.
[41] Shaw and Waldorf, 'Introduction: Localizing Transitional Justice', 3.
[42] McGonegal, *Imagining Justice: The Politics of Postcolonial Forgiveness and Reconciliation*, 34.
[43] White, *The Fiction of Narrative*, 323.

'harrowing' experiences for victims – by foregrounding victims' experiences.[44] Whereas trials 'consult victims only to illustrate the fact or scope of the defendants' guilt', and 'interrupt and truncate victim testimony' through cross examinations and objections, TRC public hearings invite testimony in a setting where the victims may speak without interruption.[45]

Even in this more open setting, the testimonies needed to be placed in particular narrative forms as a matter of expediency and interpretability. As the South African TRC report notes, the 'large volume of data required methodical and consistent treatment to ensure that each statement and amnesty application received a fair and equal evaluation'.[46] To gather victim statements, the South African TRC employed approximately 300 statement-takers.[47] Statements were taken over the course of two years, from the beginning of the Commission until December 1997. From the narrative testimonies, these statement-takers were charged with 'taxonimiz[ing] forty-eight distinct violation types' and 'three different categories of agent [victim, perpetrator, witness]'.[48] In actual practice, the statement-takers were overwhelmed by '"unstructured"' testimonies that 'relied more heavily on an individual interpretation which could not be captured by the data processing unit employed by the TRC, nor framed within the taxonomy of violations which structured agents simply into either "witnesses", "victims", or "perpetrators"'.[49] In the end,

---

[44] South Africa and Tutu, *Truth and Reconciliation Commission of South Africa Report*, 1:6.

[45] Minow, 'The Hope for Healing: What Can Truth Commissions Do?' 238. From January 1996 to December 1997, 'the Commission gathered and processed about 21,000 victims' statements'. Mack, *From Apartheid to Democracy*, 37. To manage this volume, the South African TRC 'selected those deponents who were representative of the demographic of the population of the region where the hearing was taking place and whose stories represented varied perspectives on the violence and the types of human rights violations that had occurred there'. In a sense, the patterns and types of abuse the TRC collected started to coalesce around representative or generic forms. In this way, *The Cry of Winnie Mandela* mirrors these representative victim statements, as Ndebele writes at the beginning of the novel's second part, in reference to the four waiting women characters: 'Some have names, others don't. They all come across to us like stories we've heard. Yes, there's something generic about them.' Ndebele, 39.

[46] South Africa and Tutu, *Truth and Reconciliation Commission of South Africa Report*, 1:158.

[47] Moon, *Narrating Political Reconciliation*, 82.

[48] South Africa and Tutu, *Truth and Reconciliation Commission of South Africa Report*, 1:80.

[49] Moon, *Narrating Political Reconciliation*, 82.

statements were taken through a 'highly structured questionnaire', which restricted an 'open and free narrative interpretation of the events'.⁵⁰

Through the identification of victims and perpetrators, TRCs create specific subject positions that participants inhabit, and provide an interpretative framework for understanding the relationships between individuals. The South African TRC report self-consciously acknowledged the power of these positions, and noted 'discomfort with the use of the word "victim"' for the way it may 'imply a negativity or passivity'.⁵¹ The term 'victim' was retained in contrast to the alternative 'survivor', however, because from the South African TRC's perspective 'the intention and action of the perpetrator . . . creates the condition of being a victim'. Mahmood Mamdani's oft-cited critiques of the South African TRC identify this practice as a major limitation; he argues that '[t]he TRC's version of truth was established through narrow lenses, crafted to reflect the experience of a tiny minority. This tiny minority included two groups, on the one hand perpetrators, being state-agents, and, on the other, victims, being political activists.'⁵²

While such subject positions can influence how participants view and recount their own stories, the limitations of the categories of victim and perpetrator are especially visible in the Sierra Leonean context, where the '"victim–perpetrator" dichotomy . . . fails to adequately confront the moral "gray zone" of civils wars such as Sierra Leone's'.⁵³ These narrative positions may constrain or even distort the lived experiences of participants in the armed conflict, particularly the experiences of child soldiers. As Sandra Rein reflects, the forced conscription of children into the Revolutionary United Front's army drew 'little, if any, distinction between civilians and combatants'.⁵⁴ These child soldiers' involvement in the conflict 'challenge easy distinctions between passivity and agency, or between innocence and culpability or complicity', pitting their suffering against 'the harms they have committed and their own maturation'.⁵⁵

During South Africa's TRC proceedings, gendered assumptions about victimhood additionally constrained the recognition of women's

---

⁵⁰ South Africa and Tutu, *Truth and Reconciliation Commission of South Africa Report*, 1:82.
⁵¹ Ibid., 1:59.
⁵² Mamdani, 'The Truth According to the TRC', 178.
⁵³ Shaw, 'Linking Justice with Reintegration? Ex-Combatants and the Sierra Leone Experiment', 114.
⁵⁴ Rein, 'Sierra Leone: Between the Prison-Houses of Nationalism and Transnationalism', 136.
⁵⁵ Moore, *Vulnerability and Security in Human Rights Literature and Visual Culture*, 31.

experiences of abuse under apartheid. H. Louise du Toit argues that the South African TRC 'entrenched a single-sex model of politics, i.e. one in which masculine agency and victimhood, as well as masculine biased concerns and vocabularies still pose as the universal'.[56] Specifically, she finds that 'rape was eclipsed by other forms of oppression and violation where men were the vast majority of victims', and this narrative frame relegated women to 'the road-sides of history'.[57] The language here is striking, resonating both with the Sierra Leonean TRC's language of producing 'roadmaps' for the nation's future, and with Ndebele's novel *The Cry of Winnie Mandela*, which explores the diversity of women's experiences of waiting during and after apartheid in South Africa, and concludes with the women embarking on the road together with Winnie. During the first year of the South African TRC's human rights violation hearings, it became increasingly clear that 'a gendered pattern of testimony' was occurring, wherein women testified largely as secondary rather than primary victims of abuse.[58]

To address this tendency and make women's testimonies more legible in the broader historical and national narrative, Beth Goldblatt and Sheila Meintjes recommended that the TRC 'reconsider the questionnaires used by statement takers . . . to elicit more details about women's experiences; not to probe too deeply for graphic details . . . and to offer closed hearings, staffed only by female commissioners.'[59] These recommendations paved the way for what the TRC called special Women's Hearings, which invited women to testify directly about the abuses they experienced under apartheid. The Women's Hearings in Johannesburg on 28 July 1997 opened with this explicit invitation from Thenjiwe Mtintso, the chairperson of the Commission on Gender Equality, for women '"to speak as actors, as active participants and direct survivors of the violation of human rights. Not as relatives, not as spouses, not as wives, but as themselves, those that directly suffered."'[60] These special hearings were designed to integrate the diversity of women's experiences into the South African TRC report and its larger historical narrative.

Narrative is clearly the *modus operandi* of TRC activities, but while narratives certainly shape TRC and criminal court proceedings alike – from the initial statements taken to the presentation of select testimonies

---

[56] Du Toit, 'Feminism and the Ethics of Reconciliation', 187.
[57] Ibid., 193.
[58] Mack, *From Apartheid to Democracy*, 38.
[59] Ibid., 40.
[60] Oboe, 'The TRC Women's Hearings as Performance and Protest in the New South Africa', 61.

to the public, to the final write up in report form – the role of narrative to facilitate reconciliation after conflict is much more ambivalent than advocates of TRCs tend to admit. Because TRCs aspire to achieve truth and closure through restorative justice proceedings, emphasising healing and truth over punishment, commentators have tended to focus on the advantages and disadvantages of TRC proceedings in contrast to the criminal court system, noting how the role of narrative differs in the context of transitional justice. Ndebele, for example, praised the South African TRC as '"a living example of people reinventing themselves through narrative"'.[61] In this view, the South African TRC became a transformative site for the restoration of dignity and personhood, foregrounding the power of narrative in the performance and formation of identity. Narratives, as part of a greater context of reconciliation and forgiveness, 'are places where the imperative to remember has to do with the construction of a different future', and have the potential to 'recollect the past in an attempt to bring about that which has *not yet* come'.[62] In the following sections, we will see how novels provide counterpoints to some of the TRC shortcomings outlined above – not to denigrate the important and essential work of TRCs, but rather to suggest how cultural art forms such as fiction might supplement and extend the discussion. I contend that official, state-sanctioned TRC processes and reports are not the only locations where the tensions between past and future are negotiated in a transitional present, but rather that fictional texts, such as novels, also continue such an exploration with an eye towards the 'not yet'.

Fictional Responses, Counterpoints and Supplements to TRCs

One of the most significant ways that *The Cry of Winnie Mandela* and *Radiance of Tomorrow* contrast with the official TRCs of South Africa and Sierra Leone respectively is through the expansion of the period under consideration, beyond the temporal parameters to which Commissions adhered. While the South African TRC was restricted to the years between 1960 and 1994, Ndebele's novel introduces four waiting women whose experiences establish a pattern of waiting that

---

[61] Barnard, *Apartheid and Beyond: South African Writers and the Politics of Place*, 658.
[62] McGonegal, *Imagining Justice: The Politics of Postcolonial Forgiveness and Reconciliation*, 15.

predates and extends past the TRC's mandated time frame. In the first section, 'Penelope's Descendants', the narrator explains, 'For over a century, millions of [Penelope's] South African descendants have unremittingly been put to the test by powerful social forces that caused their men to wander away from home for prolonged periods of time', starting with 'massive male labour migration to the mines and factories of South Africa'.[63] The pattern continues with men forced into exile after the banning of political organisations in 1960, as well as the 'internal exile of detention' of those who stayed behind.[64] The experiences of waiting and absence became 'the dominant African experience of home',[65] but as *The Cry of Winnie Mandela* demonstrates, waiting occupies a particularly gendered temporality with a long history in South Africa. This history was truncated by the Commission's 'temporal ambit', which 'precluded adequate assessment of the *longue durée* of certain forms of violence'.[66] When Ndebele's novel concludes in the post-apartheid present, then, with the women no longer waiting but moving together along the road to Durban, the temporality of waiting the women have reconciled with is rooted not only in the apartheid past, but also in the more distant colonial past.

Rather than extensively detail the pre-1991 past, Beah's *Radiance of Tomorrow* instead focuses exclusively on the post-TRC present. In this way, Beah's novel looks past the temporal parameters of the Sierra Leonean TRC, which was limited to 1991–9, and considers how reconciliation is an ongoing, local process whose methods might take forms other than those embodied by the TRC. While the TRC focused on reconciling combatants and non-combatants from various factions – the RUF, the Sierra Leone Army (SLA), the Armed Forces Revolutionary Council (AFRC) among other local militias – Beah's novel shows that the fragile national unity is threatened in the present by multinational mining interests and their exploitative industrial development. The first half of *Radiance of Tomorrow* depicts members of the village Imperi returning after the civil war, and their labours to reconcile with the traumatic past. The second half of the novel focuses more narrowly on the teacher Bockarie, whose struggles to provide for his family are first stymied by corruption at the elementary school, and later by the mining company.

---

[63] Ndebele, *The Cry of Winnie Mandela: A Novel*, 5–6.
[64] Ibid., 6–7.
[65] Napolitano, 'Restoring Narrative, Narrating Justice: Njabulo Ndebele's The Cry of Winnie Mandela and the Complication of Truth and Reconciliation', 337.
[66] Ross, 'An Acknowledged Failure: Women, Voice, Violence, and the South African Truth and Reconciliation Commission', 74.

The company not only requires dangerous, life-threatening work, but also conceals the deaths of its workers, pollutes the local water supply and refuses to punish sexual violence perpetrated by the white management class on the local women. The mutilations, rapes, concealments of truth, and destruction of communities that characterised the civil war are eerily restaged in the Sierra Leonean present through interactions with the exploitative mining company. The difficulty with reconciling and forgiving is compounded by the ways that the trauma recurs and repeats in a neocolonial present.

If the TRC looms large in *The Cry of Winnie Mandela*, incorporating Mandela's testimony in the second half of the text through intertextual references and explicit excerpts, the TRC as a formal structure is conspicuously absent from *Radiance of Tomorrow*. Scholars have addressed the role of the TRC in Ndebele's novel in various ways, ranging from a 'marginal yet activating presence'[67] to 'extend[ing] the most valuable aspect of the work of the South African Truth and Reconciliation Commission – the foregrounding of personal narrative and victim testimony'.[68] Joe Napolitano even observes that Ndebele's novel is structured like a truth report.[69] While Mandela testified as part of the South African TRC proceedings, none of the other waiting women in the novel would have, as the Commission would not have identified them as either victims or perpetrators of gross violations of human rights. Similarly, none of the characters in *Radiance of Tomorrow* is depicted telling her story to Commissioners. Instead, each novel demonstrates a commitment to the personal narratives of ordinary, everyday experiences of loss as well as reconciliation potentially missing from official TRC reports and histories.

In addition to extending the temporal periods beyond those delimited by TRCs, the novels implicitly interact with another critique of TRCs – one especially levelled at the South African TRC – that the official history derived from the final report elides the experiences of many who suffered. The insistence on 'everyday' experiences has a particular resonance for Ndebele, whose essays advocate the rediscovery of the ordinary in contrast to the prevalence of the spectacular in protest literature. In 'The Rediscovery of the Ordinary: Some New Writings in South Africa', Ndebele argues that protest literature focused on the 'spectacular', and was written by 'the powerless identifying the key factor responsible for

---

[67] Barnard, 'Rewriting the Nation', 659.
[68] Napolitano, 'Restoring Narrative, Narrating Justice: Njabulo Ndebele's The Cry of Winnie Mandela and the Complication of Truth and Reconciliation', 332.
[69] Ibid., 356.

their powerlessness'.[70] In contrast, the literature of the ordinary reminds readers 'that the problems of the South African social formation are complex and all-embracing', and 'that the ordinary daily lives of people should be the direct focus of political interest because they constitute the *very content* of the struggle, for the struggle involves people not abstractions'.[71] In David Medalie's view, *The Cry of Winnie Mandela* takes up this challenge in the post-apartheid era by 'cast[ing] the oppressed as "makers of the future"'.[72] Thus, while we might situate Ndebele's call for literature of the ordinary as a response to the proliferation of protest literature under apartheid, this same insistence on the ordinary proves useful even after apartheid, in post-transition times.

While the South African TRC proceedings certainly included the experiences of 'everyday' people, along with testimonies by prominent figures like Eugene de Kock and Winnie Mandela, the TRC's focus on gross violations necessarily excluded the experiences of those who suffered the ordinary humiliations and abuses endemic to life under apartheid. The South African TRC 'resolved that its mandate was to give attention to human rights violations as specific acts' rather than the general laws and policies of the apartheid government, 'however morally offensive these may have been'.[73] However, there were also good reasons, beyond the mandate's language, to justify this scope. As Albie Sachs points out, 'these individual cases of torture, assassination and violence . . . were hidden, secret and denied', as well as 'criminal even in the terms of the laws of apartheid' at the time.[74] In a sense, the ordinary experiences of apartheid were not hidden, but rather were well known; the South African TRC did not need to uncover them in the same way, yet these ordinary experiences are essential in assessing the magnitude and scope of apartheid abuses. In establishing a distinction between the spectacular and the ordinary, as well as between the South African TRC and novels like Ndebele's, my aim is not to condemn the TRC's limited purview, but rather to demonstrate that fiction here is able to expand upon the TRC's scope to consider the everyday lives precluded from the official TRC report.

---

[70] Ndebele, in *South African Literature and Culture: Rediscovery of the Ordinary*, 49.

[71] Ibid., 57.

[72] Medalie, 'The Cry of Winnie Mandela: Njabulo Ndebele's Post-Apartheid Novel', 54.

[73] South Africa and Tutu, *Truth and Reconciliation Commission of South Africa Report*, 1:64.

[74] Sachs, 'His Name Was Henry', 95.

The Cry of Winnie Mandela gives voice to four ordinary women whose individual stories emphasise the waiting that collectively structured their lives under apartheid and, in some cases, after apartheid as well. To recall the discussion of Vincent Crapanzano's *Waiting: The Whites of South Africa* in Chapter 2 in relation to *July's People*, the temporality of waiting captures the prevailing sense of the present for South African whites in the 1980s as they anxiously considered their futures in the midst of turbulent times. Derek Hook characterises this sensation from the vantage of his post-apartheid present, noting that this 'state of anxious and fearful expectancy' was 'not merely waiting, but a time of *awaiting judgement*'.[75] In the context of post-apartheid South Africa, the period in which Ndebele wrote and published *The Cry of Winnie Mandela*, this question of judgement – as least in a legal sense – had already been handled or indefinitely postponed through the hearings and amnesty proceedings of the South African TRC. Still, the waiting remains and permeates post-apartheid South African literature.

In the last twenty years, scholars of South African literature in particular have noted how waiting proliferates throughout post-apartheid fiction. Rita Barnard finds that 'the term "post-transition"', for some scholars, 'describe[s] the more disenchanted writing that has emerged in the new millennium'.[76] This disenchantment, however, is markedly different from the 'disillusionment' described in this book's Chapter 4, which tended to emphasise stasis over other temporal sensations. Hook notes that 'the temporality of South Africa's (post) apartheid period of political transition is unique', marked by 'accelerations and apparent "slow-downs" and reversals of history [that] co-exist alongside anxious periods of stasis, suspension and retroaction'.[77] While for Hook waiting may not be the dominant temporal mode that distinguishes post-apartheid temporality, it is nevertheless present as a sense of suspension that interacts with competing impressions of accelerated and backwards movements. Other scholars of South African post-apartheid fiction, such as Andrew van der Vlies, mark a lingering disappointment in South Africa that is 'a structuring affect' as well as 'a temporal condition'.[78] Similarly, Katherine Hallemeier's essay on Gordimer's 'Amnesty' and Ndebele's *The Cry of Winnie Mandela* highlights the temporality of waiting threaded throughout each text in anticipation of apartheid's end, though in her view, these 'anticipatory narratives generate the time

---

[75] Hook, 'Indefinite Delay: On (Post)Apartheid Temporality', 64.
[76] Barnard, 'Rewriting the Nation', 652.
[77] Hook, 'Petrified Life', 18.
[78] Van der Vlies, *Present Imperfect: Contemporary South African Writing*, viii.

of waiting wherein the present is experienced as stasis, as simply marking time'.[79]

My reading of waiting in Ndebele's novel suggests that the waiting that persists for the characters exhibits a variety of textures and contours such that waiting is not simply, or only, reducible to stasis. In *Present Imperfect: Contemporary South African Writing*, van der Vlies describes the aesthetics of waiting in post-apartheid South African fiction through suspension, arrested development or waithood, boredom and stasis. While he does not discuss Ndebele's *The Cry of Winnie Mandela*, he does consider other authors I have addressed throughout this book, including J. M. Coetzee and Nadine Gordimer. Although he notes that waiting appears throughout both authors' apartheid-era fictions, his focus is decidedly on the waiting that continues to pervade their post-apartheid texts. With reference to *No Time Like the Present*, Gordimer's final novel published in 2012, van der Vlies argues that the characters 'attempt to imagine another temporality in which such stasis might be overcome'.[80] My argument in this chapter, however, is that we ought not to take for granted that waiting, as it figures in both Ndebele's and Beah's novels, must be overcome in every instance. In post-apartheid fiction, waiting may not always (or only) appear as an obstacle, but may also function as an instrument.

Ndebele's women address waiting-as-obstacle in the first part of the novel, when each woman recounts the circumstances of her waiting. 'Mannete Mofolo, the first waiting woman, waits for her husband Lejone to return from the mines. Unbeknownst to her, the reason he never returns is because he has started another family. 'Mannete breaks 'Penelope's law' by refusing to wait at home, and searches for her husband. Her story resists closure, not because the narrator discloses what happened to her husband Lejone, about which 'Mannete remains ignorant, but because he lingers in her thoughts as an absent presence, even as he represses memories of her. While the narrative initially insists on her name, repeating it several times in the first few pages, by the end of her first section her name is replaced by 'she'. The final occurrence of her name in this first section occurs on page 13, when 'Mannete begins to wait anxiously after her husband's infrequent visits home stop altogether. Even as she 'begins to contemplate the meaning of a future definitively without her husband', the narrative suggests that the indefinite waiting caused by her husband's unexplained absence is self-effacing.[81]

---

[79] Hallemeier, 'Still Waiting? Writing Futurity after Apartheid', 80.
[80] Van der Vlies, *Present Imperfect: Contemporary South African Writing*, 6.
[81] Ndebele, *The Cry of Winnie Mandela: A Novel*, 15.

Her section concludes with the sensation of being unmoored in time, forgetting everything except 'the floating feeling, the medium of forgetfulness and shelter'.[82]

In the second and fourth sections of part one, Ndebele withholds the names of the descendants until later in the novel. Like 'Mannete, the fourth descendant, Marara Joyce Baloyi, confronts waiting without end when her unfaithful husband dies prematurely. While she no longer loves her husband at the time of his death, she cannot face the 'truth' and instead pays for an expensive burial. She was faithful to her husband, but notes that society expects infidelity from a waiting woman, and that '[i]f they cannot find the proof, they'll invent it'.[83] The second descendent, Deliswe Dulcie S'khosana, waits over a decade for her husband to return from his medical studies abroad. Deli's infidelity results in a child, and her husband immediately divorces her upon his return. As Deli tells it, only when she becomes pregnant and the possibility of departing to join her husband vanishes, does she begin to wait.

The third descendant, Mamello 'Patience' Molete, exemplifies the self-destructive consequences of identifying oneself wholly with the temporality of waiting. Mamello waited for her husband while he was in exile for ten years, and again when he was sentenced to fifteen years on Robben Island, but after he is released he refuses to return to her. All her life, she had considered chaste waiting to be a virtue, but her endurance goes unrewarded. Instead, her husband leaves her for a white woman, and she succumbs to a series of mental breakdowns. Mamello writes to him of her personal pain, but he responds by re-contextualising their discussion in terms of the non-racial language of post-apartheid South Africa, lecturing her on the use of the word 'coloured'.[84] While Mamello desires discussion on the personal and individual level, her husband insists on the public, national scale in his rebukes. Her section ends on a plaintive cry that the rest of the novel takes up: 'I want to reclaim my

---

[82] Ibid.,16.
[83] Ibid., 38.
[84] See Ian Goldin's 'The Reconstitution of Coloured Identity in the Western Cape' for a brief history of term in South Africa. Goldin notes that while 'coloured' was originally applied to all non-European peoples in the Western Cape in the nineteenth century, by 1904 the census 'distinguished between three "clearly defined race groups in this colony: White, Bantu, and Coloured"'. The Nationalist Party reconstituted the category 'Coloured' in the twentieth century in order to further fragment South African society and limit challenges to the state. Though used as a racial category, the grouping is multiracial in composition, and is a category many in South Africa reject. Goldin, 158, 178.

right to be wounded without my pain having to turn me into an example of woman as victim.'[85]

I have described each of the four descendants at length because they illustrate a range of different experiences of waiting during apartheid, and in my view their stories also evoke the South African TRC's project, as well as the critiques outlined earlier in this chapter. Taken together, the four descendants' stories introduce themes of closure, memory, forgetfulness, truth and victimhood explored above in my discussion of TRCs and their limitations. I will now take these concepts, so central to TRC processes and their criticisms, and identify the distinctive ways that both *The Cry of Winnie Mandela* and *Radiance of Tomorrow* address them, before turning to the texts' unique contribution of 'strategic waiting' to negotiate the temporalities of memory and reconciliation in the following section.

Through Winnie's sections in *The Cry of Winnie Mandela*, Ndebele explores the relationship between the temporality of reconciliation and the closure it posits, and the role of the South African TRC in shaping narratives of cause and effect as well as subject positions of victims and perpetrators. The connections between Winnie and reconciliation are drawn explicitly; both Winnie and the other women reference Mandela's testimony to the South African TRC. When Mandela took the witness stand at the South African TRC hearings, she famously refused to answer questions or acknowledge her involvement in a series of abuses. The report instead notes that Mandela thwarted attempts to uncover the truth, and her 'denials were complemented by a series of allegations and insinuations about individuals and structures that provided information about her role and involvement in the events of this period. She refused to take responsibility for any wrongdoing.'[86] The Commission was particularly interested in events between 1986 and 1991, during which time the Mandela United Football Club (MUFC) – a group of youths who functioned as Mandela's bodyguards – were accused of assaults, kidnappings, murder and attempted murder.[87] In 1997, the TRC subpoenaed Mandela to testify related to allegations of gross violations of human rights during the struggle, including her role in the kidnapping and murder of Stompie Seipei, who the MUFC alleged was a police informer. While the Commission found her 'politically and morally accountable for the gross violations of human rights committed by the MUFC', it

---

[85] Ndebele, *The Cry of Winnie Mandela: A Novel*, 35.
[86] South Africa and Tutu, *Truth and Reconciliation Commission of South Africa Report*, 2:578.
[87] Ibid., 2:556.

conceded that the Commission was nevertheless 'unable to arrive at a satisfactory conclusion as to what went wrong'.[88]

Ndebele's fictional exploration of Mandela's intractability focuses on this refusal to participate in reconciliation practices, and similarly resists the demanded closure as well. Mamello is the first to broach the topic of Mandela's TRC testimony. She writes to Winnie in a letter, 'Under [Tutu's] pressure, you expressed regret. But it did not really follow from the entire logic of your testimony', and she speculates that this refusal 'was the victory of image and posture, which had become fused into a compelling reality of their own'.[89] She notes that while Mandela escaped technical, criminal guilt, 'the cloud of moral doubt will hang over you without end'.[90] Mamello turns to the TRC report itself to mark Mandela's moral accountability, and Ndebele inserts some of the Commission's findings verbatim into the text. Mamello's letter to Winnie ends in the same place as the TRC: in the gap between 'fact and legal indeterminacy'.[91]

In the next section, Marara links Mandela and the TRC through a shared commitment to ambiguity and complexity. She asserts that when anti-apartheid forces 'gave up the AK-47 for negotiation, we opted for intimacy . . . We opted for complexity, ambiguity, nuance, and emergent order.'[92] Unlike Mamello, Marara is more open to the kind of contradiction Mandela represents – a representation that she views as compatible with the TRC itself. She posits,

> The Truth and Reconciliation Commission was really not about truth, but about the revelation of deliberately hidden facts so that this revelation might lead to new interpretations of our social realities and new knowledge in the public domain . . . It was not so much about judgement, but about the process of formulating judgement.[93]

For Marara, what matters more than determining Mandela's culpability, the logic might continue, is the way we formulate our judgements about her.

Ndebele's Winnie, when she does enter the text, gives fewer answers of the sort that the South African TRC sought, but does make suggestive observations with regard to the closure and truth demanded of her.

---

[88] Ibid., 1:581–2.
[89] Ndebele, *The Cry of Winnie Mandela: A Novel*, 74.
[90] Ibid., 75.
[91] Ibid., 77.
[92] Ibid., 85.
[93] Ibid., 86.

She reflects on order, and how city street 'grids of order' seem to be 'built that way for us waiting women to go through them . . . searching for our husbands'.[94] Order, she asserts, 'is one of the central features of whiteness'. As a figure of disorder and disruption, Winnie characterises her opposition to order as part of her struggle against apartheid. She hypothesises that Boer policemen understood this powerful imposition of apartheid order, and they enacted 'the disruptiveness of disorder on a mind structured into order' as a method 'to make you desire more order'.[95] Against these laws, Winnie staked out her own law: 'embrace disruption, and then rage against order instead of longing for it'. At this point, Winnie interrupts her own story, and announces that she too will address Mandela; the narrative then takes the form of the second-person as Winnie addresses herself and navigates memories, spanning from Nelson's imprisonment, to her own torture, and later his release. This experience allows Winnie to 'reclaim myself' before she discusses the TRC hearings.[96] Here, ambiguity and the rejection of reconciliation as closure manifest again. She notes that legal proceedings, even quasi-judicial proceedings like the TRC, result in a 'perilous gap between technical process and lived life'.[97] 'Would I really be expected', she asks, 'in that situation to tell the story of my life, and charm you into reconciliation?' Her section concludes with a refusal to 'be an instrument for validating the politics of reconciliation. For me, reconciliation demands my annihilation. No. *You*, all of you, have to reconcile not with me, but with the meaning of me.'[98] Here, Winnie's refusal to reconcile according to the TRC's terms demands that we – readers, as well as the Commission and its audience – wait indefinitely for an answer.

Literary scholarship has made much of Winnie's steadfast opposition to reconciliation here in the narrative. Her character embodies the anxieties and misgivings about the South African TRC project; while the possibility of amnesty could compel some to testify, it could not, in all cases, elicit the truth. Ndebele looks to Mandela specifically, Joe Napolitano suggests, because she 'represents the possible failure of both

---

[94] Ibid., 106.
[95] Ibid., 107.
[96] Ibid., 130. In his introduction to the revised 2013 edition of *The Cry of Winnie Mandela*, Ndebele explains that this narrative strategy had an additional purpose as 'a second-order distancing effect': 'I could get closer to an imagined essence as I got further and further away from the reality of the woman.' 'Introduction: Contemplating Winnie Mandela', xiv.
[97] Ndebele, *The Cry of Winnie Mandela: A Novel*, 135.
[98] Ibid., 137.

the new South Africa in general and the process begun by the Truth and Reconciliation Commission (TRC) in particular'.[99] While acknowledging that Mandela's refusal to explain in detail the circumstances and events under investigation limits the recovery of the past, Ndebele 'attempts to "exhume" this chapter of the South African past in a way that will reaffirm and reinforce the continuing healing process begun by the TRC'.[100] In this way, the narrative exhibits the paradox of fiction: that the novel 'reveals far more truth than either Winnie Mandela's trial or TRC testimony ever could'.[101] In Napolitano's view, one of the ways that the fictional text builds on the South African TRC's legacy is to refuse to fetishise the closure that would 'undermine the achievements of the TRC'.[102] Indeed, while the characters are on the road, traveling together at the conclusion of the novel, the story ends before they arrive at their destination. Penelope, on her own journey of reconciliation with women for the 'burden of unconditional fidelity [she] placed on their shoulders', is picked up as a hitchhiker but she quickly leaves the women in order to continue 'her timeless journey of consciousness'.[103] Here, Ndebele powerfully suggests that while the novel's dramatic monologues allow the women to reconcile with themselves, reconciling with others is a continual process.

Whereas each of Ndebele's waiting women, in contrast to the fragmented narratives produced by the South African TRC statement-takers' protocol and questionnaires, tells her story in full, Beah's characters choose to share what seems necessary in the moment, deciding at other times to let the past go unspoken in the service of forging new relationships. In this way, Beah's novel restructures the relationship between reconciliation, disclosure, and closure in a different form from Ndebele's novel and the Sierra Leonean TRC process. The novel opens with one of the elders, Mama Kadie, returning to the village of Imperi after years of civil war. As characters elect to remember parts of their past, the omniscient narrator slowly recounts the destruction of the village and the violence inflicted on its inhabitants. Each memory is tentative; Mama Kadie 'managed to conjure the memory of what the town had looked like the day before she began running away for her life', but the reverie stops abruptly as soon as she arrives at the moment when 'gunshots rang through the town

---

[99] Napolitano, 'Restoring Narrative, Narrating Justice: Njabulo Ndebele's The Cry of Winnie Mandela and the Complication of Truth and Reconciliation', 346.
[100] Ibid., 355.
[101] Ibid., 356.
[102] Ibid., 357.
[103] Ndebele, *The Cry of Winnie Mandela: A Novel*, 145–6.

and chaos ensued'.[104] Like TRCs more generally, *Radiance of Tomorrow* underscores the restorative role of storytelling; here, storytelling is also a method of approaching painful truths less directly. In an author's note at the beginning of the novel, Beah remarks that the oral tradition of storytelling in Sierra Leone taught him 'that stories are the most potent way of seeing anything we encounter in our lives, and how we can deal with living'.[105] The phrase 'deal with living' points to the struggle to come to terms with the hardships and memories following violence and trauma, a struggle the novel's characters exemplify.

Within *Radiance of Tomorrow*, oral storytelling becomes an intimate method of processing the past, as Mama Kadie adjusts old stories for the present. All gather at the town's square to hear Mama Kadie's story about the water spirits, who are blamed when a young man does not heed warnings about the treacherous river and drowns. A boy interrupts the story to ask whether the hunter seeking revenge used arrows or guns, pointing out, '"He could do more with guns and grenades"', while his 'eyes [were] redder than the flames and memories of the recent past in his imagination'.[106] Without a pause, Mama Kadie sits closer to the boy and explains 'how in those days there were no guns or grenades . . . and how the act of one person whose heart had been quickly consumed by negative fire had caused the water spirits to hide from humans forever'. The narrative contextualises the moment for the reader in terms of what it accomplishes for former child soldiers seeking to be reconciled with their communities:

> It was an important point that needed to be made about the nature of distrust and how it can spiral into violence. It was also a story to reassure some of the younger ones that their innocence was not to be feared any longer, as it had come to be during the time of war.[107]

The epigraph that frames the novel is also repeated at the text's conclusion, and emphasises not only the regenerative power of stories, but also the continuities storytelling can forge between women. The italicised text reads, '*It is the end, or maybe the beginning, of another story. / Every story begins and ends with a woman, a mother,/ a grandmother, a girl, a child./ Every story is a birth.*'[108] In returning the reader to the novel's opening and linking endings and beginnings, the text resists the

---

[104] Beah, *Radiance of Tomorrow*, 6.
[105] Ibid., vii.
[106] Ibid., 48.
[107] Ibid., 49.
[108] Ibid., 3, 240.

closure we might expect from an otherwise chronologically ordered narrative. By linking women closely with storytelling, the novel shares with *The Cry of Winnie Mandela* an interest in creating community through shared and gendered experiences of storytelling. Though Ndebele's novel eschews dates, the women's experiences in *Radiance of Tomorrow* situate them roughly in the same generation of waiting women living under and through apartheid in *The Cry of Winnie Mandela*. In *Radiance of Tomorrow*, we see Mama Kadie sharing stories for the whole community, but also transferring stories directly and intimately inter-generationally to Ouma,[109] Bockerie's daughter.

In both novels, then, waiting is essential for the transmission of stories. Ndebele's women are linked through their experiences of waiting, but by unmooring the women in time during their monologues and apostrophes to Winnie Mandela, the narrative re-enacts a suspension of time that recalls the temporal experience of waiting as well. In *Radiance of Tomorrow*, Mama Kadie informs Ouma,

> 'It isn't about knowing the most stories, child. It is about carrying the ones that are most important and passing them along . . . You have to be *patient*, though, for the stories can only remain in the mind and veins of a *patient* person.'[110]

Patience here registers an orientation in time that is open, deliberate and unrushed. Ouma returns to Mama Kadie periodically for more stories, and through her patience is able to retain and process each story in turn. Ouma understands the importance of timing and storytelling; as Mama Kadie demonstrates, when told at the right time, the right story can lend powerful insight even in new contexts. To achieve the desired effect, reconciling old stories and new contexts, sometimes one has to wait.

'Strategic Waiting' and the Temporalities of Reconciliation

Thus far, I have discussed the two novels and the ways they interact with the TRC hearings and reports' formulations of closure, storytelling

---

[109] I am grateful to Stephen Clingman for pointing out that this word means 'grandmother' in Afrikaans and Dutch; I have been unable to determine any Mende lineage for the word; it remains, then, an interesting and provocative link between *The Cry of Winnie Mandela*'s South African context and *Radiance of Tomorrow*'s Sierra Leonean one.

[110] Beah, *Radiance of Tomorrow*, 35, emphasis mine.

and narrative. I now turn to the novels to identify terms and concepts central to their explorations of time and reconciliation, but that are not obviously central to the reconciliation process structured by TRCs in South Africa and Sierra Leone. In rebuilding the social fabric, both texts exhibit 'strategic waiting', but Ndebele's novel additionally explores waiting in opposition to victimhood. Beah's novel, on the other hand, establishes the relationship between waiting and silence, where declining to speak affords one additional time to process even as it compels others to wait indefinitely.

For many of the women in *The Cry of Winnie Mandela*, waiting appears to foster further pain and uncertainty, and none of their experiences as recounted in the novel's first half seems to suggest waiting as a source of empowerment. Yet it is the shared experience of waiting that forms the basis for their incorporation first into an *ibandla* (a gathering) of women, and second into the larger narrative of South Africa. The novel opens with 'the blurb of an imaginary book about a South African woman during the long years of apartheid', and asserts, '*Departure, waiting, and return: they define her experience of the past, present and future.*'[111] While Crapanzano's study on waiting and South Africans in the 1980s focused almost exclusively on the experiences of whites, Ndebele here makes the case for waiting to be central, albeit in different forms, to the experiences of black South African women as well.

The state of waiting, as well as the women's reflections on it, facilitates a transformation of their senses of time, space, and agency that resists reduction to passivity. Even as 'Mannete resigns herself to indefinite waiting for her husband's return from the mines, she 'contemplate[s] the meaning of a future definitively without her husband', as well as the 'notion of independence' that 'push[es] her towards independent decision-making'.[112] In a similar vein, waiting and its tribulations force Deli to act. At first, 'the hope of departing one day' is 'a way of managing the state of waiting'.[113] Hopeful anticipation quickly turns to dread after she becomes pregnant with another man's child, which forces her to confront 'the reality of her situation' that she would never depart to join her husband.[114] Nevertheless, she realises now that there is '[n]o more time to waste. She acts fast' and opens a shop to meet her family's basic needs.[115] Importantly, this time of waiting is not a time of

---

[111] Ndebele, *The Cry of Winnie Mandela: A Novel*, 1.
[112] Ibid., 15.
[113] Ibid., 17.
[114] Ibid., 22.
[115] Ibid., 19.

idleness, or dead time. Despite the circumstances of her husband's absence, which pit his mobility against her immobility as she stays behind, Deli demonstrates that her waiting is not her sole occupation, and neither is 'Mannete wholly limited by her waiting. As much as the novel reflects a gendered history of labour, exile, detention, and jail in South Africa, Deli's swelling belly subtly suggests that this gendered history's assumptions – that waiting is all women do, that waiting is unproductive time – are misplaced.

Winnie's section, as a response to the women who have addressed her in order to work through what Deli calls the 'minefield of ambiguities' that is the life of waiting,[116] embodies the contradictions and complexities of waiting in a way that makes space for all of the women's myriad experiences to coexist. Together, they are, as Dorothy Driver argues, 'more than simply waiting women' and while 'the novel seems to retain some difference between herself and the other women, [Winnie] finally occupies – as they all do – an intersection of order and disorder, as indeed of waiting and not waiting'.[117] Winnie's relationship with other waiting women, even as she waits for Nelson to be released from prison, is complicated. She admits, 'From time to time I created more of them by taking their men' and claims, 'They had nothing for me.'[118] This assertion is belied by the reconciliation with herself that is enacted within the text through the women's evocation of, and addresses to, Winnie. While embracing her own status as a symbol of the waiting woman, Winnie nevertheless proclaims, 'Winnie does not wait. She goes and gets what she wants.'[119] Waiting, here, is a double bind; while she can leverage the image of the waiting woman to empower herself in the public domain, she finds that waiting also 'empties out your life'.[120]

Throughout the novel, as Driver observes, 'the women's two states – of waiting and not waiting – are simultaneously held in place, despite the overall shift in focus from waiting to travelling'.[121] To recall the discussion of the gendered construction of waiting in the previous chapter, this move undoes the association of waiting with immobility, as well as with static passivity. Waiting, and reflections on the lived experiences

---

[116] Ibid., 51.
[117] Driver, '"On these premises I am the government': Njabulo Ndebele's The Cry of Winnie Mandela and the Reconstructions of Gender and Nation', 8.
[118] Ndebele, *The Cry of Winnie Mandela: A Novel*, 125.
[119] Ibid., 105.
[120] Ibid., 106.
[121] Driver, '"On these premises I am the government": Njabulo Ndebele's The Cry of Winnie Mandela and the Reconstructions of Gender and Nation', 14.

of waiting, can be a transformative temporal modality that forces her to confront her anticipations of what the future will be, and the values that underpin these expectations. Waiting, in other words, encourages an opening-up of experience, giving temporal experience more time, volume and texture. Their shared experiences of waiting – waiting that they experienced in the past as well as in the unspecified present moment of the text – suggest that 'the women's waiting may come to mean something more than the moribund condition of victimhood, that the power of agency may not be lost after all'.[122] Each of the women is better able to identify the oppressive dimensions of waiting by the novel's end, yet their shared experiences suggest that 'waiting', when strategically and consciously inhabited, can also empower and build community.

In his 2001 essay 'South Africans in Search of Common Values', Ndebele argues that time is an essential dimension to formulating community. He observes, 'Missing in our social calendar are the symbols necessary for expressing a vital sense of community life as South Africans', and then suggests that the 'answers might lie in the cycles of daily life in our communities'.[123] In addition to imposing a divided sense of space, apartheid also created an abbreviated sense of time:

> The calendar of life in a typical township in the worst days of apartheid was all too short. It was a 24-hour calendar. Designed to obliterate any sense of history beyond yesterday, any sense of the future beyond tomorrow. The township was little more than a dormitory, a place of limited social growth.[124]

Ndebele's characters in *The Cry of Winnie Mandela*, published two years after this essay, identify waiting as a facet of apartheid temporality that also worked to truncate the future; as Deli describes, hope and uncertainty produce the monotony of days that 'begin and end without a definitive future . . . Waiting. Not waiting. But waiting.'[125] However, I contend that the novel is also an imaginary exploration of what might make South Africans gravitate towards a collective. Turning to the mundane, everyday experiences of waiting, Ndebele demonstrates that the 'strategic waiting' inhabited by the waiting women as they recount their diverse experiences may shape their sense of community, even after they exit the temporality of waiting at the novel's conclusion. This is not to

---

[122] Medalie, 'The Cry of Winnie Mandela: Njabulo Ndebele's Post-Apartheid Novel', 62.
[123] Ndebele, 'South Africans in Search of Common Values', 75, 77.
[124] Ibid., 77.
[125] Ndebele, *The Cry of Winnie Mandela: A Novel*, 17.

elevate waiting as ideal state of being, because the characters' pain, anxiety, and loss speak as much to the detrimental effects of waiting.

Yet these experiences of waiting, which would not be incorporated otherwise in the TRC narratives of life under apartheid, are in *The Cry of Winnie Mandela* essential to theorising reconciliation. This insistence on the centrality of waiting, in all its uncertainty, dread, anticipation and expectation, offers an explanation as to why Ndebele's Winnie places herself in opposition to the form of reconciliation as outlined by the South African TRC. To return to the temporality of reconciliation described by Christodoulidis and Veitch above, reconciliation '"overdetermines" the past' by 'project[ing] onto it the origin of a common future'. In Winnie's view, her refusal to 'validat[e] the politics of reconciliation' is a 'defense of the future'.[126] To understand how this might work, it is essential to read further in the paragraph, where Winnie explains, 'For my meaning is the endless human search for the right thing to do.' This language contrasts significantly with Mandela's statement to the TRC hearings, where she admitted that '"things had gone horribly wrong"'.[127] Unlike the temporality of reconciliation, which projects onto the past the seeds of later reconciliation, Winnie resists the temporality of inevitability. Rather than 'proclaim a truce between old lives', she emphasises a 'distrust of reconciliation' and a commitment to continue to wrestle with the past and its meaning in the present and for a future yet to come.

Reconciliation threatens to erase retroactively the coexisting opposites Winnie embodies – she lists solutions and mistakes, beauty and ugliness, hell and heaven, honour and humiliation, to which I add right and wrong – in service of a common, collective future. Citing Christodoulidis, Andrew Schaap writes that 'political reconciliation refers to a future anterior, an imagined "not yet" that is "brought into the present to become constitutive of the experience of the present"'.[128] In creating this narrative, the extraneous elements that might impede the realisation of this future, or at the very least appear irrelevant, risk being omitted. Whereas the South African TRC's theory of reconciliation

---

[126] 137.

[127] South Africa and Tutu, *Truth and Reconciliation Commission of South Africa Report*, 2:578. The distinction between right and wrong in the context of the struggle against apartheid continued to be debated by the TRC. Combatants in the struggle objected that they need not seek amnesty because theirs was a 'just war'. At the very least, the ANC argued, 'abuses committed by its members could not be equated with those of the apartheid state'. Campbell, 'The Truth and Reconciliation Commission (TRC): Human Rights and State Transitions – The South Africa Model', 42.

[128] Schaap, 'The Time of Reconciliation and the Space of Politics', 15.

involved 'constructing victims that it can then proceed to heal, Ndebele's novel constructs subjects who want to redefine their past experience and escape the confines of victimization'.[129] In this way, Ndebele's Winnie redefines the past and victimhood at odds with the South African TRC, as well as the TRC's temporality of reconciliation.

The Cry of Winnie Mandela and *Radiance of Tomorrow* share departure, waiting and return as framing temporal experiences, and in both texts, they are not easily pried apart. Departures can signal the beginning of a time of waiting, and returns can take on the temporality of waiting for changes to register or manifest. When the elders of *Radiance of Tomorrow* return to Imperi in order to rebuild, their spatial return overlaps with the temporality of waiting. Mama Kadie and Pa Moiwa are the first to return, and they are joined shortly after by Pa Kainesi. As Mama Kadie walks the miles from the town to the village, she notes that the tree 'branches grew towards the ground, burying the leaves in the soil to blind their eyes so the sun would not promise them tomorrow with its rays'.[130] Given the novel's title and eventual endorsement of the radiance of tomorrow, this opening paragraph depicts the difficulty of facing the future when the past has not been sufficiently dealt with.

In negotiating the time between pain and reconciliation, Mama Kadie and the elders also strategically inhabit waiting in order to suspend the need to speak or to reconcile before the time is right. The paths Mama Kadie traverses are 'now ready to shed their old skins for new ones, and such occurrences take time with the necessary interruptions. Today, her feet began one of those interruptions'.[131] The temporality of waiting can also be inhabited as an interruption, as a modality that will eventually facilitate the shedding of old pain for new hope, given the requisite time. Pa Moiwa relates a familiar proverb to Mama Kadie to underscore the same message:

> 'The spider sometimes runs out of webs to spin, so it waits in the one it has spun.' Pa Moiwa used the saying to assure his friend that more words would come to her and she might be able to dwell on things other than the horrors of the past.[132]

The waiting embodied and practised by the elders who return first to Imperi generates a temporality that is expressly linked to (re)creating

---

[129] Liatsos, 'Truth, Confession and the Post-Apartheid Black Consciousness in Njabulo Ndebele's The Cry of Winnie Mandela', 126.
[130] Beah, *Radiance of Tomorrow*, 3.
[131] Ibid., 3.
[132] Ibid., 13.

the lost community. Pa Kainesi reflects on the next steps to rebuild, and remarks, '"We still have laughter among us, my friends, and hopefully some of those we have shared it with so deeply will return and we will be waiting."'[133] Although waiting, the elders are not idle; as they walk through 'the ruins of their town', they kick up 'a small tornado of dust as though cleansing the air for the possibility of life again'. While slowly burying the exposed skeletons of villagers killed during the war, the elders orient themselves in time through waiting, inhabiting waiting strategically to process the immense trauma produced by the civil war.

The novel then complicates the temporality of waiting by drawing attention to how it can reproduce, through the economic and environmental devastation wrought by the mining company, the dynamics of the powerless and powerful. The productive and strategic waiting that the elders choose and that predominates in the first half of the novel is replaced in the second half by the pressures of progress and development embodied by the mining company. Following his friend Benjamin's death in a mining accident, Bockarie laments, '"We cannot wait any longer. We must leave Imperi tomorrow."'[134] Bockarie and his family fled during the civil war, and their flight here is occasioned by circumstances that mirror the earlier conflict. Most strikingly, the mining company represses news of workers' deaths, leaving families without bodies to bury or truth to bring closure. Benjamin calls Bockarie from the mining dredge, where an iron bucket collapsed and pinned him along with five co-workers. '"Three have already died,"' he confesses, '"and it is just a matter of time."'[135] Beah then describes a conversation between the workers and a loyal company driver, toeing the company line. In response to their desperate inquiries about Benjamin, they are told, '"Haven't you heard that no one was harmed? The dredge just fell and everyone working at that time is safe."' Stunned, Bockarie is helpless because he

> couldn't go to the police and he had no way of spreading the truth – no money to pay for a radio announcement or a notice in the newspapers. He and the families of the other men couldn't even recover the bodies – the company stuck by its story, which was that no one had died.[136]

The company even falsifies the scheduling rosters to substantiate its claim that none of the men who died was working that day. By restaging cover-ups, denials and the manipulation of written documents to

---

[133] Ibid., 18.
[134] Ibid., 172.
[135] Ibid., 168.
[136] Ibid., 170.

obscure the truth, this moment, which also pivots the narrative from village to city, as the family subsequently moves to Freetown for work, evokes the TRC without ever naming the institution. These kinds of buried truths were precisely the targets of TRC investigations. Through direct references to the civil war, the novel makes an oblique connection to the circumstances that necessitated the Sierra Leonean TRC, as the narrator observes, 'The incident reminded people of the war, when they'd suffered the same emotional and psychological toll, burying people without their bodies or graveyards.'

Radiance of Tomorrow ultimately depicts waiting in three ways. First, the elders inhabit the temporality of waiting in order to process their pain; second, the mining company imposes the temporality of waiting on the villagers in order to defer indefinitely the truth of workers' fates. The novel reformulates the temporality of waiting a third time when Bockarie's family moves to the city. The jobs that Bockarie and his wife Kula acquire are disheartening; Bockarie discovers that rather than correcting student papers, his job actually requires him to write essays on commission for wealthy students. Kula then loses her job at a hotel reception desk abruptly because of a turnover in management, leaving them both with 'the worries of a broken tomorrow'.[137] Their experiences with under- and unemployment are prevalent among the city's population. Here, people are 'waiting in vain for something. After they had waited for so long, anything, even the devil, became an opportunity.'[138] Just when the waiting and the despair threatens to overpower them, a former boy soldier, Colonel, who has had to flee Imperi for retaliating against the company on behalf of the elders, reappears. To Ouma, he gives a basket of food and a message. She announces to her family, '"The one who gave me the food told me to tell you that the world is not ending today and that you must cheer up if you want to continue living in it."'[139] Sated by the meal, Kula tells a story about two boys who accidentally leave their hearts behind before they embark on a journey. When the boys hasten back to retrieve their hearts, they discover that ants have eaten pieces of them. Kula concludes, '"The brothers washed the hearts and put them back in their places, but they could no longer experience things the way they had."' Into the silence, Ouma adds new lines to the story, adjusting its message: '"So they must find a way to repair their broken hearts by relighting the fire that is now dull within them.

---

[137] Ibid., 236.
[138] Ibid., 177.
[139] Ibid., 239.

They should live for that.'"[140] Before the epigraph that both begins and concludes the novel, the narrative's final line reads, 'That is what happens when old wisdom and new wisdom merge, and find room in the young.'

By locating the possibilities of reconciliation, renewal and adaptation in the young, the novel addresses one of the defining features of Sierra Leone's civil war, reconciliation and reconstruction: the reintegration of child soldiers. Beah's first book, the 2007 memoir *A Long Way Gone*,[141] recounts his personal experiences as a teenaged soldier conscripted by army forces, and describes in brutal detail the violent acts he witnessed as well as perpetrated. In the novel, Beah moves the timeframe forwards, declining to depict the events of the civil war as they occurred, and focusing instead on the challenges of reconciliation and rebuilding that face small communities. While Colonel's storyline, out of all the child soldiers who return, is the most straightforwardly redemptive, another former child soldier, Ernest, underscores the difficulty many children had in coming to terms with their dual positions of perpetrators and victims. Glimpses of Ernest's coerced role in a roving armed squad are revealed early on in the text, when Sila and his children return to Imperi. The elders quickly note the family's amputations, which were a widespread mechanism of violence and abuse during the war. Neither Sila nor Ernest describe the amputations that Ernest inflicted on the family. Instead, the omniscient third-person narrator fills in these blanks, noting that Ernest, who had 'been forced at gunpoint to do his first cutting [amputation] when he was nine years old' on his relatives, is called upon to amputate the family's hands.[142] We learn that Sila and his children unnerve Ernest because they endure the amputations in silence, which 'made him hear the sound that the machete made when it went through the flesh, the bone, and then the flesh again, finally hitting the log'.[143]

The silence that triggers remorse in the otherwise hardened Ernest recurs throughout the novel's early chapters that depict return and rebuilding, and in my view establishes silence as an important aspect of reconciliation that tends to be overlooked in the TRC's emphasis on testimony. This is not to discount the vital work that public testimony accomplished in Sierra Leone for reconciliation at a national level, but it does point to how individuals may *wait* in silence until and unless they choose to speak. Mahawa, a teenaged girl who returns with a two-year-old son,

---

[140] Ibid., 240.
[141] Beah, *A Long Way Gone: Memoirs of a Boy Soldier*.
[142] Beah, *Radiance of Tomorrow*, 25.
[143] Ibid., 26.

'dread[s] having to explain how this child had come to this world, a story she didn't want to remember, not yet, perhaps ever. She wanted people to make their own assumptions and leave her out of it.'[144] Mahawa is a minor character in the narrative, and is taken in by Mama Kadie to create a new family unit. Her past is never elaborated any further.

Likewise, silence is integral to Ernest's reconciliation with Sila and his family. To the elders, Ernest's story is contained 'in his eyes' but they are aware that 'more needed to be done to mend what had been broken'.[145] Ernest's overtures of reconciliation involve secretly watching over the family at night, and then protecting the family when foreigners associated with the mining company throw a bottle that inadvertently hits Sila's son. While Sila 'learned what Ernest had done and wanted to thank him . . . he still needed time to be able to shake Ernest's hands'.[146] Eventually, the text suggests, the time may come when the silence can be broken, but in the meantime, silence can be a refuge. At the same time, however, Beah notes that silence, when combined with the temporality of waiting, does not necessary entail forgetting or burying the past; as the occupants of Imperi look for activities to fill the 'silence of that waiting, memories of war were awakened, bringing restlessness and irritability'.[147] The silence characteristic of the waiting in Imperi is maintained strategically, not in an effort to silence others who want or need to talk about what happened, but rather as a mode of recuperation and healing. Kula's advice to her children on how to navigate their own friendships with Sila's children is instructive here: '"It is an accident that people do not want to speak about just yet. So don't ask questions, okay. In time you will know if necessary."'[148] The narrator continues, 'They laughed and stood together for a while, holding each other to gather the strength that was needed for this day, *another day of waiting*.'[149]

Silence as Receptive Waiting

In contrast to the TRCs' emphasis on the cathartic power of testimony, *Radiance of Tomorrow* centres silence and waiting as important strategies for coming to terms with the past and with one's neighbours,

---

[144] Ibid., 22.
[145] Ibid., 30.
[146] Ibid., 122.
[147] Ibid., 38.
[148] Ibid., 42.
[149] Ibid., emphasis mine.

especially after a traumatic conflict that blurred the lines between victims and perpetrators. In a critical reading of novels that include *Radiance of Tomorrow*, Alexandra Moore notes that child soldiers are 'paradoxical figures of death and the future . . . poised at the limit', and in Beah's novel specifically the child soldiers are 'side characters who signify the depth of destruction of social bonds and the difficulty of their reconstruction'.[150] By turning to the post-conflict era, she argues, 'Beah tries to imagine a local alternative to the therapeutic promise articulated within IHL [international humanitarian law].'[151] TRCs are implicated here too, though Moore does not address them. In addition to civil rights violations, TRCs investigate violations of international humanitarian law, and both TRCs and international humanitarian law strive to put an end to armed conflict. Thus, I would argue that the novel's imaginative exploration of reconciliation outside the parameters of TRCs also resists the therapeutic promises so often associated with them as well.

Critical studies of Sierra Leone's TRC echo Beah's representation of the strategic roles of silence and waiting for reconciliation after armed conflict. The authors of 'Stay the Hand of Justice: Whose Priorities Take Priority?' make two observations that resonate with my reading of Beah's novel via-à-vis the Sierra Leonean TRC. First, they note that in assessing the success or failure of the Sierra Leonean TRC, 'the "official view" at the international level' might not match the impressions of 'Sierra Leoneans, especially since many reported a lack of "genuine partnership" with local civil society organizations'.[152] The Sierra Leone Working Group on Truth and Reconciliation observed in 2006 that 'Sierra Leonean voices are heard at the international level, where criteria for assessing the success and failures of the "experiment" may be different from those locally and where different agendas may shape the conclusion reached.'[153] Electing to be silent can be a restorative, empowering strategy for recently traumatised parties after armed conflict, but the assessment at the international level of the TRC's outcomes and accomplishments risks perpetuating further institutional violence by silencing experiences that may challenge the narrative promoted on an international scale. Second, the authors point to Rosalind Shaw's 2005 assessment, commissioned by the United States Institute of Peace, which found that 'there was little popular support for bringing such a commission

---

[150] Moore, *Vulnerability and Security in Human Rights Literature and Visual Culture*, 34, 60.
[151] Ibid., 60.
[152] Weinstein et al., 'Stay the Hand of Justice: Whose Priorities Take Priority?', 29.
[153] Ibid., 29.

[TRC] to Sierra Leone, since people preferred a "forgive and forget" approach.'[154] One explanation for the appeal of this approach is that 'close-knit communities have to learn to live together', and an extended process of sifting through truth and blame – especially in conflicts where child soldiers are involved – might not serve the reconstitution of the social fabric.[155] Indeed, such strategies have been labelled practices of 'social forgetting' in Sierra Leone, or in Rwanda, 'chosen amnesia'.[156]

By demonstrating the strategic possibilities of silence and waiting, Beah's novel illustrates techniques that, while at first glance appear utterly at odds with the mechanisms and goals of public testimonies and TRCs, can also address devastation and social disintegration following armed conflict. Child soldiers, he suggests, might be reconciled not only through public hearings and acknowledgements, but also slowly, through small acts and meaningful silences. As Mahawa also expresses, silence – refusing to tell one's story – can be leveraged to make someone else wait and to assert oneself by withholding speech. From this standpoint, we might connect her with Winnie Mandela, who famously refused to disclose her involvement in human rights violations, and who in Ndebele's fictional rendering maintains her intransigence. Though the silences of both characters are obviously employed for different ends, the two instances nevertheless crystallise the relationship between silence, waiting, and power.

Silence, these novels suggest, is an undertheorised but integral aspect of theorising reconciliation in relation to TRCs. While silences during the 'post-Cold War phase of transitional justice' may have indexed 'repressive political silencing', in post-conflict areas like Sierra Leone it may be truth, rather than silence, that 'subverts the process of living together'.[157] In fact, Shaw and Waldorf find that silences may be 'shape[d] . . . into a modality of reintegration'. Concerning the South African TRC, Fiona Ross proposes, 'There is a temporal dimension to the expression and reception of harsh experience; it may take time for events to settle in such a way that they can be narrated.'[158] While official TRCs operate within a given timeframe, and focus on a designated time span, the work of reconciliation and repair, narration and knowledge, must continue in order to accommodate new voices when the time comes. Turning to

---

[154] Ibid. 30.
[155] Gready, *The Era of Transitional Justice*, 53.
[156] Ibid., 53.
[157] Shaw and Waldorf, 'Introduction: Localizing Transitional Justice', 13.
[158] Ross, 'An Acknowledged Failure: Women, Voice, Violence, and the South African Truth and Reconciliation Commission', 86.

feminist scholar Tillie Olsen, Ross points to the productive interplay of silence and waiting: While silences can certainly manifest in forms ranging from censorship to oppression, silences may also be natural, in that they mark '"that necessary time for renewal, lying fallow, gestation, in the natural cycle of creation"; "a receptive waiting."'[159]

Charting waiting and silence as important concepts to theorise alongside TRCs' philosophies of narration and reconciliation has allowed us to complete a full revolution, back to Ndebele's 'The Revolution of the Aged' and the themes of timing and agency. Strategies of waiting – to speak, to address, to recount – may syncopate with the tempos of reconciliation on a national scale, but may also be necessary temporal modalities from which to stage reconciliation with oneself as well as others. As a result, 'waiting for' transforms into 'waiting with', creating bonds through a shared temporality of waiting that shifts from a focus on vertical lines of power and oppression to horizontal lines of comradeship. Neither novel suggests that waiting should be inhabited indefinitely, but both depict important community-building work being accomplished while waiting. *The Cry of Winnie Mandela* is structured like a waiting room for Penelope's descendants, where they can analyse their personal histories of waiting until they are ready to embark together on a journey out of the unspecified present moment and into the future.[160] The novel notes the shortcomings of the temporal ambit of the South African TRC while also modelling waiting as a strategic temporality, despite the ways that waiting limited the women's lives during apartheid. Likewise, the elders of *Radiance of Tomorrow* wait as they rebuild, where waiting produces time to heal even as it facilitates reconciliation through small, deliberate silences. But waiting also produces vulnerable populations, as Bockerie navigates first the mining company's deception and then restless urban unemployment. In this way, *Radiance of Tomorrow* additionally gestures towards the complications of neocolonial 'progress' and industrial development in postcolonial societies: a reminder that the struggles produced in and by waiting are very much still here in the present.

---

[159] Ibid., 86.

[160] Ndebele remarks that readers shared this process as well; in South Africa, he writes, 'the overwhelming view was that the novel pried open some space for a more honest and potentially healing public reflection ... The stories of unknown, ordinary women who tell their own stories enabled many readers to reflect intimately on the privacy of their own lives.' 'Introduction: Contemplating Winnie Mandela', xxvi.

Conclusion

'He moves too slow for me, Daddy Joe; I'm tired waiting so . . . If a thousand years with us is but a day with God, do you think I'm required to wait all that time? . . . That's no talk for me, Daddy Joe; I've been "standing still" long enough – I'll "stand still" no longer.'
　　　　Martin R. Delaney, *Blake; or The Huts of America: A Novel* (1859)

At the Black Entertainment Television (BET) Awards on 26 June 2016, activist and actor Jesse Williams accepted the Humanitarian Award with a powerful speech, decrying the inability of police in the United States to de-escalate conflicts with the Black community in the same way that they do for whites, and calling for urgent organisation and resistance: 'Now, freedom is always coming in the hereafter but, you know what, though, the hereafter is a hustle. We want it now . . . We've been floating this country on credit for centuries, yo. And we're done watching, and waiting while this invention called whiteness uses and abuses us.'[1] The Awards ceremony closed with Beyoncé and Kendrick Lamar's surprise performance of 'Freedom', which for the show was remixed to include a sample from Martin Luther King Jr's 'I Have a Dream' speech. From the emphasis on urgency and waiting, to freedom and resistance, the BET speeches and performances certainly echoed and underscored the sampling of King's speech, which criticised the United States for signing and subsequently defaulting on a 'promissory note' of 'unalienable Rights'. The excerpted sample from King's speech ended just before King proclaims, 'We have also come to this hallowed spot to remind America of the fierce urgency of Now' – a line which instead is substituted by the rest of the anthem 'Freedom'.

---

[1] Toney, 'Jesse Williams Gave One of the Most Memorable Speeches in Award Show History'.

At the time of this writing, the Black Lives Matter movement has been reignited by the videotaped death of George Floyd, and calls for justice link Floyd with Breonna Taylor, Stephon Clark, Philando Castile, Alton Sterling, Tamir Rice, Sandra Bland, Rekia Boyd, Atatiana Jefferson and countless others both known and unknown murdered by police in the United States. The larger Black Lives Matter movement responds to the 'typical origins of black leadership' embodied in figures like King, and 'represents a move from a singular political organizing centered on racial justice to an intersectional agenda'.[2] With a more expansive, inclusive and decentralised organisational structure, the Black Lives Matter political and cultural movement organises in response to some of the same issues that animated the 1960s civil rights movement: institutional racism, police brutality and the persistent deferral of freedom. The 2020 protests are set against the backdrop of the global COVID-19 pandemic; in defiance of stay-at-home orders, protestors from every US state and many other cities across the globe occupied streets, parks and even police precincts in a dramatic refusal to wait for justice that will never come from a criminal justice system as currently constituted. So urgent are the protestors' demands that activism cannot wait for the pandemic to end first – and indeed, communities of colour have been devastated not only by the institutional racism of American policing, but also by uneven economic investment, healthcare and social services that contribute to disproportionately stark outcomes for COVID-19 patients of colour.

The language of waiting and urgency is striking in both sermon and speech, King's in 1963 and Williams's in 2016 respectively, that bookend this study of the temporalities of waiting. At the same time, the tactics and strategies of each movement has played with the power of waiting: from refusing to vacate seats at lunch counters, forcing the establishments to choose to either wait on them or wait for the police to intervene with arrests, to contemporary highway 'sit-ins', disrupting commutes and insisting that others wait. These strategies of direct action mobilise 'waiting' to accomplish two goals. First, the tactics underscore the ways that the status quo of racial oppression has been maintained through waiting; second, the tactics render that waiting visible by appropriating the temporal strategy for the aims of social justice. The doubleness that attends to waiting – a doubleness I have tracked throughout the chapters of this book – can be understood as what Julius Fleming calls 'black patience' in his study of grassroots theatre in Mississippi during

---

[2] Black Lives Matter, 'Two Years Later, Black Lives Matter Faces Critique, But It Won't Be Stopped'.

the 1960s. While black patience is 'a racialized system of waiting that has historically produced and vitalized antiblackness and white supremacy by compelling black people to wait and to capitulate to the racialized terms and assumptions of these forced performances of waiting', he notes that 'black people have historically recast black patience as a tool of black political and ontological possibility'.[3] These dramatic embodiments of black patience produce 'a challenge to black patience qua black patience – a performative attempt to unsettle "the wait" in and through a radical performance of waiting'.[4]

In its occupation of both space and time, the Black Lives Matter movement in the United States stresses the enduring dialectic of waiting and urgency in the struggle for social justice progress, not only in the United States but also elsewhere as well. As Alicia Garza, one of the co-founders of the Black Lives Network acknowledges, '[W]e understand that we're in a moment that is different from ones in the past. It is informed by them, but it is not the same . . . Our approach at this point is to experiment and innovate, boldly and courageously.'[5] Likewise, the waiting that is named and created in these settings shifts in response to new concerns in new moments, informed by the past but not reducible to a reproduction of it. Throughout this book study, waiting reappears in diverse settings and times, and different actors inhabit and invoke the temporal modalities of waiting for oppressive and resistive purposes alike. The Introduction to this book discussed Kwame Nkrumah's midnight independence speech and Martin Luther King Jr's *Why We Can't Wait*, and in some ways, their words continue to reverberate for the 'global Black family' named on the Black Lives Matter website and other communities marginalised in the still-decolonising world. Yet, as each of the subsequent book chapters have shown, the temporal dimensions of waiting interact with specific settings, histories and circumstances, producing possibilities for action and resistance – as well as passivity and capitulation – that are informed by the colonial history of waiting, power and politics, but not the same.

In drawing this book to a close, I want to dwell in the tension, the doubleness this book has explored, of the temporality of waiting as a weapon that reproduces temporal violence, as well as its possibilities as a tool of arrhythmic temporal disjuncture. In what remains of this conclusion, I observe how waiting continues to structure the contemporary

---

[3] Fleming, 'Transforming Geographies of Black Time: How the Free Southern Theater Used the Plantation for Civil Rights Activism', 589.
[4] Ibid., 590.
[5] Fletcher, 'From Hashtag to Strategy: The Growing Pains of Black Lives Matter'.

geopolitical landscape, and especially how waiting has been leveraged within and by the United States. While the fiction analysed throughout this book largely focused on the past, or offered a vision of future liberation through waiting as resistance, here I want explicitly to address the present, or the 'now'. In addition to pointing to this book's potential interlocutors outside literary studies, I hope that this conclusion can serve as a model for how we read these times – our times, the contemporary moment. Thus, instead of ending with a close reading of novels, I draw out this book's impact and implications beyond literary studies by examining the rhetoric of waiting as it has been articulated by the George W. Bush administration and the then-Presidential candidate Donald J. Trump in 2016, and the ways that the temporalities of waiting shape attitudes towards asylum seekers and refugees. While the leap between Black Lives Matter and the US American state's campaigns against terror may, at first blush, seem too far, the juxtaposition reveals the imbrication of white supremacy and 'national security' as it is practised both domestically and abroad. As the Black Lives Matter protests in summer 2020 swelled, Trump was quick to scapegoat 'antifa', a 'diffuse movement of left-wing protesters who engage in more aggressive techniques like vandalism', and label them domestic terrorists.[6] While critics quickly pointed out that the federal government has the authority to designate foreign groups and not domestic ones as terroristic, Trump nevertheless participated in the long US American practice of designating agitators for change as threats to national security interests.[7] In what follows, I present several vignettes that identify the United States as exemplar for the entanglement of the temporalities of waiting and 'national security', especially in the aftermath of 9/11. It has been my contention that the temporal dimensions of waiting in literature respond to postcolonial conditions outside the novels' pages, and this concluding analysis of waiting in the speeches, declarations and descriptions of post-9/11 experiences underscores the relationship between text and greater context. Lastly, though I have been examining waiting as a distinctive temporality of postcoloniality, this final discussion of contemporary waiting suggests provocative overlaps between 'postcolonial' and 'post-9/11' temporal modalities.

---

[6] Haberman and Savage, 'Trump, Lacking Clear Authority, Says U.S. Will Declare Antifa a Terrorist Group'.
[7] See especially the FBI's programme 'COINTELPRO', described in detail in Nelson Blackstock's *Cointelpro: The FBI's Secret War on Political Freedom*, which targeted Martin Luther King Jr, the Black Panther Party and other civil rights leaders.

The choice to pivot to the United States[8] is deliberate for several reasons, not least because of the United States's influential role in brokering trade deals and imposing sanctions, waging war and negotiating peace, employing what many identify as neocolonial practices through interventions in the function and affairs of countries around the world. Additionally, I aim to underscore the multivalent function of waiting, especially at the level of the state, where waiting can be simultaneously mobilised by a government to disenfranchise populations within a state's territorial boundaries, even as refusals to wait are exhibited in its interactions between other states. As Anthony Reed argues in *Freedom Time*, 'regimes of governmentality are also temporal orders, referring to a shared set of myths of the past that set the terms of imagining the future'.[9] The temporal signatures of the War on Terror, I argue, include both waiting and pre-emption, but there is not a single, homogeneous way that powerful entities engage the temporal dimensions of waiting for political ends. And finally, in turning towards my own country of origin, I want to disrupt any impression that the vicissitudes of waiting are navigated only elsewhere, in an isolated 'postcolonial' world. Waiting, as this book has argued, has a particular resonance with colonial discourse and anticolonial nationalist movements, taking on additional textures in conjunction with post-independence disillusionment, truth and reconciliation commissions, and other temporalities in complex timescapes. Contemporary evocations of waiting by representatives of the US government are informed by these colonial and postcolonial discourses, but interact with what Ben Anderson calls 'catastrophic futures' – projections of future catastrophes, 'from terrorism to transspecies epidemics' – that produce 'the present [as] . . . a prefiguration of the future disaster' and make 'catastrophic futures . . . part of an already tensed present'.[10] Waiting, Anderson finds, is directly opposed to that urgent state of emergency called forth by these catastrophic futures. These insights indicate a renewed sense in which 'waiting' is an approach to being in time and in the world.

---

[8] Though beyond the scope of this conclusion, the US remains a complicated site for postcolonial theorising. For a history of American Studies and postcolonial theory, see Malini Schueller's review of two anthologies on the topic, titled 'Postcolonial American Studies'. If, as I have argued, waiting is especially characteristic of postcolonial temporalities and colonial time regimes, then the way waiting permeates the US's execution of power globally indirectly makes a case for the US as a (post)colonial site.

[9] Reed, *Freedom Time*, 212.

[10] Anderson, 'Emergency Futures: Exception, Urgency, Interval, Hope', 467.

Waiting and the George W. Bush Administration

In his Address to the Joint Session of the 107th Congress on 20 September 2001, former President George W. Bush indicated the scope and indeterminate duration of what would become the US-led global War on Terror:

> Our war on terror begins with al Qaeda, but it does not end there. It will not end until every terrorist group of global reach has been found, stopped and defeated ... Our response involves far more than instant retaliation and isolated strikes. Americans should not expect one battle, but a lengthy campaign, unlike any other we have seen.[11]

The pre-emptive military strikes that would become characteristic of the War on Terror campaign, as well as the ratcheting up of surveillance within the United States, are foreshadowed as well, as Bush promised:

> We will come together to give law enforcement the additional tools it needs to track down terror here at home. We will come together to strengthen our intelligence capabilities to know the plans of terrorists before they act, and find them before they strike.[12]

Put another way, we might read the grammar of Bush's simple-future statement as declaring, 'We will not wait for them to act first': an assertion of pre-emption and a pronouncement of preparedness. Here, Bush asserts a complicated relationship between the present and the future, insofar as the future is not only anticipatable, but also able to be circumvented in advance to usher in its alternative; we will know when terrorists *will* strike so that we can act in such a way that this future will never be realised. The pre-emption of Empire in Coetzee's *Waiting for the Barbarians*, discussed briefly in Chapter 3, is not dissimilar from the discourses of pre-emption mobilised by Bush. Just as the perception of future threat justifies the Empire's torture of the 'barbarians' captured in Coetzee's novel – and let us not overlook the persistence of the clash of civilisations rhetoric popularised by Samuel Huntington here[13] – so too does this utilitarian logic underpin the Bush administration's justification

---

[11] Bush, 'Selected Speeches of President George W. Bush, 2001–2008', 68–9.
[12] Ibid., 71–2.
[13] Huntington, *The Clash of Civilizations and the Remaking of World Order*. While the original essay was published in 1993, the argument was expanded into a book in 1998 with a new edition in 2003 – the same year that the War on Terror expanded into Iraq.

of 'enhanced interrogation techniques', and the country's invasion of Afghanistan and Iraq.

More than any other, the temporality of waiting has characterised the politics and strategies associated with the War on Terror. In *Qualified Hope: A Postmodern Politics of Time*, Mitchum Huehls observes that the rhetoric of preparedness and pre-emption stems from the way that 'the future's unpredictability' is posited as the United States' 'primary enemy'.[14] Rather than the 'patient justice' Bush promised at the conclusion of his speech on 20 September, the United States has increasingly followed the path of impatient action.[15] In subsequent speeches to the nation, Bush insistently characterised US operations in Afghanistan and Iraq as 'patient': 'we will win this conflict by the patient accumulation of successes', 'no cave is deep enough to escape the patient justice of the United States of America', '[we] will continue to be steadfast and patient and persistent in the pursuit of two great objectives', 'America is a patient nation, and Iraq can count on our partnership', and 'the families of those murdered that day have waited patiently for justice'.[16] Huehls points out that this radically open future does not guarantee a realisation of the liberatory politics, but instead presents a

> stark, all-or-nothing choice: it can subscribe to a real-time model of temporal experience, a wait-and-see approach that might get everyone killed; or it can preempt time, acting in the present to make sure that the future plays out according to its plans and desires.[17]

At the same time, would-be terrorists in waiting evoke the temporality of waiting differently. Strategically, terrorists 'wait-out preemption (hence the phrase "sleeper cells"), wielding the specter of the unknown next attack as their strongest weapon'.[18] While domestic 'lone-wolf' plots such as the 2015 San Bernardino attacks and the New York and New Jersey bombings in 2016 were nowhere close to the scale of destruction that characterised 9/11, these attacks can shore up support for subsequent pre-emptive, precautionary measures. For example, during the 2016 presidential campaign, Donald Trump repeatedly called for a ban on Muslims entering the United States, a proposal he reiterated in various forms from December 2015 to July 2016, and changed with chimeric frequency from an indefinite to a temporary ban, to a

---

[14] Huehls, *Qualified Hope*, 7.
[15] Ibid., 73.
[16] Bush, 'Selected Speeches', 76, 92, 105, 386, 418.
[17] Huehls, *Qualified Hope*, 7.
[18] Ibid., 83.

religious test, to a values assessment, to restrictions based on national origins. As Beth Reinhard and Damian Paletta observed in *The Wall Street Journal*, Trump's first television ad, in January 2016, 'depicted images of the suspects in the San Bernardino attacks and of Islamic State militants and said, "That's why he's calling for a temporary shutdown of Muslims entering the United States."'[19] Measures like immigration bans or restrictions, however unconstitutional and racist, aim to prevent a capricious threat by emphasising prevention and pre-emption. Instead of waiting for a threat to materialise (the 'retroactive temporality of representation'), the logic of pre-emption imposes 'the immanent temporality of performance . . . forcing [time] ahead of itself to determine the future before it has a chance to occur'.[20] In this way, the temporality of waiting continues to 'affect our political interactions with the world and with each other'.

In contrast to some of this book's chapters, which focus on waiting as anticipation alongside hope, anxiety and disillusionment, here the dominant emotion provoked by the temporality of waiting is fear. 'Responses to terrorism', Sara Ahmed argues, 'work as "an economy of fear", in which the figure of the terrorist gets associated with some bodies (and not others), at the same time as the terrorist "could be" anyone or anywhere'.[21] Importantly, fear has a 'temporal dimension':

> Fear, like pain, is felt as an unpleasant form of intensity. But while the lived experience of fear may be unpleasant in the present, the unpleasantness of fear also relates to the future. Fear involves an *anticipation* of hurt or injury. Fear projects us from the present into a future. But the feeling of fear presses us into that future as an intense bodily experience in the present . . . So the object that we fear is not simply before us, or in front of us, but impresses upon us in the present, as an anticipated pain in the future.[22]

Trump has given voice to a particular framing of the multivalent temporality of waiting in relation to security and the future. On the one hand, the US government cannot afford to wait and see whether immigrants from conflict areas will plan terrorist acts in the US. In this fearful present, avoiding future harm serves to legitimise extraordinary measures, such as the suspension of civil liberties, indefinite detention and, of course, pre-emptive strikes. As Elizabeth Povinelli describes, 'specific

---

[19] Reinhard and Paletta, 'Donald Trump Back-Pedals on Banning Muslims from U.S.'.
[20] Huehls, *Qualified Hope*, 83.
[21] Ahmed, *The Cultural Politics of Emotion*, 15.
[22] Ibid., 65.

arrangements of tense, eventfulness, and ethical substance make affectively and cognitively sensible and practical, late liberal distributions of life and death, or hope and harm, and of endurance and exhaustion across social difference'.[23] The War on Terror mobilises fear in service of the future perfect tense: before the terrorists strike, we will have prevented this possibility from manifesting.

On the other hand, the government can use the temporality of waiting, as embodied in temporary bans, or as I write in 2021, concentration camps on the southern US border, ostensibly to postpone these anticipated acts indefinitely. To pantomime the emergent US homeland security talking points, immigrants, asylum seekers and refugees must wait until we can figure out what is going on. By 'asserting control over the unfolding of the future through anticipatory actions in the present', Liam Stockdale argues, pre-emption strategies 'mitigate the potentially pernicious effects' of 'radical uncertainty'.[24] In turn, according to Stockdale, this 'implies that a pre-emptive politics of security hinges on the exercise of the imagination by relevant decision makers, since this is the only way politically actionable "knowledge" about the ultimately unknowable future can be generated'.[25] Yet pre-emption strategies tend to reproduce rather than eliminate vulnerability and risk; as Stockdale observes, 'vulnerability to the threat posed by a radically uncertain future' is replaced with 'vulnerability to a state security apparatus that can act arbitrarily and violently in an attempt to govern those uncertainties'. In this landscape of fear and uncertainty, vulnerability and risk, the present, Ahmed concludes, 'becomes preserved by defending the community against imagined others, who may take form in ways that cannot be anticipated, a "not-yet-ness" which means the work of defence is never over'.[26]

Waiting for Refuge

Immigration restrictions appeal to this logic of fear and uncertainty, to assessments of vulnerability and risk, and to the defence of the

---

[23] Povinelli, *Economies of Abandonment*, 5.
[24] Stockdale, 'Imagined Futures and Exceptional Presents: A Conceptual Critique of 'Pre-Emptive Security',' 90.
[25] Ibid., 91.
[26] Ahmed, *The Cultural Politics of Emotion*, 79. I give a fuller account of the relationship between postcolonial fiction and temporalities of preemption in my article 'Terrorist Plots: Temporality, the Politics of Preemption, and the Postcolonial Novel'.

community over the potential threat of 'unknown' others. The Syrian conflict has underscored the refugee as an emblematic political figure for the twenty-first century, a figure who cannot wait but must flee. While theorists from Georgio Agamben to Hannah Arendt have discussed the camp as a prevailing image of the twentieth century,[27] the contemporary camp's parameters have become more amorphous: whole countries and smaller enclaves, temporary holdings for indeterminate lengths of time, sanctioned officially as well as unofficially by the global community. Even before the Syrian refugee crisis, refugees' protracted waiting was on the rise; the wait time for refugees 'has increased from nine years in 1993 to 17 years in 2003', and the contemporary refugee crisis will continue to exacerbate the conditions of asylum seeking.[28] On the US/Mexico border, the Trump administration's 'zero tolerance' policy was rationalised by 'the false perception . . . that lax immigration enforcement allows gang members and terrorists to pour into the US from Mexico'.[29] While that border has long been a site of imperial violence, the 'warlike tactics' deployed by border agents increased after 11 September 2001.[30] In the 'aftermath of 9/11', Maria Cristina Morales writes, 'policy and public perceptions of immigrants, particularly undocumented border crosses, started to be framed in terms of possible terrorism'.[31]

Immigrant and refugee experiences at the border are punctuated by waiting: waiting to make a claim, then waiting in 'temporary' facilities, camps, or detention centres while their cases move slowly.[32] The association of refugees and immigrants with the temporal dimensions of waiting, however, extends beyond the way that waiting characterises their own temporal experience; waiting itself has become a condition through which countries in the Global North assess mobility risk. As Hyndman and Giles explain, from the perspective of the Global North, refugee

---

[27] See Arendt, *The Origins of Totalitarianism*, part 3 chapter 12, and Georgio Agamben, *Homo Sacer: Sovereign Power and Bare Life*.
[28] Hyndman and Giles, 'Waiting for What? The Feminization of Asylum in Protracted Situations', 361. According to the US State Department, 'Protracted Refugee Situations', the average wait time for refugees in protracted refugee situations is now twenty-six years.
[29] Gokee, Stewart and De León, 'Scales of Suffering in the US–Mexico Borderlands'.
[30] Morales, 'The Manufacturing of the US–Mexico Border Crisis', 5.
[31] Ibid., 6.
[32] The Transactional Records Access Clearinghouse produced at Syracuse University reports that the average time pending cases have been waiting in immigration courts, as of April 2020, is over 700 days – or two years. TRAC Immigration, 'Average Time Pending Cases Have Been Waiting in Immigration Courts as of April 2020'.

populations are divided into two groups, and 'those who stay still are viewed as genuine, immobile, depoliticised, feminised, while those on the move are potential liabilities at best, and security threats at worst'.[33] Paradoxically for the waiting refugee, the ability to wait characterises 'non-threatening' behaviour, but this patient waiting will not impress urgency upon the countries of asylum to accelerate repatriation or resource-allocation. As we saw in Chapter 4 through Baako and Maya's experiences of patience and urgency, an external demand to wait that is in conflict with one's impression of urgency can be self-destructive. In this contemporary moment as well, 'space and waiting come together to produce and maintain potentially abusive and harmful arrangements of power and inequality'.[34]

Increasingly, as governments debate and navigate crises of civil war and large-scale global movement, the 'end' of one period of waiting tends to beget another. As Elizabeth Olson notes, the urgency of state security 'creates new scales and new temporal orders of response ... many of which treat the urgent body as impulsive and thus requiring management'.[35] As a result, 'the urgent body is at best an assumed eventuality, one that will likely require another state of waiting, such as triage'.[36] More and more, the urgency of managing the threat of terrorism from abroad overrides the urgency of attending to humanitarian need elsewhere. These 'contemporary geographies' are constructed and maintained 'in the name of preempting, preparing for, or preventing threats to liberal-democratic life'.[37] Refusing to wait in the twenty-first century thus posits an uncertain and indeterminate future that 'will radically differ from the here and now', shaping the discourse as well as policies on issues ranging from climate change to the war on terror.[38] The future is increasingly viewed as 'ungovernable, radically uncertain and dangerous'.[39] An openness of the future, discussed in Chapter 3 in relation to marronage and embodied in Michael K's flight from camps, is here tainted with an ominous, apocalyptic cast.

---

[33] Hyndman and Giles, 'Waiting for What? The Feminization of Asylum in Protracted Situations', 353.
[34] Olson, 'Geography and Ethics 1: Waiting and Urgency', 517.
[35] Ibid., 520.
[36] Ibid., 521.
[37] Anderson, 'Preemption, Precaution, Preparedness: Anticipatory Action and Future Geographies', 777.
[38] Ibid., 780.
[39] Amin, 'Surviving the Turbulent Future', 140.

Recognising that the temporality of waiting in the twenty-first century is imbricated with discourses of pre-emption, precaution and preparedness, to borrow the three logics of contemporary anticipatory action that Ben Anderson identifies, is a starting point for thinking new forms of critical response and resistance. It is clear that '[t]o protect, save and care for certain forms of life' – those who cannot wait – 'is to potentially abandon, dispossess and destroy others'.[40] Refusals to grant refugees asylum in the name of pre-empting threats depend precisely on this assessment and management of risk. With regard to the United States, we can identify this calculation in the government's response to terroristic threats from without its borders, as well as its response to disasters within. While various crises, such as terrorist attacks or civil wars, can prompt governments to respond with measures designed to prepare for and pre-empt a future recurrence, individual responses can counter this compressed temporality by insisting on the temporality of waiting to organise their lived experiences. This waiting may go by other names; in Povinelli's hands, it is endurance, which 'is not a singularity', nor is it 'a homogeneous space . . . [it] is shot through with multiple and incommensurate configurations of tense, eventfulness, and ethical substance and aggregations of life'.[41] As this book has endeavoured to show, waiting also is not a singularity. Povinelli insists that endurance in a 'durative present' does not mean that those dispatched to waiting rooms, physical and material, political and existential, endure passively. Rather, 'the condition in which they endure has the temporal structure of limbo – an edge of life located somewhere between given and new social positions and roles, and between the conditions of the past and the promise of the future'.[42] Likewise, Arjun Appadurai remarks that one strategy communities employ to 'oppose the politics of catastrophe, exception, and emergency . . . is frequently the politics of patience, which can even more accurately be called the politics of waiting'.[43] Regarding slum dwellers in Mumbai, he observes that waiting can be agentive; he finds that 'organized hope mediates between emergency and patience and produces in bare citizens the internal resources to see themselves as

---

[40] Anderson, 'Preemption, Precaution, Preparedness: Anticipatory Action and Future Geographies', 791.
[41] Povinelli, *Economies of Abandonment*, 32. Here, Povinelli explicitly links her discussion to Dipesh Chakrabarty's 'imaginary waiting room of history', discussed in detail in this book's Introduction and Chapter 2.
[42] Ibid., 77–8.
[43] Appadurai, *The Future as Cultural Fact*, 126.

active participants in the very process of waiting'.[44] Echoing the insights of Chapter 5, whether configured as endurance or patience, 'waiting for' transforms into 'waiting with', creating bonds through a shared temporality of waiting that can prove both agentive and reparative.

Waiting for Now

Though spanning a long twentieth century, the fiction in *Postcolonial Fiction and Colonial Time: Waiting for Now* has urgent potential for showing the utility of waiting – now. Connecting disparate geographies and discrete contexts, waiting as resistance links US protest movements to struggle elsewhere, as we saw in Chapter 3 that waiting can disrupt the temporal regimes of colonial or apartheid states. Both Ti Noël and Michael K demonstrate that flight, labour and 'idleness' can be mobilised as strategies of resistive waiting. Similarly, the elders of Imperi in Chapter 5 reflect and rebuild through strategic waiting, which is inhabited in the service of reconciliation. The elders in *Radiance of Tomorrow* suggest that important community-building work can be accomplished while waiting. Likewise, Nadine Gordimer's Maureen Smales in Chapter 2 shows that waiting can disrupt the relationship between time and lived patterns, such that Maureen is able to re-evaluate herself in relation to others. At the same time, the temporality of waiting carries its own risks. As Chapter 2 also demonstrates, V. S. Naipaul's rendering of the eponymous bend in the river as a waiting room for Salim and other African citizens suggests that, notwithstanding political independence, 'not yet' will never become 'now'. With a cyclical African history of destruction doomed to repeat itself indefinitely, any 'refusal to wait', in Naipaul's hands, is emptied of its urgency.

The temporal impression of urgency has also been threaded throughout this book study of the temporal dimensions of waiting. As this conclusion's brief examination of pre-emptive military strikes in the global War on Terror suggests, urgency can compel precautionary actions designed to circumvent a feared and anticipated future; at the same time, the safety and security of some necessitates the abandonment or destruction of others. Yet even urgency is contingent on circumstance; Maya in Chapter 4 eschews patience and embraces a 'fierce urgency of now' to reject her untenable condition. The language of 'fierce urgency' returns us once again to Martin Luther King Jr and mid-twentieth-century

---

[44] Ibid., 127.

rejections of waiting. King's promotion of what Mario Feit calls 'democratic impatience' can incite 'a political crisis' that hastens action and manufactures urgency for the movement's demands; at the same time, 'operational patience' – what Feit describes as 'strategic delays and long-term programs of transformation' – also has a role in the realisation of a more just future.[45] While US American discourses of pre-emptive military strikes as 'refusals to wait' in the War on Terror might appropriate the radical rhetoric of mid-century independence and civil rights movements' opposition to waiting, the novels surveyed in this book remind us that waiting continues to have multiple valences. Waiting can be re-appropriated as a cultural practice, a way of marking and managing time with the potential to trouble the structures of power that seek to dichotomise the powerful and powerless.

Theorists of globalisation and modernity from David Harvey to Lynn Hunt have posited that the contemporary experience of time is impacted by the sensation that space too has been compressed.[46] At the turn of the twenty-first century, Harvey influentially argued that 'we have been experiencing, these last two decades, an intense phase of time-space compression that has had a disorienting and disruptive impact upon political-economic practices, the balance of class power, as well as upon cultural and social life'.[47] But he clarifies: 'the maelstrom of ephemerality has provoked an explosion of opposed sentiments and tendencies' designed to protect 'against future volatility'.[48] Harvey's observations pinpoint acceleration and speed as dominant temporal modes of the later twentieth century. My argument, however, is slightly different; it is not that the impression of acceleration has provoked temporal modes such as waiting in response, but rather, that waiting is a constitutive element of acceleration. As we have seen, for example, in Baako's 1970s Accra, accelerating 'progress' and prosperity is not evenly distributed, and economic mobility for some may depend on others' continued waiting in destitution. Waiting and acceleration are two sides of the same coin.

A book study that draws from such a range of places and times risks giving the impression that waiting is simply too ubiquitous to be useful as an analytic. I want to stress that the analytic of waiting draws our attention to unevenness and counter-temporalities, asynchronies and arrhythmias that characterise waiting as a condition of postcoloniality

---

[45] Feit, 'Democratic Impatience: Martin Luther King, Jr. on Democratic Temporality', 3, 12.
[46] Hunt, 'Globalisation and Time'.
[47] Harvey, 'Time-Space Compression and the Postmodern Condition', 98.
[48] Ibid., 105.

itself that shifts across literary histories of colonial and anticolonial writing. Even more specifically, as a structuring affect of postcolonial fiction and a temporal mode, waiting is integral to the weaponisation of time by colonial time regimes as well as an unruly disruption to its functioning; it is both a temporal expression of subordination as well as a challenge to hegemonic time. Despite the pervasiveness of waiting in quotidian life, the history of discourses of idleness, belatedness, backwardness or stasis to describe (post)colonial spaces and peoples mark waiting as a specifically postcolonial temporality. The temporal dimensions of waiting interact with specific settings, histories and circumstances, producing possibilities for action and resistance, as well as passivity and capitulation, that are informed by colonial histories of waiting, power and politics, but not the same. Waiting, this book has argued, has a particular resonance with colonial discourse and anticolonial nationalist movements, taking on additional textures in conjunction with post-independence disillusionment, truth and reconciliation commissions, and other temporalities in complex timescapes. Attention to the 'postcolonial' temporality of waiting exposes how powerful entities continue the colonisation of time – what Charles Mills describes as 'White times, the particular temporal topographies and chronological colonizations imposed on Africa and the Americas, and their inhabitants'[49] – through time theft, unequal distribution of time, prolonged or indefinite deferral and, as this conclusion shows, through foreclosing the future preemptively. Still, time is also evidently a scene of struggle, a weapon that can be retooled by the otherwise disempowered to force others to wait.

The insights of critical time studies have allowed us to identify waiting as a prevailing temporal mode of the twentieth century and today, and its prevalence prompts us to reconsider the way concepts like 'modernity' have been framed. If modernity is not simply defined, as Reinhardt Koselleck would have it, 'by an experience of acceleration of time that is philosophically grounded in an original gesture of reduction of the plurality of traditional histories to the "collective singular" of History',[50] but *also* defined by the experience of waiting, then the premise of unidirectional, linear history is also unsettled through a critical time framework. More work remains to be done on the impact of 'waiting' on studies of time and globalisation, as well as time and modernity.

---

[49] Mills, 'White Time: The Chronic Injustice of Ideal Theory', 30–1.
[50] Mezzadra and Rahola, 'The Postcolonial Condition: A Few Notes on the Quality of Historical Time in the Global Present', 49.

Jean-François Bayart describes the paradoxical relationship between waiting and speed in relation to globalisation this way:

> the processes of globalization create states, and even, to an increasing degree, 'states of emergency' or 'of exception', which are states in which peoples are stockpiled and forced into latency . . . It is at the heart of the reactor of globalization that they wait.[51]

Bayart warns, 'Intoxicated by speed, we neglect waiting.'[52] This study has been an effort to compensate for that neglect.

Though waiting has been used to defer justice and to distort a lived sense of historicity in colonial and postcolonial settings, this book has argued that waiting can also be a tactic adopted by the politically, socially and economically disenfranchised as part of a larger strategy of protest and perseverance. Although it has become commonplace to describe the twentieth century as an era of intensifying speed, this book has shown that the temporal dimensions of waiting paradoxically characterise this temporal experience of acceleration. From the Belgian Congo to Sierra Leone, and from Ghana to the United States, waiting is not only integral in the discourses of colonial administration and anticolonial nationalisms, but also deployed in strategic and political expressions of resistance. In this way, the temporal dimensions of waiting remain central to the formation of geopolitical realities.

---

[51] Bayart, *Global Subjects*, 269.
[52] Ibid., 290.

Bibliography

Achebe, Chinua. 'An Image of Africa: Racism in Conrad's Heart of Darkness'. *Massachusetts Review* 57, no. 1 (2016): 14–27.
Adam, Barbara. *Time*. Key Concepts. Cambridge, UK; Malden, MA: Polity, 2004.
Adam, Barbara. *Timescapes of Modernity: The Environment and Invisible Hazards*. London; New York: Routledge, 1998.
Adib, and Paul Emiljanowicz. 'Colonial Time in Tension: Decolonizing Temporal Imaginaries'. *Time & Society* 28, no. 3 (2018): 1221–38.
Adjaye, Joseph K. 'Time, Identity, and Historical Consciousness in Akan'. In *Time in the Black Experience*, edited by Joseph K. Adjaye, 55–77. Contributions in Afro-American and African Studies 167. Westport, CT: Greenwood Press, 1994.
Adjaye, Joseph K. 'Time in Africa and Its Diaspora: An Introduction'. In *Time in the Black Experience*, edited by Joseph K. Adjaye, 1–16. Contributions in Afro-American and African Studies 167. Westport, CT: Greenwood Press, 1994.
Afzal-Khan, Fawzia. *Cultural Imperialism and the Indo-English Novel: Genre and Ideology in R. K. Narayan, Anita Desai, Kamala Markandaya, and Salman Rushdie*. University Park, PA: Pennsylvania State University Press, 1993.
Agacinski, Sylviane. *Time Passing: Modernity and Nostalgia*. New York: Columbia University Press, 2003.
Agamben, Giorgio. *Homo Sacer: Sovereign Power and Bare Life*. Translated by Danielle Heller-Roazen. Stanford, CA: Stanford University Press, 1995.
Ahmed, Sara. *The Cultural Politics of Emotion*. Second edition. Edinburgh: Edinburgh University Press, 2014.
Alie, Joe A. D. 'A Price for Peace? Justice and Reconciliation in Post-War Sierra Leone'. In *Bound to Cooperate: Conflict, Peace and People in Sierra Leone*, edited by Anatole N. Ayissi, Robin Poulton and United Nations Institute for Disarmament Research, 165–83. Second edition. Geneva: United Nations Institute for Disarmament Research, 2006.
Amin, Ash. 'Surviving the Turbulent Future'. *Environment and Planning D: Society and Space* 31 (2013): 140–56.
Amin-Khan, Tariq. *The Post-Colonial State in the Era of Capitalist Globalization: Historical, Political and Theoretical Approaches to State*

Formation. Routledge Studies in Social and Political Thought 74. New York: Routledge, 2012.

Andersen, Morten Koch. 'Time-Use, Activism and the Making of Future'. *South Asia: Journal of South Asian Studies* 39, no. 2 (2016): 415–29.

Anderson, Ben. 'Emergency Futures: Exception, Urgency, Interval, Hope'. *The Sociological Review* 65, no. 3 (2016): 463–77.

Anderson, Ben. 'Preemption, Precaution, Preparedness: Anticipatory Action and Future Geographies'. *Progress in Human Geography* 34, no. 6 (2010): 777–98.

Anderson, Benedict. *Imagined Communities: Reflections on the Origin and Spread of Nationalism*. London; New York: Verso, 2006.

Appadurai, Arjun, ed. *The Future as Cultural Fact: Essays on the Global Condition*. London: New York : Verso Books, 2013.

Arendt, Hannah. *The Origins of Totalitarianism*. New York: Harcourt, Brace & World, 1966.

Armah, Ayi Kwei. *Fragments*. African Writers Series 154. London: Heinemann, 1974.

Ashar, Meera. 'Decolonizing What? Categories, Concepts and the Enduring "Not Yet"'. *Cultural Dynamics* 27, no. 2 (2015): 253–65.

Assmann, Aleida. 'Transformations of the Modern Time Regime'. In *Breaking up Time: Negotiating the Borders between Present, Past and Future*, edited by Chris Lorenz and Berber Bevernage, 39–56. Bristol, CT: Vandenhoeck & Ruprecht LLC, 2013.

Attwell, David. *Rewriting Modernity: Studies in Black South African Literary History*. Athens: Ohio University Press, 2006.

Austen, Ralph A. 'Struggling with the African Bildungsroman'. *Research in African Literatures* 46, no. 3 (2015): 214–31.

Auyero, Javier. *Patients of the State: The Politics of Waiting in Argentina*. Durham, NC: Duke University Press, 2012.

Awoonor, Kofi. *The Breast of the Earth: A Survey of the History, Culture, and Literature of Africa South of the Sahara*. Garden City, NY Anchor Press, 1976.

Azim, Firdous. *The Colonial Rise of the Novel*. London; New York: Routledge, 1993.

Baldwin, Lewis V. 'General Introduction'. In *'In a Single Garment of Destiny': A Global Vision of Justice*, xix–xxviii. The King Legacy Series. Boston, MA: Beacon Press, 2012.

Balfour, Robert. 'Home as Postcolonial Trope in the Fiction of V. S. Naipaul'. *Journal of Literary Studies* 26, no. 3 (2010): 16–33.

Bangura, Ahmed S. *Islam and the West African Novel: The Politics of Representation*. Boulder, CO: L. Rienner, 2000.

Barak, On. *On Time: Technology and Temporality in Modern Egypt*. Berkeley: University of California Press, 2013.

Barnard, Rita. *Apartheid and Beyond: South African Writers and the Politics of Place*. Oxford: Oxford University Press, 2007.

Barnard, Rita. 'Rewriting the Nation'. In *The Cambridge History of South African Literature*, edited by David Attwell and Derek Attridge, 652–75. Cambridge; New York: Cambridge University Press, 2012.

Barnard, Rita. 'Tsotsis: On Law, the Outlaw, and the Postcolonial State'. *Contemporary Literature* 49, no. 4 (2008): 541–72.

Barnard, Rita, and Andrew van der Vlies, eds. 'Introduction'. In *South African Writing in Transition*, 1–32. New York: Bloomsbury Academic, 2019.
Barrows, Adam. *The Cosmic Time of Empire: Modern Britain and World Literature*. Flashpoints 3. Berkeley: University of California Press, 2011.
Bashir, Shahzad. 'On Islamic Time: Rethinking Chronology in the Historiography of Muslim Societies'. *History the Theory* 53 (2014): 519–44.
Bayart, Jean-François. *Global Subjects: A Political Critique of Globalization*. Translated by Andrew Brown. Cambridge: Polity, 2007.
Beah, Ishmael. *A Long Way Gone: Memoirs of a Boy Soldier*. New York: Farrar, Straus and Giroux, 2007.
Beah, Ishmael. *Radiance of Tomorrow: [A Novel]*. New York: Sarah Crichton Books, Farrar, Straus and Giroux, 2014.
Beck, Ulrich, and Daniel Levy. 'Cosmopolitanized Nations: Re-Imagining Collectivity in World Risk Society'. *Theory, Culture & Society* 30, no. 2 (2013): 3–31.
Benjamin, Walter. *Illuminations*. New York: Schocken Books, 1986.
Benjamin, Walter, and Rolf Tiedemann. *The Arcades Project*. Cambridge, MA: Belknap Press, 1999.
Berger, Roger A. 'Writing Without a Future: Colonial Nostalgia in V. S. Naipaul's "A Bend in the River"'. *Essays in Literature* 22, no. 1 (Spring 1995): 144–56.
Berlant, Lauren Gail. *Cruel Optimism*. Durham, NC: Duke University Press, 2011.
Bernstein, J. A. '"No audible tick": Conrad, McTaggart, and the Revolt Against Time'. *Conradian: Journal of the Joseph Conrad Society* 37, no. 1 (2012): 32–45.
Bevernage, Berber, and Chris Lorenz. 'Breaking up Time: Negotiating the Borders between Present, Past and Future. An Introduction'. In *Breaking up Time: Negotiating the Borders between Present, Past and Future*, 7–35. Bristol, CT: Vandenhoeck & Ruprecht LLC, 2013.
Bhabha, Homi K. '"Race", Time and the Revision of Modernity'. *Oxford Literary Review* 13, nos 1/2 (1991): 193–219.
Bhabha, Homi K. *The Location of Culture*. Routledge Classics. London; New York: Routledge, 2004.
Bilby, Kenneth M. *True-Born Maroons*. New World Diasporas. Gainesville: University Press of Florida, 2005.
Birth, Kevin K. *Objects of Time: How Things Shape Temporality*. Culture, Mind, and Society. New York: Palgrave Macmillan, 2012.
Bissell, David. 'Animating Suspension: Waiting for Mobilities'. *Mobilities* 2, no. 2 (2007): 277–98.
Black Lives Matter. 'Two Years Later, Black Lives Matter Faces Critique, But It Won't Be Stopped'. Black Lives Matter. Available at <http://blacklivesmatter.com/two-years-later-black-lives-matter-faces-critiques-but-it-wont-be-stopped> (last accessed 27 June 2016).
Blackstock, Nelson. *Cointelpro: The FBI's Secret War on Political Freedom*. New York: Pathfinder Press. 2018.
Boehmer, Elleke. *Colonial and Postcolonial Literature*. New York: Oxford University Press, 1995.
Boehmer, Elleke. 'Postcolonial Writing and Terror'. In *Terror and the Postcolonial: A Concise Companion*, edited by Elleke Boehmer and Stephen

Morton, 141–50. Concise Companions to Literature and Culture. Malden, MA: Wiley-Blackwell, 2010.

Boehmer, Elleke. *Stories of Women: Gender and Narrative in the Postcolonial Nation*. Manchester; New York: Manchester University Press, 2005.

Bourdieu, Pierre. *Pascalian Meditations*. Stanford, CA: Stanford University Press, 2000.

Brantlinger, Patrick. '"Heart of darkness": Anti-Imperialism, Racism, or Impressionism?' *Criticism* 27, no. 4 (1985): 363–85.

Braudel, Fernand. 'History and the Social Science: The Longue Duree'. In *The Longue Durée and World-Systems Analysis*, edited by Richard E. Lee, translated by Immanuel Wallerstein, 725–53. Fernand Braudel Center Studies in Historical Social Science. New York: State University of New York Press, 2012.

Bruyneel, Kevin. *The Third Space of Sovereignty*. NED-New edition. Minneapolis: University of Minnesota Press, 2007.

Buck-Morss, Susan. *Hegel, Haiti and Universal History*. Illuminations. Pittsburgh, PA: University of Pittsburgh Press, 2009.

Bush, George W. 'Selected Speeches of President George W. Bush, 2001–2008'. National Archives and Records Administration, 30 April 2003. Available at <https://georgewbush-whitehouse.archives.gov/infocus/bushrecord/documents/Selected_Speeches_George_W_Bush.pdf> (last accessed 5 October 2016).

Caminero-Santangelo, Byron. *African Fiction and Joseph Conrad: Reading Postcolonial Intertextuality*. Albany: State University of New York Press, 2005.

Campbell, Patricia J. 'The Truth and Reconciliation Commission (TRC): Human Rights and State Transitions – The South Africa Model'. *African Studies Quarterly* 4, no. 3 (2000): 41–63.

Campt, Tina. *Listening to Images*. Durham, NC: Duke University Press, 2017.

Caplan, Marc. 'Nos Ancêtres, Les Diallobés: Cheikh Hamidou Kane's Ambiguous Adventure and the Paradoxes of Islamic Negritude'. *Modern Fiction Studies* 51, no. 4 (2005): 936–57.

Carpentier, Alejo. *The Kingdom of This World*. Translated by Harriet de Onís. New York: Farrar, Straus and Giroux, 2006.

Carr, David. *Time, Narrative, and History*. Studies in Phenomenology and Existential Philosophy. Bloomington: Indiana University Press, 1986.

Chakrabarty, Dipesh. *Provincializing Europe: Postcolonial Thought and Historical Difference*. Princeton, NJ: Princeton University Press, 2008.

Chakrabarty, Dipesh. 'The Legacies of Bandung: Decolonization and the Politics of Culture'. In *Making a World After Empire: The Bandung Moment and Its Political Afterlives*, edited by Christopher J. Lee, 45–68. Athens: Ohio University Press, 2010.

Chatterjee, Partha. 'Anderson's Utopia'. *Diacritics* 29, no. 4 (1999): 128–34.

Chatterjee, Partha. *The Nation and Its Fragments: Colonial and Postcolonial Histories*. Princeton Studies in Culture/Power/History. Princeton, NJ: Princeton University Press, 1993.

Chaudhuri, Amit. 'In the Waiting-Room of History'. *London Review of Books* 26, no. 12 (24 June 2004). Available at <http://www.lrb.co.uk/v26/n12/amit-chaudhuri/in-the-waiting-room-of-history> (last accessed 4 March 2022).

Cheah, Pheng. *What Is a World? On Postcolonial Literature as World Literature.* Durham, NC: Duke University Press, 2016.
Christodoulidis, Emilios, and Scott Veitch. 'Introduction'. In *Law and the Politics of Reconciliation*, edited by Scott Veitch, 1–8. Edinburgh Centre of Law and Society Series. Aldershot, UK; Burlington, VT: Ashgate, 2007.
Clingman, Stephen. *The Grammar of Identity: Transnational Fiction and the Nature of the Boundary.* Oxford, UK: Oxford University Press, 2012.
Clingman, Stephen. *The Novels of Nadine Gordimer: History from the Inside.* Second edition. Amherst: University of Massachusetts Press, 1992.
Coetzee, J. M. *Life & Times of Michael K.* New York: Viking Press, 1984.
Coetzee, J. M. *Waiting for the Barbarians.* Harmondsworth, UK; New York: Penguin Books, 1982.
Coetzee, J. M. *White Writing: On the Culture of Letters in South Africa.* New Haven, CT: Yale University Press, 1988.
Cole, Ernest. 'Nadine Gordimer and Post-Apartheid Interregnum: An Analysis of "July's People"'. *Journal of the African Literature Association* 2, no. 1 (2008): 60–82.
Conlon, Deirdre. 'Waiting: Feminist Perspectives on the Spacings/Timings of Migrant (Im)Mobility'. *Gender, Place and Culture* 18, no. 3 (2011): 353–60.
Conrad, Joseph. *Heart of Darkness and Other Tales.* Borders Classics. Ann Arbor, MI: Borders Classics, 2004.
Conteh-Morgan, John. 'Beyond Race: Class Conflict and Tragic Vision in an African Novel'. *Race and Class* 19, no. 2 (1987): 17–23.
Coovadia, Imraan. 'Authority and Misquotation in V. S. Naipaul's A Bend in the River'. *Postcolonial Text* 4, no. 1 (2008): 1–12.
Crais, Clifton C. *White Supremacy and Black Resistance in Pre-Industrial South Africa: The Making of the Colonial Order in the Eastern Cape, 1770–1865.* African Studies Series 72. Cambridge, UK; New York: Cambridge University Press, 1992.
Crapanzano, Vincent. *Waiting: The Whites of South Africa.* New York: Random House, 1985.
Cudjoe, Selwyn Reginald. *V. S. Naipaul: A Materialist Reading.* Amherst: University of Massachusetts Press, 1988.
Czarnota, Adam. 'Sacrum, Profanum and Social Time: Quasi-Theological Reflections on Time and Reconciliation'. In *Law and the Politics of Reconciliation*, edited by Scott Veitch, 147–62. Edinburgh Centre of Law and Society Series. Aldershot, UK; Burlington, VT: Ashgate, 2007.
De Lange, Johnny. 'The Historical Context, Legal Origins and Philosophical Foundation of the South African Truth and Reconciliation Commission'. In *Looking Back, Reaching Forward: Reflections on the Truth and Reconciliation Commission of South Africa*, edited by Charles Villa-Vicencio and Wilhelm Verwoerd, 14–31. Cape Town; London; New York: University of Cape Town Press; Zed Books, 2000.
Delany, Martin R. *Blake or The Huts of America: A Novel.* Boston, MA: Beacon Press, 1996.
Desai, Anita. *Cry, the Peacock.* Orient Paperbacks 318. New Delhi: Orient Paperbacks, 2004.
Doyle, Laura. 'Inter-Imperiality and Literary Studies in the Longer *Durée*'. *PMLA* 130, no. 2 (2015): 336–47.

Driver, Dorothy. '"On these premises I am the government": Njabulo Ndebele's The Cry of Winnie Mandela and the Reconstructions of Gender and Nation'. In *Africa Writing Europe: Opposition, Juxtaposition, Entanglement*, edited by Maria Olaussen and Christina Angelfors, 105:1–38. Cross/Cultures – Readings in the Post/Colonial Literatures in English. Amsterdam: Rodopi, 2009.

du Toit, H. Louise. 'Feminism and the Ethics of Reconciliation'. In *Law and the Politics of Reconciliation*, edited by Scott Veitch, 185–213. Edinburgh Centre of Law and Society Series. Aldershot, UK; Burlington, VT: Ashgate, 2007.

Echevarría, Roberto Gonzalez. *Alejo Carpentier: The Pilgrim at Home*. Austin: University of Texas Press, 1990.

English, Daylanne K. *Each Hour Redeem: Time and Justice in African American Literature*, 2013.

Fabian, Johannes. *Time and the Other: How Anthropology Makes Its Object*. New York: Columbia University Press, 1983.

Fanon, Frantz. *The Wretched of the Earth*. New York: Grove Press, 1963.

Feit, Mario. 'Democratic Impatience: Martin Luther King, Jr. on Democratic Temporality'. *Contemporary Political Theory* (2016): 1–24.

Figueroa, Víctor. *Prophetic Visions of the Past: Pan-Caribbean Representations of the Haitian Revolution*. Transoceanic Studies. Columbus: Ohio State University Press, 2015.

Figueroa, Víctor. 'The Kingdom of Black Jacobins: C. L. R. James and Alejo Carpentier on the Haitian Revolution'. *Afro-Hispanic Review* 25, no. 2 (2006): 55–71.

Fischer, Sibylle. *Modernity Disavowed: Haiti and the Cultures of Slavery in the Age of Revolution*. Durham, NC: Duke University Press, 2004.

Fleming Jr, Julius B. 'Transforming Geographies of Black Time: How the Free Southern Theater Used the Plantation for Civil Rights Activism'. *American Literature* 91, no. 3 (2019): 587–617.

Fletcher Jr, Bill. 'From Hashtag to Strategy: The Growing Pains of Black Lives Matter'. In These Times, 23 September 2015. Available at <http://inthesetimes.com/article/18394/from-hashtag-to-strategy-the-growing-pains-of-black-lives-matter> (last accessed 27 June 2016).

Freeman, Elizabeth. *Time Binds: Queer Temporalities, Queer Histories*. Perverse Modernities. Durham, NC: Duke University Press, 2010.

Friedman, Susan Stanford. *Planetary Modernisms: Provocations on Modernity across Time*. Modernist Latitudes. New York: Columbia University Press, 2015.

Gadjigo, Samba. 'Literature and History: The Case of Cheikh Hamidou Kane's Ambiguous Adventure'. *Research in African Literatures* 22, no. 4 (1991): 29–38.

Ganguly, Keya. 'Temporality and Postcolonial Critique'. In *The Cambridge Companion to Postcolonial Literary Studies*, edited by Neil Lazarus, 162–79. Cambridge Companions to Literature. Cambridge, UK; New York: Cambridge University Press, 2004.

Geggus, Patrick. *Haitian Revolutionary Studies*. Bloomington: Indiana University Press, 2002.

Gellar, Sheldon. *Senegal: An African Nation between Islam and the West*. Nations of the Modern World Africa. Second edition. Boulder, CO: Westview Press, 1995.

Gikandi, Simon. *Reading the African Novel*. London: Currey, 1988.
Gillman, Susan. 'Oceans of "Longues Durees"'. *PMLA* 127, no. 2 (2012): 328–34.
Glissant, Édouard. *Caribbean Discourse: Selected Essays*. Translated by J. Michael Dash. CARAF Books. Charlottesville: University Press of Virginia, 1989.
Gokee, Cameron, Haeden Stewart and Jason De León. 'Scales of Suffering in the US–Mexico Borderlands'. *International Journal of Historical Archaeology* 24 (3 January 2020): 823–51.
Goldin, Ian. 'The Reconstitution of Coloured Identity in the Western Cape'. In *The Politics of Race, Class, and Nationalism in Twentieth Century South Africa*, edited by Shula Marks and Stanley Trapido, 156–81. Harlow, UK: Longman Group, 1987.
Gordimer, Nadine. *July's People*. New York: Penguin Books, 1982.
Gordimer, Nadine, and Stephen Clingman. *The Essential Gesture: Writing, Politics, and Places*. Edited by Stephen Clingman. New York: Penguin Books, 1989.
Gready, Paul. *The Era of Transitional Justice: The Aftermath of the Truth and Reconciliation Commission in South Africa and Beyond*. A GlassHouse Book. Abingdon, UK: Routledge, 2011.
Gupta, R. K. 'Trends in Modern Indian Fiction'. *World Literature Today* 68, no. 2 (1994): 299–307.
Haberman, Maggie, and Charlie Savage. 'Trump, Lacking Clear Authority, Says U.S. Will Declare Antifa a Terrorist Group'. *New York Times*, 31 May 2020. Available at <https://www.nytimes.com/2020/05/31/us/politics/trump-antifa-terrorist-group.html> (last accessed 16 June 2020).
Hall, Stuart. 'When Was "the Post-Colonial"? Thinking at the Limit'. In *The Post-Colonial Question: Common Skies, Divided Horizons*, edited by Iain Chambers and Lidia Curti, 242–60. London: Routledge, 1996.
Hallemeier, Katherine. 'Still Waiting? Writing Futurity After Apartheid'. In *South African Writing in Transition*, edited by Rita Barnard and Andrew van der Vlies, 77–97. New York: Bloomsbury Academic, 2019.
Hamann, Byron Ellsworth. 'How to Chronologize with a Hammer, Or, The Myth of Homogeneous, Empty Time'. *HAU: Journal of Ethnographic Theory* 6, no. 1 (2016): 261–92.
Hanchard, Michael. 'Afro-Modernity: Temporality, Politics, and the African Diaspora'. In *Alternative Modernities*, edited by Dilip Parameshwar Gaonkar, 272–98. Durham, NC: Duke University Press, 2001.
Harrow, Kenneth W. 'An African Reading of Naipaul's "A Bend in the River"'. *Journal of South Asian Literature* 26, no. 1/2 (1991): 322–35.
Harrow, Kenneth W., ed. *Faces of Islam in African Literature*. Studies in African Literature. Portsmouth, NH; London: Heinemann ; J. Currey, 1991.
Hartman, Saidiya. 'The Time of Slavery'. *The South Atlantic Quarterly* 101, no. 4 (2002): 757–77.
Harvey, David. 'Time-Space Compression and the Postmodern Condition'. In *Modernity: Critical Concepts in Sociology*, edited by Malcolm Waters, vol. IV:98–118. London: Routledge, 1999.
Hayes, Patrick. *J. M. Coetzee and the Novel: Writing and Politics after Beckett*. Oxford English Monographs. Oxford, UK; New York: Oxford University Press, 2010.

Hayward, Helen. *The Enigma of V. S. Naipaul: Sources and Contexts*. Basingstoke, UK; New York: Palgrave Macmillan, 2002.
Hegel, G. W. F. *The Philosophy of History*. Translated by J. Sibree. New York: American Dome Library Company, 1902.
Heider, Sarah Dove. 'The Timeless Ecstasy of Michael K'. *Bucknell Review* 37, no. 1 (1993): 83–98.
Helgesson, Stefan. 'Radicalizing Temporal Difference: Anthropology, Postcolonial Theory, and Literary Time'. *History and Theory* 53 (2011): 545–62.
Honwana, Alcinda Manuel. *The Time of Youth: Work, Social Change, and Politics in Africa*. Sterling, VA: Kumarian Press Pub, 2012.
Hook, Derek. *A Critical Psychology of the Postcolonial: The Mind of Apartheid*. New York: Routledge, 2012.
Hook, Derek. 'Indefinite Delay: On (Post)Apartheid Temporality'. In *Psychosocial Imaginaries: Perspectives on Temporality, Subjectivity, and Activism*, edited by Stephen Frosh, 48–71. Basingstoke, UK; New York: Palgrave Macmillan, 2015.
Hook, Derek. 'Petrified Life'. *Social Dynamics*, 2015, 1–23.
Hoy, David Couzens. *The Time of Our Lives: A Critical History of Temporality*. Cambridge, MA: MIT Press, 2009.
Huebener, Paul. *Timing Canada: The Shifting Politics of Time in Canadian Literary Culture*, 2016. Available at <http://deslibris.ca/ID/450374> (last accessed 5 July 2019).
Huehls, Mitchum. *Qualified Hope: A Postmodern Politics of Time*. Columbus: Ohio State University Press, 2009.
Hunt, Lynn. 'Globalisation and Time'. In *Breaking up Time: Negotiating the Borders between Present, Past and Future*, 199–215. Bristol, CT: Vandenhoeck & Ruprecht LLC, 2013.
Huntington, Samuel P. *The Clash of Civilizations and the Remaking of World Order*. New York: Simon & Schuster, 2003.
Hyndman, Jennifer, and Wenona Giles. 'Waiting for What? The Feminization of Asylum in Protracted Situations'. *Gender, Place and Culture* 18, no. 3 (2011): 361–79.
Ilmonen, Kaisa. 'Talking Back to the Bildungsroman: Caribbean Literature and the Dis/Location of the Genre'. *Journal of West Indian Literature* 24, no. 1 (2017): 60–76.
Insko, Jeffrey. 'Prospects for the Present'. *American Literary History* 26, no. 4 (2014): 836–48.
James, C. L. R. *The Black Jacobins: Toussaint L'Ouverture and the San Domingo Revolution*. Second edition. New York: Vintage, 1989.
James, Cynthia. *The Maroon Narrative: Caribbean Literature in English across Boundaries, Ethnicities, and Centuries*. Studies in Caribbean Literature. Portsmouth, NH: Heinemann, 2002.
Jameson, Frederic. 'Third-World Literature in the Era of Multinational Capitalism'. *Social Text* 15 (1986): 65–88.
Jamkhandi, Sudhakar R. 'The Artistic Effects of the Shifts in Point of View in Anita Desai's Cry, the Peacock'. *The Journal of Indian Writing in English* 9, no. 1 (1981): 35–46.

Jeffrey, Craig. *Timepass: Youth, Class, and the Politics of Waiting in India*. Stanford, CA: Stanford University Press, 2010.
Jensen, Steffen. 'This House Is Not My Own . . . ! Temporalities in a South African Homeland'. *Journal of Southern African Studies* 41, no. 5 (2015): 991–1004.
Jessop, Bob. 'Time and Space in the Globalization of Capital and Their Implications for State Power'. *Rethinking Marxism: A Journal of Economics, Culture and Society* 14, no. 1 (2002): 97–117.
Johnson, Erica L. '"Provincializing Europe": The Postcolonial Urban Uncanny in V. S. Naipaul's A Bend in the River'. *Journal of Narrative Theory* 40, no. 2 (Summer 2010): 209–30.
Jussawalla, Feroza F., ed. *Conversations with V. S. Naipaul*. Literary Conversations Series. Jackson: University Press of Mississippi, 1997.
Kamalu, Chukwunyere. *Person, Divinity & Nature: A Modern View of the Person and the Cosmos in African Thought*. London: Karnak House, 1998.
Kane, Hamidou. *Ambiguous Adventure*. Translated by Katherine Woods. African Writers Series 119. London: Heinemann, 1972.
Kargbo, Abubakar. 'The Long Road to Peace: 1991–1997'. In *Bound to Cooperate: Conflict, Peace and People in Sierra Leone*, edited by Anatole N. Ayissi, Robin Poulton and United Nations Institute for Disarmament Research, 37–48. Second edition. Geneva: United Nations Institute for Disarmament Research, 2006.
Keating, Christine. *Decolonizing Democracy: Transforming the Social Contract in India*. University Park: Pennsylvania State University Press, 2011.
Keeling, Kara. *The Witch's Flight: The Cinematic, the Black Femme, and the Image of Common Sense*. Durham, NC: Duke University Press, 2008.
Kelley, Elleza. '"Follow the tree flowers": Fugitive Mapping in Beloved'. *Antipode* 53, no. 1 (2021): 181–99.
Kermode, Frank. *The Sense of an Ending: Studies in the Theory of Fiction: With a New Epilogue*. Oxford, UK; New York: Oxford University Press, 2000.
Kertzer, J. M. 'Joseph Conrad and the Metaphysics of Time'. *Studies in the Novel* 11, no. 3 (1979): 302–17.
Kher, Inder N. 'Madness as Discourse in Anita Desai's Cry, the Peacock'. *Commonwealth Novel in English* 5, no. 2 (1992): 16–25.
King, Bruce. *V. S. Naipaul*. Modern Novelists. New York: St Martin's Press, 1993.
King Jr, Martin Luther. *'In a Single Garment of Destiny': A Global Vision of Justice*. The King Legacy Series. Boston, MA: Beacon Press, 2012.
King Jr, Martin Luther. *Why We Can't Wait*. New York: Harper & Row, 1963.
Klostermaier, Klaus K. *A Survey of Hinduism*. Third edition. Albany: State University of New York Press, 2007.
Kumar, Radha. *The History of Doing: An Illustrated Account of Movements for Women's Rights and Feminism in India, 1800–1990*. New Delhi: Kali for Women, 1993.
Kwon, June Hee. 'The Work of Waiting: Love and Money in Korean Chinese Transnational Migration'. *Cultural Anthropology* 30, no. 3 (2015): 477–500.
Lagji, Amanda. 'Terrorist Plots: Temporality, the Politics of Preemption, and the Postcolonial Novel'. *Studies in the Novel* 52, no. 4 (2020): 403–18.

Lalla, Barbara. *Defining Jamaican Fiction: Marronage and the Discourse of Survival*. Tuscaloosa: University of Alabama Press, 1996.
Laski, Gregory. *Untimely Democracy: The Politics of Progress after Slavery*. New York: Oxford University Press, 2018.
Lawson, William. *The Western Scar: The Theme of the Been-to in West African Fiction*. Athens: Ohio University Press, 1982.
Lazarus, Joyce Block. 'Islam and the West in the Fiction of Cheikh Hamidou Kane'. *Symposium* 58, no. 3 (2004): 179–90.
Lazarus, Neil. *Resistance in Postcolonial African Fiction*. New Haven, CT: Yale University Press, 1990.
Leavis, F. R. *The Great Tradition*. New York: New York University Press, 1948.
Liatsos, Yianna. 'Truth, Confession and the Post-Apartheid Black Consciousness in Njabulo Ndebele's The Cry of Winnie Mandela'. In *Modern Confessional Writing: New Critical Essays*, edited by Jo Gill, 115–36. Routledge Studies in Twentieth-Century Literature 2. London; New York: Routledge, 2006.
Little, J. P. 'Autofiction and Cheikh Hamidou Kane's "L'aventure Ambigue"'. *Research in African Literatures* 31, no. 2 (2000): 71–90.
Mack, Katherine Elizabeth. *From Apartheid to Democracy: Deliberating Truth and Reconciliation in South Africa*. Rhetoric and Democratic Deliberation 11. University Park: Pennsylvania State University Press, 2014.
Mackie, Erin Skye. 'Welcome the Outlaws: Pirates, Maroons, and Caribbean Countercultures'. *Cultural Critique* 59 (2005): 24–62.
Majumdar, Saikat. *Prose of the World*. New York: Columbia University Press, 2013.
Mamdani, Mahmood. 'The Truth According to the TRC'. In *The Politics of Memory: Truth, Healing, and Social Justice*, edited by Ifi Amadiume and ʿAbd Allāh Aḥmad Naʿīm, 176–83. London; New York: Zed Books, 2000.
Masquelier, Adeline. 'Teatime: Boredom and the Temporalities of Young Men in Niger'. *Africa: The Journal of the International African Institute* 83, no. 3 (2013): 385–402.
Masterton, Rebecca. 'Islamic Mystical Readings of Cheikh Hamidou Kane's Ambiguous Adventure'. *Journal of Islamic Studies* 20, no. 1 (2008): 21–45.
Mazrui, Alamin, and Lupenga Mphande. 'Time and Labor in Colonial Africa: The Case of Kenya and Malawi'. In *Time in the Black Experience*, edited by Joseph K. Adjaye. Contributions in Afro-American and African Studies 167. Westport, CT: Greenwood Press, 1994.
Mbembe, Achille. *On the Postcolony*. Studies on the History of Society and Culture 41. Berkeley: University of California Press, 2001.
Mbiti, John S. *African Religions & Philosophy*. Second revised and enlarged edition. Oxford, UK; Portsmouth, NH: Heinemann, 1990.
McGonegal, Julie. *Imagining Justice: The Politics of Postcolonial Forgiveness and Reconciliation*. Montreal: McGill-Queen's University Press, 2009.
McKittrick, Katherine. 'Plantation Futures'. *Small Axe* 17, no. 3 (2013): 1–15.
McKittrick, Katherine. 'Wait Canada Anticipate Black'. *The CLR James Journal* 20, nos 1–2 (2014): 243–49.
Medalie, David. 'The Cry of Winnie Mandela: Njabulo Ndebele's Post-Apartheid Novel'. *English Studies in Africa* 49, no. 2 (2006): 51–65.
Mehta, Uday S. 'Indian Constitutionalism: The Articulation of a Political Vision'. In *From the Colonial to the Postcolonial: India and Pakistan in*

Transition, edited by Dipesh Chakrabarty, Rochona Majumdar and Andrew Sartori, 13–30. Oxford: Oxford University Press, 2007.

Melas, Natalie. *All the Difference in the World: Postcoloniality and the Ends of Comparison*. Cultural Memory in the Present. Stanford, CA: Stanford University Press, 2007.

Mezzadra, Sandro, and Federico Rahola. 'The Postcolonial Condition: A Few Notes on the Quality of Historical Time in the Global Present'. In *Reworking Postcolonialism: Globalization, Labour and Rights*, edited by Pavan Kumar Malreddy, Birte Heidemann and Ole Birk Lauresen, 2:36–54. Basingstoke, UK: Palgrave Macmillan, 2015.

Mignolo, Walter. *Local Histories/Global Designs: Coloniality, Subaltern Knowledges, and Border Thinking*. Princeton Studies in Culture/Power/History. Princeton, NJ; Woodstock, UK: Princeton University Press, 2012.

Mills, Charles W. 'White Time: The Chronic Injustice of Ideal Theory'. *Du Bois Review* 11, no. 1 (2014): 27–42.

Minow, Martha. 'The Hope for Healing: What Can Truth Commissions Do?' In *Truth V. Justice: The Morality of Truth Commissions*, edited by Robert I. Rotberg and Dennis F. Thompson, 235–60. Princeton, NJ: Princeton University Press, 2000.

Monson, Tamlyn. 'An Infinite Question: The Paradox of Representation in Life & Times of Michael K'. *Journal of Commonwealth Literature* 38, no. 3 (2003): 87–106.

Moon, Claire. *Narrating Political Reconciliation: South Africa's Truth and Reconciliation Commission*. Lanham, MD: Lexington Books, 2008.

Moon, Claire. 'Reconciliation as Therapy and Compensation: A Critical Analysis'. In *Law and the Politics of Reconciliation*, edited by Scott Veitch, 163–84. Edinburgh Centre of Law and Society Series. Aldershot, UK; Burlington, VT: Ashgate, 2007.

Moore, Alexandra Schultheis. *Vulnerability and Security in Human Rights Literature and Visual Culture*. Routledge Interdisciplinary Perspectives on Literature 56. New York: Routledge, Taylor & Francis Group, 2016.

Morales, Maria Cristina. 'The Manufacturing of the US–Mexico Border Crisis'. In *The Oxford Handbook of Migration Crises*, edited by Cecilia Menjívar, Marie Ruiz and Immanuel Ness, 1–18. New York: Oxford University Press, 2019.

Moten, Fred. *Stolen Life. Consent Not to Be a Single Being*, vol. 2. Durham, NC: Duke University Press, 2018.

Moten, Fred. 'The Case of Blackness'. *Criticism* 50, no. 2 (2008): 177–218.

Mudimbe, V. Y. *The Idea of Africa*. African Systems of Thought. Bloomington; London: Indiana University Press ; J. Currey, 1994.

Mudimbe, V. Y. *The Invention of Africa: Gnosis, Philosophy, and the Order of Knowledge*. African Systems of Thought. Bloomington: Indiana University Press, 1988.

Mullin, Michael. *Africa in America: Slave Acculturation and Resistance in the American South and the British Caribbean, 1736–1831*. Blacks in the New World. Urbana: University of Illinois Press, 1992.

Munro, Martin. 'Haitian Novels and Novels of Haiti: History, Haitian Writing, and Madison Smartt Bell's Trilogy'. *Small Axe* 11, no. 2 (2007): 163–76.

Murphy, Laura. 'The Curse of Constant Remembrance: The Belated Trauma of the Slave Trade in Ayi Kwei Armah's Fragments'. *Studies in the Novel* 40, no. 1 (2008): 52–71.

Mustafa, Fawzia. *V. S. Naipaul*. Cambridge Studies in African and Caribbean Literature. Cambridge, UK; New York: Cambridge University Press, 1995.

Nadkarni, Asha. *Eugenic Feminism: Reproductive Nationalism in the United States and India*. Minneapolis: University of Minnesota Press, 2014.

Naipaul, V. S. *A Bend in the River*. New York: Vintage Books, 1980.

Naipaul, V. S. *In a Free State*. London: Deutsch, 1971.

Naipaul, V. S. *Literary Occasions: Essays*. New York: Alfred A. Knopf, 2003.

Naipaul, V. S. *The Middle Passage: Impressions of Five Societies – British, French, and Dutch – in the West Indies and South America*. New York: Vintage Books, 1981.

Nakai, Asako. 'Journey to the Heart of Darkness: Naipaul's "Conradian Atavism" Reconsidered'. *The Conradian* 23, no. 2 (1998): 1–16.

Nanni, Giordano. *The Colonisation of Time: Ritual, Routine and Resistance in the British Empire*. Studies in Imperialism. Manchester, UK; New York: Manchester University Press, 2012.

Napolitano, Joe. 'Restoring Narrative, Narrating Justice: Njabulo Ndebele's The Cry of Winnie Mandela and the Complication of Truth and Reconciliation'. In *Migrations and Creative Expressions in Africa and the African Diaspora*, edited by Toyin Falola, Niyi Afolabi and Aderonke Adesola Adesanya, 331–60. Durham, NC: Carolina Academic Press, 2008.

Ndebele, Njabulo S. 'Introduction: Contemplating Winnie Mandela'. In *The Cry of Winnie Mandela: A Novel*, x–xl. Johannesburg: Picador Africa, 2013.

Ndebele, Njabulo S. 'Of Lions and Rabbits: Thoughts on Democracy and Reconciliation'. In *After the TRC: Reflections on Truth and Reconciliation in South Africa*, edited by Wilmot James and Linda Van De Vijver, 143–56. Athens: Ohio University Press, 2001.

Ndebele, Njabulo S. *South African Literature and Culture: Rediscovery of the Ordinary*. Edited by Njabulo S Ndebele. Manchester, UK; New York: Manchester University Press, 1994.

Ndebele, Njabulo S. 'South Africans in Search of Common Values'. *Pretexts: Literary and Cultural Studies* 10, no. 1 (2001): 75–81.

Ndebele, Njabulo S. *The Cry of Winnie Mandela : A Novel*. Banbury, UK: Ayebia Clarke Pub., 2004.

Ndebele, Njabulo S. 'The Revolution of the Aged'. In *Ten Years of Staffrider, 1978–1988*, edited by Andries Walter Oliphant and Ivan Vladislavic, 241–2. Johannesburg: Raven Press, n.d.

Nicholls, Brendon, ed. *Nadine Gordimer's July's People*. Routledge Guides to Literature. London; New York: Routledge, 2011.

Niekerk, Marlene van. 'The Literary Text in Turbulent Times: An Instrument of Social Cohesion or an Eruption of "Critical" Bliss. Notes on J M Coetzee's Life and Times of Michael K'. *Acta Academia* 45, no. 4 (2013): 1–39.

Nightingale, Peggy. *Journey through Darkness: The Writing of V. S. Naipaul*. St Lucia, Australia; New York: University of Queensland Press, 1987.

Nixon, Rob. *London Calling: V. S. Naipaul, Postcolonial Mandarin*. New York: Oxford University Press, 1992.

Nkrumah, Kwame. *I Speak of Freedom*. London: Panaf Books Limited, 1973.

Nnaemeka, Obioma. 'Exile(s), Choice, and the Burden of Memory in Cheikh Hamidou Kane's Ambiguous Adventure'. In *Challenging Hierarchies: Issues and Themes in Colonial and Postcolonial African Literature*, edited by Leonard A Podis and Saaka Yakubu, 229–41. New York: Peter Lang, 1998.

Nwankwo, Ifeoma Kiddoe. *Black Cosmopolitanism: Racial Consciousness and Transnational Identity in the Nineteenth-Century Americas*. Philadelphia: University of Pennsylvania Press, 2005.

Nyatetũ-Waigwa, Wangari wa. *The Liminal Novel: Studies in the Francophone-African Novel as Bildungsroman*. American University Studies, vol. 6. New York: Peter Lang, 1996.

Obi Jr, Joe E. 'A Critical Reading of the Disillusionment Novel'. *Journal of Black Studies* 20, no. 4 (1990): 399–413.

Oboe, Analisa. 'The TRC Women's Hearings as Performance and Protest in the New South Africa'. *Research in African Literatures* 38, no. 3 (2007): 60–76.

O'Brien, Anthony. *Against Normalization: Writing Radical Democracy in South Africa*. Post-Contemporary Interventions. Durham, NC: Duke University Press, 2001.

O'Connell, Hugh Charles. 'A Weak Utopianism of Postcolonial Nationalist Bildung: Re-Reading Ayi Kwei Armah's The Beautyful Ones Are Not Yet Born'. *Journal of Postcolonial Writing* 48, no. 4 (2012): 371–83.

Ogle, Vanessa. *The Global Transformation of Time: 1870–1950*. Cambridge, MA: Harvard University Press, 2015.

Olson, Elizabeth. 'Geography and Ethics 1: Waiting and Urgency'. *Progress in Human Geography* 39, no. 4 (2015): 517–26.

Omelsky, Matthew. 'African Fugitivities'. *The Black Scholar: Journal of Black Studies and Research* 50, no. 1 (2020): 56–69.

Oxford English Dictionary. 'patience, n.1 (and Int.)'., n.d. Available at <http://www.oed.com/view/Entry/138816?rskey=Gpgyiw&result=1> (last accessed 25 January 2016).

Oxford English Dictionary. 'suffer, v.', n.d. Available at <http://www.oed.com/view/Entry/193523?redirectedFrom=suffer> (last accessed 31 March 2016).

Oxford English Dictionary. 'Wait, v. 1'. n.d. Available at <https://www.oed.com/view/Entry/225136?rskey=HJ5DKa&result=3> (last accessed 11 August 2016).

Paravisini-Gebert, Lizabeth. 'The Haitian Revolution in Interstices and Shadows: A Re-Reading of Alejo Carpentier's "The Kingdom of This World"'. *Research in African Literatures* 35, no. 2 (2004): 114–27.

Parker, Andrew, Mary Russo, Doris Sommer and Patricia Yaeger, ed. *Nationalisms and Sexualities*. New York: Routledge, 1992.

Penfold, Tom. 'Volume, Power, Originality: Reassessing the Complexities of Soweto Poetry'. *Journal of Southern African Studies* 41, no. 4 (2015): 1–19.

Penn, Nigel. 'Drosters of the Bokkeveld and the Roggeveld, 1770–1800'. In *Slavery in South Africa: Captive Labor on the Dutch Frontier*, edited by Elizabeth A. Eldredge and Fred Morton, 41–65. African Modernization and Development Series. Boulder, CO; Pietermaritzburg, South Africa: Westview Press; University of Natal Press, 1994.

Peteet, Julie. 'The Work of Comparison: Israel/Palestine and Apartheid'. *Anthropological Quarterly* 89, no. 1 (2016): 247–81.

Peters, John G. 'Joseph Conrad's "Sudden Holes" in Time: The Epistemology of Temporality'. *Studies in the Novel* 32, no. 4 (2000): 420–41.

Posel, Deborah. 'What's in a Name? Racial Categorisations under Apartheid and Their Afterlife'. In *History Workshop*, 59–82. Johannesburg: University of the Witswatersrand, 2001.

Povinelli, Elizabeth A. *Economies of Abandonment: Social Belonging and Endurance in Late Liberalism*. Durham, NC: Duke University Press, 2013.

Pugh, Judy F. 'Astrology and Fate: The Hindu and Muslim Experiences'. In *Karma: An Anthropological Inquiry*, edited by Charles F. Keyes and E. Valentine Daniel, 131–46. Berkeley: University of California Press, 1983.

Quayson, Ato. *Oxford Street, Accra: City Life and the Itineraries of Transnationalism*. Durham, NC: Duke University Press, 2014.

Ray, Sangeeta. *En-Gendering India: Woman and Nation in Colonial and Postcolonial Narratives*. Durham, NC: Duke University Press, 2000.

Reed, Anthony. *Freedom Time: The Poetics and Politics of Black Experimental Writing*. The Callaloo African Diaspora Series. Baltimore, MD: Johns Hopkins University Press, 2014.

Rege, Josna. 'Codes in Conflict: Post-Independence Alienation in Anita Desai's Early Novels'. *Journal of Gender Studies* 5, no. 3 (1996): 317–28.

Rege, Josna. *Colonial Karma: Self, Action, and Nation in the Indian English Novel*. New York: Palgrave Macmillan, 2004.

Rein, Sandra. 'Sierra Leone: Between the Prison-Houses of Nationalism and Transnationalism'. In *Globalizing Africa*, edited by Malinda Smith, 127–46. Trenton, NJ: Africa World Press, 2003.

Reinhard, Beth, and Damian Paletta. 'Donald Trump Back-Pedals on Banning Muslims from U.S'. *Wall Street Journal*. 28 June 2016, Online edition, sec. Politics. Available at <https://www.wsj.com/articles/donald-trump-back-pedals-on-banning-muslims-from-u-s-1467058774> (last accessed 5 October 2016).

Richardson, Bonham C. *The Caribbean in the Wider World, 1492–1992: A Regional Geography*. Geography of the World-Economy. Cambridge, UK; New York: Cambridge University Press, 1992.

Rifkin, Mark. *Beyond Settler Time: Temporal Sovereignty and Indigenous Self-Determination*. Durham, NC; London: Duke University Press, 2017.

Roberts, Neil. *Freedom as Marronage*. Chicago: University of Chicago Press, 2015.

Ross, Fiona C. 'An Acknowledged Failure: Women, Voice, Violence, and the South African Truth and Reconciliation Commission'. In *Localizing Transitional Justice: Interventions and Priorities after Mass Violence*, edited by Rosalind Shaw, Lars Waldorf and Pierre Hazan, 69–91. Stanford Studies in Human Rights. Stanford, CA: Stanford University Press, 2010.

Rotberg, Robert I., and Dennis F. Thompson, ed. *Truth v. Justice: The Morality of Truth Commissions*. University Center for Human Values Series. Princeton, NJ: Princeton University Press, 2000.

Sachs, Albie. 'His Name Was Henry'. In *After the TRC: Reflections on Truth and Reconciliation in South Africa*, edited by Wilmot Godfrey James and Linda van de Vijver, 94–100. Athens: Ohio University Press, 2001.

Said, Edward W. *Beginnings : Intention and Method*. New York: Basic Books, 1975.

Said, Edward W. *Culture and Imperialism*. New York: Vintage Books, 1994.
Said, Edward W. *Orientalism*. New York: Vintage Books, 1994.
Sanders, Mark. *Ambiguities of Witnessing: Law and Literature in the Time of a Truth Commission*. Meridian: Crossing Aesthetics. Stanford, CA: Stanford University Press, 2007.
Sawyer, Stephen W. 'Time after Time: Narratives of the Longue Duree in the Anthropocene'. *Transatlantica* 1 (2015): 1–18.
Schaap, Andrew. 'The Time of Reconciliation and the Space of Politics'. In *Law and the Politics of Reconciliation*, edited by Scott Veitch, 9–31. Edinburgh Centre of Law and Society Series. Aldershot, UK; Burlington, VT: Ashgate, 2007.
Schueller, Malini Johar. 'Postcolonial American Studies'. *American Literary History* 16, no. 1 (2004): 162–75.
Schwartz, Barry. 'Waiting, Exchange, and Power: The Distribution of Time in Social Systems'. *American Journal of Sociology* 79, no. 4 (1974): 841–70.
Schweizer, Harold. *On Waiting*. Thinking in Action. London ; New York: Routledge, 2008.
Scott, David. *Conscripts of Modernity: The Tragedy of Colonial Enlightenment*. Durham, NC: Duke University Press, 2004.
Scott, David. *Omens of Adversity: Tragedy, Time, Memory, Justice*. Durham, NC: Duke University Press, 2014.
Scott, James C. *The Art of Not Being Governed: An Anarchist History of Upland Southeast Asia*. New Haven, CT: Yale University Press, 2009.
Sharma, Som. P, and Kamal N. Awasthi. 'Anita Desai's Cry the Peacock: A Vindication of the Feminine'. In *Perspectives on Anita Desai*, edited by Ramesh K. Srivastava, 138–49. Delhi: Vimal Prakash Gupta, 1984.
Sharpe, Christina Elizabeth. *In the Wake: On Blackness and Being*. Durham, NC; London: Duke University Press, 2016.
Shaw, Rosalind. 'Linking Justice with Reintegration? Ex-Combatants and the Sierra Leone Experiment'. In *Localizing Transitional Justice: Interventions and Priorities after Mass Violence*, edited by Rosalind Shaw, Lars Waldorf and Pierre Hazan, 111–32. Stanford Studies in Human Rights. Stanford, CA: Stanford University Press, 2010.
Shaw, Rosalind, and Lars Waldorf. 'Introduction: Localizing Transitional Justice'. In *Localizing Transitional Justice: Interventions and Priorities after Mass Violence*, edited by Rosalind Shaw, Lars Waldorf and Pierre Hazan, 3–26. Stanford Studies in Human Rights. Stanford, CA: Stanford University Press, 2010.
Sierra Leone and Truth and Reconciliation Commission. *Witness to Truth: Report of the Sierra Leone Truth and Reconciliation Commission, Volume 1*. Accra, Ghana: GPL Press, 2004. Available at <http://www.sierraleonetrc.org/index.php/view-the-final-report/download-table-of-contents/volume-one/item/witness-to-the-truth-volume-one-chapters-1-5?category_id=11> (last accessed 4 April 2016).
Silenieks, Juris. 'The Maroon Figure in Caribbean Francophone Prose'. In *Voices from under: Black Narrative in Latin America and the Caribbean*, edited by William Luis, 115–25. Westport, CT: Greenwood Press, 1984.
Simone, Abdoumaliq. 'Waiting in African Cities'. In *Indefensible Space: The Architecture of the National Insecurity State*, edited by Michael Sorkin, 97–109. New York: Routledge, 2008.

Singh, Elangbam Hemanta. 'Utopian and Dystopian Visions of the Future in Nadine Gordimer's July's People'. *The Atlantic Literary Review* 12, no. 2 (2011): 55–65.

South Africa, and Desmond Tutu, ed. *Truth and Reconciliation Commission of South Africa Report*. Vol. 1. Cape Town: The Commission, 1998.

South Africa, and Desmond Tutu, ed. *Truth and Reconciliation Commission of South Africa Report*. Vol. 2. Cape Town: The Commission, 1998.

Spivak, Gayatri Chakravorty. *A Critique of Postcolonial Reason: Toward a History of the Vanishing Present*. Cambridge, MA: Harvard University Press, 1999.

Srivastava, Ramesh K. 'Introduction'. In *Perspectives on Anita Desai*, edited by Ramesh K. Srivastava, xiii–xlvii. Delhi: Vimal Prakash Gupta, 1984.

Stinchcombe, Arthur L. *Sugar Island Slavery in the Age of Enlightenment: The Political Economy of the Caribbean World*. Princeton, NJ: Princeton University Press, 1995.

Stockdale, Liam. 'Imagined Futures and Exceptional Presents: A Conceptual Critique of "Pre-Emptive Security"'. In *Time, Globalization, and Human Experience*, edited by Paul Huebener, Liam Stockdale, Susie O'Brien, Yanqiu Rachel Zhou and Tony Porter, 87–109, 2017.

Sunder Rajan, Rajeswari. *The Scandal of the State: Women, Law, and Citizenship in Postcolonial India*. Next Wave. Durham, NC: Duke University Press, 2003.

Toney, Veronica. 'Jesse Williams Gave One of the Most Memorable Speeches in Award Show History'. *Washington Post*, 27 June 2016. Available at <https://www.washingtonpost.com/news/arts-and-entertainment/wp/2016/06/27/jesse-williams-gave-one-of-the-most-memorable-speeches-in-award-show-history-full-transcript> (last accessed 27 June 2016).

TRAC Immigration. 'Average Time Pending Cases Have Been Waiting in Immigration Courts as of April 2020'. Transactional Records Assess Clearinghouse, April 2020. Available at <https://trac.syr.edu/phptools/immigration/court_backlog/apprep_backlog_avgdays.php> (last accessed 4 March 2022).

Trouillot, Michel-Rolph. *Silencing the Past: Power and the Production of History*. Boston, MA: Beacon Press, 2015.

US State Department. 'Protracted Refugee Situations'. Government website. Protracted Refugee Situations. Available at <https://www.state.gov/j/prm/policyissues/issues/protracted> (last accessed 3 March 2017).

Van Zyl, Paul. 'Dilemmas of Transitional Justice: The Case of South Africa's Truth and Reconciliation Commission'. *Journal of International Affairs* 52, no. 2 (1999): 647–67.

Vlies, Andrew van der. *Present Imperfect: Contemporary South African Writing*. Oxford: Oxford University Press, 2017.

Waller, Richard. 'Rebellious Youth in Colonial Africa'. *Journal of African History* 47, no. 1 (2006): 77–92.

Walunywa, Joseph. 'The "Non-Native Native" in V.S. Naipaul's A Bend in the River'. *Postcolonial Text* 4, no. 2 (2008): 1–25.

Warnes, Christopher. 'Magical Realism and the Legacy of German Idealism'. *The Modern Language Review* 101, no. 2 (2006): 488–98.

Warren, Calvin. 'Black Time: Slavery, Metaphysics, and the Logic of Wellness'. In *The Psychic Hold of Slavery: Legacies in American Expressive Culture*,

edited by Soyica Diggs Colbert, Robert J. Patterson and Aida Levy-Hussen, 55–68. New Brunswick, NJ: Rutgers University Press, 2016.
Watt, Ian P. *Conrad in the Nineteenth Century*. Berkeley: University of California Press, 1981.
Webb, Barbara J. *Myth and History in Caribbean Fiction: Alejo Carpentier, Wilson Harris, and Edouard Glissant*. Amherst: University of Massachusetts Press, 1992.
Weeks, Kathi. *The Problem with Work: Feminism, Marxism, Antiwork Politics, and Postwork Imaginaries*. Durham, NC: Duke University Press, 2011.
Wehrs, Donald R. *Islam, Ethics, Revolt: Politics and Piety in Francophone West African and Maghreb Narrative*. Lanham, MD: Lexington Books, 2008.
Weik, Terry. 'The Archeology of Maroon Societies in the Americas: Resistance, Cultural Continuity, and Transformation in the African Diaspora'. *Historical Archeology* 31, no. 2 (1997): 81–92.
Weinstein, Harvey M., Laurel E. Fletcher, Patrick Vinck and Phuong N. Pham. 'Stay the Hand of Justice: Whose Priorities Take Priority?' In *Localizing Transitional Justice: Interventions and Priorities after Mass Violence*, edited by Rosalind Shaw, Lars Waldorf and Pierre Hazan, 27–48. Stanford Studies in Human Rights. Stanford, CA: Stanford University Press, 2010.
Weiss, Timothy. *On the Margins: The Art of Exile in V. S. Naipaul*. Amherst: University of Massachusetts Press, 1992.
Wenzel, Jennifer. *Bulletproof: Afterlives of Anticolonial Prophecy in South Africa and Beyond*. Chicago; London: University of Chicago Press, 2009.
West-Pavlov, Russell. *Temporalities*. The New Critical Idiom. New York: Routledge, 2013.
White, Hayden V. *The Fiction of Narrative: Essays on History, Literature, and Theory, 1957–2007*. Baltimore, MD: Johns Hopkins University Press, 2010.
Wright, Derek. 'African Literature and Post-Independence Disillusionment'. In *Cambridge History of African and Caribbean Literature*, edited by Abiola Irele and Simon Gikandi, 2:797–808. Cambridge: Cambridge University Press, 2004.
Wright, Derek. 'Fragments: The Akan Background'. *Research in African Literatures* 18, no. 2 (1987): 176–91.
Wright, Laura. *Writing 'Out of All the Camps': J. M. Coetzee's Narratives of Displacement*. Studies in Major Literary Authors. New York: Routledge, 2006.
Wright, Michelle M. *Physics of Blackness: Beyond the Middle Passage Epistemology*. Minneapolis: University of Minnesota Press, 2015.
Wright, Timothy. 'The Art of Evasion: Writing and the State in J.M. Coetzee's Life & Times of Michael K'. *JLS/TLW* 28, no. 3 (2012): 55–76.
Zabus, Chantal. *The African Palimpsest: Indigenization of Language in the West African Europhone Novel*. Vol. 2. Cross/Cultures 4. Amsterdam: Rodopi, 2007.

Index

acceleration, 14, 17, 31, 36, 51, 56, 61, 134, 178, 212–14
Achebe, Chinua, 59, 122
Adam, Barbara, 125, 126
Adjaye, Joseph, 12, 137
Africa
   African cosmologies, 131–2
   Africanist interpretations of time, 11–13, 17, 125
   association with timelessness, 12, 58–9, 65–6
   disillusionment novels in African fiction, 30, 121–2
   see also *Bend in the River, A* (Naipaul); Ghana; *Heart of Darkness* (Conrad); Senegal; Sierra Leone; South Africa
Agamben, Giorgio, 110, 208
Ahmed, Sara, 10, 123, 134, 151, 206
Ambiguous Adventure (Kane)
   as *bildungsroman*, 48–9
   colonial time, 29, 43–4, 51–2, 53
   in dialogue with *Heart of Darkness*, 29, 36, 55–7
   disillusionment in, 52
   longue durée of time and history, 35–6, 43, 46–8, 52, 54, 55–6
   modern/traditional time dualities, 44–6, 50–1, 52–3, 55
   narrative, 29, 35, 43
   pre-Islamic worldview, 43, 46–8, 52–4, 55–6
   role of generational time, 52–4
   Senegal's histories of trade and empire, 43–4
   temporalities of waiting, 51–2, 56–7
   twilight in, 35, 48, 49–52, 54–5, 59

Anderson, Benedict, 26, 89, 111–12, 126, 129, 143, 203, 210
Armah, Ayi Kwei, 27, 122; see also *Fragments* (Armah)
Attwell, David, 6, 107
Auyero, Javier, 22–4
Awoonor, Kofi, 122

Bangura, Ahmed, 43, 46
Barnard, Rita, 111, 116, 178
Bashir, Shahzad, 56
Bayart, Jean-François, 214
Beah, Ishmael, 2, 31, 194; see also *Radiance of Tomorrow* (Beah)
Bend in the River, A (Naipaul)
   aimless waiting, 67, 69–70, 73–4, 75, 76
   helicopter imagery, 78–9
   Indian-African ethnicity, 64–5, 68, 72–8
   intertextuality with *Heart of Darkness*, 59, 62
   longue durée view of history, 64–5, 68–71
   motifs of light and darkness, 67–8
   past-future tensions, 74, 75–6
   pessimism over Africa's postcolonial future, 60, 64, 66–8, 72, 78, 89–90
   relationship to Western historical time, 64–5, 66–7, 68–72, 77–8, 79
   timelessness of Africa, 65–6
   use of 'outsider' perspectives, 63–4, 73–6
   waiting rooms of history model, 29–30, 59–60, 67–8, 72, 75, 76–8
Berlant, Lauren, 123
Bernstein, J. A., 34

Bhabha, Homi, 18, 121, 127, 156
Bissell, David, 127–8, 140
Black Lives Matter movement, 199–201, 202
Black studies, 4–7
Boehmer, Elleke, 3, 25–6, 129, 142, 144, 145
Bourdieu, Pierre, 24, 117
Bush, George W., 204–7

Campt, Tina, 96, 97
Carpentier, Alejo, 102, 106; see also *Kingdom of This World, The* (Carpentier)
Carr, David, 19, 20
Chakrabarty, Dipesh, 10, 17–18, 39, 59, 60–1, 77, 89, 102, 143
Chatterjee, Partha, 126 n.19, 142, 143
Cheah, Pheng, 7, 18, 47
Christodoulidis, Emilios, 169–70, 190
Clingman, Stephen, 86, 88
Coetzee, J. M.
  political engagement in the works of, 106–7, 111
  as a postcolonial writer, 3
  Waiting for the Barbarians, 107–9, 110, 116, 204
  waiting's multivalent function in the works of, 107–9, 116
  White Writing: On the Culture of Letters in South Africa, 109, 112, 116–17, 131
  see also *Life & Times of Michael K* (Coetzee)
colonial regimes of time
  in *Ambiguous Adventure*, 29, 43–4, 51–2, 53
  in *A Bend in the River*, 64
  concept of, 14
  as homogenising and universalising, 12–16, 39
  longue durée view of, 36, 41, 46–8, 54, 55–6
  modern/traditional dualities, 7, 12–13, 14–15, 18, 31–2, 36, 39, 44–6, 50–1, 55, 125
  the production of time lags, 18–19
  revolutionary ruptures of, 61–2
  waiting within, 3, 15–16, 36
  see also waiting room model
Conlon, Deirdre, 128
Conrad, Joseph, 2, 3, 34–5, 62–3
  see also *Heart of Darkness* (Conrad)
Crais, Clifton, 112–13

Crapanzano, Vincent, 30, 82–4, 85, 178, 187
critical time studies, 6, 7, 213–14
Cry, the Peacock (Desai)
  concept of karma, 146–7
  disillusionment in, 140–1
  as an exploration of female consciousness, 141
  gendered dimensions of waiting, 124, 125, 127, 129, 151–2, 156–8
  gendered discourses of nationalism, 142–3, 144, 145, 146–7, 149
  narrative, 141–2, 145
  patience and urgency in waiting, 30, 125, 129, 142, 146, 148, 151–4
  temporality of fate, 146–8, 149–50, 152–5
  themes of mental distress, 140, 141, 142, 145–6, 155–6
  woman/tradition bind, 130, 142, 148–51, 152–3
Cry of Winnie Mandela, The (Ndebele)
  gendered dimensions of waiting, 161, 173, 175, 187–9
  as literature of the ordinary, 176–7, 178
  narrative, 160–1
  Penelope tradition of waiting, 161, 174–5
  post-apartheid waiting, 178–9
  reconciliation-disclosure-closure relationship, 161, 161–2, 181–4, 185, 190–1, 197
  as a response to the TRC proceedings, 163–4, 176, 181–4, 190–1
  strategic waiting, 31, 164, 187–8, 189–90, 198
  victimhood and waiting, 181, 187
  waiting during apartheid, 179–81, 189
Cuba, 102, 106
Cudjoe, Selwyn, 77

Delaney, Martin R., 199
Desai, Anita, 27, 141, 146–7; see also *Cry, the Peacock* (Desai)
Dessalines, Jean-Jacques, 94, 102, 105, 106
disillusionment novels
  affects of, 122–4
  in African fiction, 30, 121–2
  gendered dimensions of waiting, 124, 127

genre, 30, 124
  in Indian fiction, 30, 122
  role of waiting in, 124
  and the wait for national belonging, 122–3
  see also *Cry, the Peacock* (Desai); *Fragments* (Armah)
Doyle, Laura, 47, 54

English, Daylanne, 4

Fanon, Frantz, 18–19, 130–1
Feit, Mario, 154, 212
Figueroa, Víctor, 94
Fleming, Julius B., 5, 200–1
Fragments (Armah)
  cargo cult mentality, 132–4
  disillusionment in, 27, 122, 130–1, 133, 139, 140–1
  gendered dimensions of waiting, 124, 125, 127, 129, 130, 138–40, 156–8
  images of the slave trade, 133–4
  moments of temporal arrhythmias, 131, 136–8
  patience and urgency in waiting, 30, 125, 129, 130, 132–3, 138–40, 142
  productive time, 130, 131–2, 134, 135, 140
  themes of mental distress, 131, 132–3, 136, 139, 140
  traditional temporalities, 135–8
  waiting as stasis, 131, 138
Freeman, Elizabeth, 121, 127, 156

Garza, Alicia, 201
gender
  assumptions about victimhood during TRCs, 172–3
  gendered dimensions of waiting, 30, 124, 125, 127–9, 138–40, 151–2, 156–8, 187–9
  gendered nationalisms, 142–5, 146–7, 149
  gendering of nation states, 129–30
  notions of patience and urgency, 30, 125, 127–9, 130, 132–3, 138–40, 142, 146, 148, 151–4
  Penelope tradition of waiting, 161, 174–5
  woman/tradition bind, 130, 142, 148–51, 152–3

Ghana
  gymmers, 8–9, 22, 132
  independence ceremony, 1–2
  see also *Fragments* (Armah)
Gilroy, Paul, 13 n.61
Glissant, Édouard, 13, 99–100, 119
Gonzalez Echevarría, Roberto, 100
Gordimer, Nadine
  imagery of the broken watch, 87–8, 89
  'Living in the Interregnum,' 80, 82, 83
  No Time Like the Present, 179
  as a postcolonial writer, 3
  see also *July's People* (Gordimer)
Haitian Revolution, 91–2, 94, 100, 102; see also *Kingdom of This World, The* (Carpentier)
Hamann, Byron Ellsworth, 126–7
Hanchard, Michael, 16
Hartman, Saidya, 5, 92–3, 133
Harvey, David, 212
Hayes, Patrick, 108, 116
Heart of Darkness (Conrad)
  in dialogue with *Ambiguous Adventure*, 29, 36, 55–7
  'fantastic invasion' phrase, 40–2
  intertextuality with *A Bend in the River*, 59, 62
  intertextuality with *July's People*, 59, 79
  longue durée view of, 43, 65
  motifs of light and darkness, 34, 35, 37, 67–8
  narrative, 58
  patience and waiting, 39, 41, 42
  representations of Africa, 40, 42, 58–9
  storytelling and waiting connections, 33–4, 35
  temporalities of waiting, 29, 33–4, 35, 36–42, 56–7, 58–9
  waiting as frustration and futility, 37–41
  waiting as survival, 40–2
Hegel, Georg Wilhelm Friedrich, 12, 13, 21, 64
history
  critiques of Western time and history, 6–7, 10–13, 17–18
  erasure of precolonial history, 12–13, 17

longue durée concept, 35–6
longue durée in *A Bend in the River*, 64–5, 68–71
longue durée in *Ambiguous Adventure*, 35–6, 43, 46–8, 52, 54, 55–6
perceptions of linearity, 14–15
see also modernity
Hook, Derek, 9, 84 n.101, 85, 178
Huebener, Paul, 7
Huehls, Mitchum, 205
Humper, Joseph Christian, 165–6

India
concept of karma, 146–7
the Constitution, 62
disillusionment novels in Indian fiction, 30, 122
Hindu Code Bill, 143
Indian-African ethnicity in *A Bend in the River*, 64–5, 68, 72–8
legacies of gendered nationalism, 143–5
nationalist movements, 17, 60–1
postcolonial fiction, 30–1
revolutionary moment, 61–2
waiting room model, post-Independence, 61, 143–4
waiting room model, pre-Independence, 60–1
see also *Cry, the Peacock* (Desai)
Islam
pre-Islamic worldview in *Ambiguous Adventure*, 43, 46–8, 52–4, 55–6
in Senegal, 43, 44
studies of Islamic history and time, 56

James, C. L. R., 91–2, 93
James, Cynthia, 95, 98, 99
July's People (Gordimer)
apartheid temporality, 60, 80, 81–2, 84–6, 88–9
helicopter imagery, 79, 80, 87, 88
intertextuality with *Heart of Darkness*, 59, 79
Maureen's waiting/self-reflection, 79, 81–2, 83, 84, 85–6, 88, 90
narrative, 79
obsolescence of the clock and calendar, 87–8, 89
past-present-future relationship and, 86–8

temporality of the interregnum, 79–82, 83, 87–8, 89–90
views of the postcolonial future of Africa, 79, 89–90
waiting rooms of history model, 29–30, 59–60

Kane, Cheikh Hamidou, 29, 42–3
Keating, Christine, 143
Keeling, Kara, 18–19
Kermode, Frank, 20
Kher, Inder, 155
King, Bruce, 65, 73
King Jr, Martin Luther
Black Lives Matter movement and, 200
at Ghana's independence ceremony, 1–2
'I Have a Dream' speech, 199
'Letter from Birmingham Jail,' 1, 2
links between civil rights and freedom movements, 1–2
rejections of waiting, 1–2, 4, 129, 154, 199, 201, 211–12
Kingdom of This World, The (Carpentier)
freedom and resistance through marronage, 93, 99, 102–5, 118–19
Macandal character, 103–4, 105–6
marronage's association with waiting, 118–20
narrative, 102–6
role of the maroon, 30, 93, 103
Ti Noël character, 100, 102–6

labour
gymmers in Accra, 8–9, 22, 132
idleness and the refusal to work, 30, 99, 112–14, 116, 117, 118
idleness on the Cape, 109, 112, 116–17, 131
productive time, 131–2
Western capitalist modernity, 7, 9, 131–2, 136
Laski, Gregory, 5–6
Lazarus, Joyce Block, 45
Lazarus, Neil, 138, 140
Life & Times of Michael K (Coetzee)
discourse of waiting, 109, 116
freedom and resistance through marronage, 30, 114–16, 117–19
idleness and the refusal to work, 30, 99, 112–14, 116, 117, 118

marronage's association with waiting, 118–20
Michael K as a maroon figure, 93, 107
past-present-future relationship and, 110, 111–12, 113–14
political critique and, 110–11
rejection of state time, 111–12, 114, 116
L'Ouverture, Toussaint, 91–2

McKittrick, Katherine, 5, 100–1
McTaggart, J. M. E., 34
Majumdar, Saikat, 9, 27–8
Mandela, Winnie, 181–2
maroons
 in Caribbean literature, 95–6, 97
 etymology, 94–5
 figure of/as non-state actors, 96, 97–9, 105
 François Mackandal, 103
 models of fugitivity and, 93, 96–7, 99, 103–4, 105, 106
 in relation to history and time, 98–9
 relationship with the plantations, 95–6, 100–1
 Ti Noël, 102–6
 see also *Kingdom of This World, The* (Carpentier); *Life & Times of Michael K* (Coetzee)
marronage
 association with waiting, 118–20
 flight, 93, 94, 95, 96–7, 98, 119
 freedom and resistance in *Life & Times of Michael K*, 114–16, 117–19
 freedom as a state of flight, 99–100
 idleness as resistive waiting, 94, 118–20
 importance of place/topography, 95, 99
 in *The Kingdom of This World*, 102–5, 118
 labour, 94, 99, 112–14, 116, 117, 118
 literary representations of, 98–9
 in opposition to the modern nation-state, 119–20
 rhizomatic marronage, 99–100
 temporal difference and, 100–2
 term, 97
Mazrui, Alamin, 131
Mbembe, Achille, 16
Mehta, Uday, 30, 58, 61–2, 143

Mills, John Stuart, 17
modernity
 contradictory temporalities of, 18
 heterogeneous forms of, 16
 marronage in opposition to, 119–20
 modern/traditional dualities, 7, 12–13, 14–15, 18, 31–2, 36, 39, 44–6, 50–1, 55, 125
 not-yet European discourses, 11, 17–18, 24, 39, 60, 102
 revolutionary ruptures of, 91–2
 time-lag of, 18–19
 Western capitalist modernity, 7, 9, 131–2, 136
 see also waiting room model
Moon, Claire, 169
Mphande, Lupenga, 131
Mudimbe, V. Y., 11, 12, 125
Murphy, Laura, 133, 134
Mustafa, Fawzia, 64

Nadkarni, Asha, 144–5
Naidu, Sarojini, 144
Naipaul, V. S.
 'In a Free State,' 63–4, 66, 69, 78, 89
 imagery of the broken watch, 63, 64, 78, 89
 links with Conrad, 62–3
 Nobel Prize for Literature, 62
 pessimism over Africa's postcolonial future, 64, 78
 on writing history, 69
 see also *Bend in the River, A* (Naipaul)
Napolitano, Joe, 183–4
narrative
 and experience, 19–20
 and fiction, 3, 42
 frames, 35, 40, 58
 and history, 13, 17, 21, 60, 71
 of Orientalism, 11
 of Romance, 91–2, 100, 106
 and the state, 111, 119, 145
 and Truth and Reconciliation Commissions, 161, 164, 167, 169–74, 181
nation states
 disillusionment and the wait for national belonging, 122–3
 gendering of, 129–30
 the maroon as a non-state actor, 96, 97–9, 105
 multivalent function of waiting, 203

rejection of state time, 111–12, 114, 116, 119, 126, 130, 189
response to civil agitation, 202
nationalist movements
  end of the wait for freedom and independence, 1–2, 17–18
  gendered nationalisms, 142–5, 146–7, 149
  in India, 17, 60–1
  links between civil rights and freedom movements, 1–2
  rejection of the waiting room model, 10, 17, 59, 60–1
  see also revolution
Ndebele, Njabulo
  'The Rediscovery of the Ordinary: Some New Writings in South Africa,' 176–7
  'The Revolution of the Aged,' 159–60, 198
  on the South African TRC, 174
  'South Africans in Search of Common Values,' 189
  see also Cry of Winnie Mandela, The (Ndebele)
Nkrumah, Kwame, 1, 2, 4, 201

O'Connell, Hugh, 122
Olson, Elizabeth, 129
Omelsky, Matthew, 5, 97

patience
  black patience, 5, 200–1
  gendered patience and urgency in waiting, 30, 125, 127–9, 130, 132–3, 138–40, 142, 146, 148, 151–4
  not-yet European discourses, 11, 17, 24, 39, 60–1
  politics of patience, 210–11
  pre-emption strategies of the War on Terror, 203, 204–7, 210
  suffering within, 160
  waiting as, 22
  and waiting in *Heart of Darkness*, 39, 41, 42
postcolonial fiction
  comparative methodology, 27–9
  cultural time regimes, 15–16
  genre, 3–4
  time and temporality in, 2–3, 25–6
  waiting in, 2, 7–8, 16, 26–8, 31–2, 212–14
  see also disillusionment novels

postcolonial studies
  critiques of Western time and history, 6–7, 10–13, 17–18
  scholarship on time and temporality, 5–7
  time and, 10–16
power
  from mathematical and scientific time, 20–1
  over the waiting subject, 21, 22–4, 117, 158, 197–8, 200–3, 212–13
  rhizomatic marronage, 100
progress, 40, 79

Quayson, Ato, 8, 9, 22, 132

Radiance of Tomorrow (Beah)
  healing function of silence, 163, 191, 194–8
  ongoing trauma in the postcolonial present, 175–6, 192–3
  oral storytelling, 184–6
  reintegration of child soldiers, 185, 194–5, 196, 197
  as a response to the TRC proceedings, 163–4, 176, 184–6
  strategic waiting, 31, 161, 164, 179, 187, 192, 196–8
  temporalities of waiting, 193–4
  themes of reconciliation and rebuilding, 161–2, 163, 175–6, 191–5
Ravenscroft, Arthur, 121–2
Rege, Josna, 141, 145, 146
revolution
  Haitian Revolution, 91–2, 94, 100, 102
  open-ended temporality, 92
  revolutionary ruptures of colonialism, 61–2
  romantic narratives of overcoming, 91–2, 100, 106
  see also *Kingdom of This World, The* (Carpentier)
Roberts, Neil, 96, 97, 99, 119
Ross, Fiona, 197, 198

Said, Edward, 11–12, 26, 163
Sanders, Mark, 163–4
Scott, David, 6, 7, 14, 91–2, 100, 105, 119
Senegal, 43–4; see also *Ambiguous Adventure* (Kane)
Sierra Leone
  Lomé Peace Agreement, 166

reintegration of child soldiers, 162, 172, 185, 194
Truth and Reconciliation Commissions (TRCs), 31, 162–3, 165–8, 172, 196–7
see also *Radiance of Tomorrow* (Beah)
slavery
  Haitian Revolution, 91–2, 94, 100, 102
  images of the slave trade in *Fragments*, 133–4
  Muslim resistance organisations in Senegal, 44
  power dynamics of, 92
  redemptive narratives, 92
  temporalities of, 5
  see also maroons; marronage
South Africa
  discourse of idleness, 109, 112, 116–17, 131
  Penelope tradition of waiting, 161, 174–5
  refugees from the Theopolis settlement, 112–13
  'The Revolution of the Aged' (Ndebele), 159–60, 198
  sense of time during apartheid, 189
  Truth and Reconciliation Commissions (TRCs), 31, 162–3, 165–73, 177, 181–2, 190–1
  waiting during the apartheid era, 9
  waiting during the interregnum, 82–3
  waiting in post-apartheid fiction, 178–9
  see also *Cry of Winnie Mandela, The* (Ndebele); *July's People* (Gordimer); *Life & Times of Michael K* (Coetzee)
South African literary studies, 7, 9, 27, 28
Soyinka, Wole, 122, 170

temporality
  affect and, 9–10
  apartheid temporality, 60, 80, 81–2, 84–6, 88–9
  Black studies scholarship on, 4–7
  critiques of Western time and history, 6–7
  of fate, 146–8, 149–50, 152–5
  of the interregnum in South Africa, 79–82, 83, 87–8, 89–90
  multiple temporalities of waiting, 3, 4, 7, 10, 19–25
  of the nation-state, 111–12, 114, 116, 119, 126, 130, 189
  in postcolonial fiction, 2–3, 25–6
  of slavery, 5
  temporal arrhythmias, 131, 136–8
  temporal differences of marronage, 100–2
  temporal heterogeneity, 127
  temporalities of waiting and 'national security,' 202
  temporalities of waiting in *Heart of Darkness*, 29, 33–4, 35, 36–42, 56–7, 58–9
  term, 20
  traditional temporalities, 135–8
time
  Africanist interpretations, 11–13, 17, 125
  clocks and calendars, 63, 64, 78, 87–8, 89, 126–7, 189
  in Conrad's works, 34–5
  contemporary compression of, 212
  critiques of Western time and history, 6–7, 10–13, 17–18
  Islamic history and time, 56
  narrative devices, 19–20
  Orientalist interpretations of, 11–12, 17, 125
  postcolonial studies and, 10–16
  racial time, 16
  rejection of state time, 111–12, 114, 116, 119, 126, 130, 189
  term, 20
  watch imagery, 63, 64, 78, 87–8, 89
  see also colonial regimes of time
timescapes
  concept of, 125
  temporal heterogeneity, 15, 16, 36, 40, 127
  Western temporality and, 126–7
Trump, Donald J.
  'antifa' movement and, 202
  immigration restrictions, 205–6, 208–9
  threats to national security, 202
Truth and Reconciliation Commissions (TRCs)
  absence of 'everyday' experiences, 176–7
  emphasis on remembering and recounting, 169, 170–2, 173–4

as an end to waiting, 162–3
fictive responses to, 163–4
gendered assumptions about victimhood during, 172–3
interregnum temporalities of, 168
mandates of, 162–3, 165–9, 177
and narrative, 161, 164, 167, 169–74, 181
past-present-future relationship and, 165–6, 168–70
restorative justice and, 166–8
in Sierra Leone, 31, 162–3, 165–8, 172, 196–7
in South Africa, 31, 162–3, 165–73, 177, 181–2, 190–1
temporal limits of, 167, 174, 197–8
Tutu, Desmond, 165–6

United States of America (USA)
Black Lives Matter movement, 199–200, 202
civil rights movements, 1–2
global geopolitics and, 203
immigration restrictions, 205–8
pre-emption strategies of the War on Terror, 203, 204–7, 210
temporalities of waiting and 'national security,' 202
see also slavery

Veitch, Scott, 169–70, 190
Vlies, Andrew van der, 9, 178, 179

waiting
affect and, 9–10
boredom and, 9, 21
in the contemporary geopolitical landscape, 201–3
definitions, 4
for freedom and independence, 1–2
multiple temporalities of, 3, 4, 7, 10, 19–25
past-present-future relationship and, 83–4, 85
politics and strategies of the War on Terror, 204–7
in postcolonial fiction, 2, 7–8, 16, 26–8, 31–2, 212–14
power dynamics of, 21, 22–4
refugee experiences, 112–13, 128, 202, 207–10
rhetoric of the Donald Trump, 202
temporality of waiting in *Heart of Darkness*, 29, 33–4, 35, 36–42, 56–7
as an urban practice, 8–9
urgency and, 1–2, 200–1, 202, 211–12
waiting room model
anticolonial nationalist rejections of, 10, 17, 59, 60–1
in *A Bend in the River*, 29–30, 59–60, 67–8, 72, 75, 76–8
in India, 60–1, 143–4
in *July's People*, 29–30, 59–60
not-yet European discourses, 11, 17, 24, 39, 60–1
revolutionary temporality and, 61–2
Walunywa, Joseph, 67, 77
watch imagery, 63, 64, 78, 87–8, 89
Wehrs, David, 45, 46, 47
Weiss, Timothy, 69, 70, 71
Wenzel, Jennifer, 160
Williams, Jesse, 199, 200
Wright, David, 135

EU representative:
Easy Access System Europe
Mustamäe tee 50, 10621 Tallinn, Estonia
Gpsr.requests@easproject.com